Goethe in German-Jewish Culture

Studies in German Literature, Linguistics, and Culture

Edited by James Hardin
(*South Carolina*)

Goethe
in German-Jewish Culture

Edited by
Klaus L. Berghahn
and
Jost Hermand

CAMDEN HOUSE

First published 2001
by Camden House

Camden House is an imprint of Boydell & Brewer Inc.
PO Box 41026, Rochester, NY 14604–4126 USA
and of Boydell & Brewer Limited
PO Box 9, Woodbridge, Suffolk IP12 3DF, UK

ISBN: 1–57113–323–2

Library of Congress Cataloging-in-Publication Data

Goethe in German-Jewish Culture / edited by Klaus L. Berghahn and Jost
Hermand.
    p. cm. – (Studies in German literature, linguistics, and culture)
Includes bibliographical references and index.
Papers presented at the 31st Wisconsin Workshop, held in Madison,
Wisconsin from 28 to 30 Oct., 1999.
    ISBN 1–57113–323–2 (alk. paper)
    1. Goethe, Johann Wolfgang von, 1749–1832 — Political and social views —
Congresses. 2. Goethe, Johann Wolfgang von, 1749–1832 — Views on Jews. 3.
Jews — Germany — Congresses. 4. Antisemitism — Germany — Congresses.
I. Berghahn, Klaus L. II. Hermand, Jost. III. Wisconsin Workshop (31st: 1999:
Madison, Wis.) IV. Studies in German literature, linguistics, and culture (Un-
numbered)

PT2200.J4 G64 2001
831'.6—dc21

                                                                    00–065088

A catalogue record for this title is available from the British Library.

This publication is printed on acid-free paper.
Printed in the United States of America

In memoriam: George L. Mosse

Contents

Preface

THE SUCCESS OF DANIEL GOLDHAGEN'S *Hitler's Willing Execution-
ers* (1996) and the heated debates that followed its publication exposed once again Germany's long history of anti-Semitism as one of the
main causes of Hitler's "Final Solution." Goldhagen, like others before
him,[1] drew a direct and irresistible line from Luther's pamphlets against
the Jews to Hitler's attempted annihilation of European Jewry. Employing the perspective of a universal anti-Semitism in Germany, Goldhagen did not differentiate between old anti-Judaism and modern
forms of anti-Semitism, and he also overlooked or neglected all those
texts from the Enlightenment through the nineteenth century up to
the Weimar Republic that opposed anti-Semitism. Nevertheless, Goldhagen's moral indignation and his harsh accusations are important, because they force us to reexamine a significant segment of Germany's
cultural tradition: How tolerant were the famous German philosophers
and poets of the eighteenth and early nineteenth centuries? In general,
less tolerant than one would expect or hope. A case in point is Johann
Wolfgang von Goethe, whose 250th birthday we celebrated last year.

The aim of this collection of essays is to examine the thesis of a universal anti-Semitism in Germany by focusing on its greatest author,
Goethe, whom both Adolf Hitler and Léon Poliakov have claimed as
an enemy of the Jews.[2] Since he was used by Hitler to legitimate his
ideology of racism and by Poliakov to demonstrate the anti-Jewish sentiments of the German Enlightenment, one begins to wonder whether
Goethe was, indeed, an anti-Semite. It is, however, not our intention
to construct an apology by balancing all of Goethe's utterances for or
against the Jews, as many have already done;[3] instead, we want to high-
light the reception of Goethe's works in a broader historical context:
Goethe's relationship to Judaism and the Jews; the reception of
Goethe's works and his concept of Bildung[4] by a Jewish elite in Germany; the Goethe cult and criticism of it by prominent Jewish authors;
the Jewish contribution to Goethe philology; and Goethe's heritage in
exile during the Third Reich. In demonstrating the tremendous influence Goethe's works and his concept of Bildung had on his Jewish
audience in Germany and by underscoring the great contributions of
Jewish authors and scholars to Goethe's fame, we hope to shed new

light on a neglected chapter of Goethe's reception by German Jews. Instead of returning to the tired question of whether Goethe was either an anti-Semite or a philo-Semite, as a recent article did,[5] we want to show the complexity of the German-Jewish symbiosis in which the reception of Goethe's works by a Jewish audience played an important role. In transforming the exhausted theme "Goethe and the Jews" into the more interesting one of "the German Jews and Goethe," we hope to establish a new perspective on the German-Jewish heritage and Goethe's exemplary role in it.

The first part of the book concentrates on Goethe's relationship to Judaism and the contemporary Jews, his concept of Bildung, and the enthusiastic reception of his works by members of the first Jewish salons in Berlin. Goethe's most famous text about the Jews is his childhood memory of the Frankfurt ghetto, which is — for two reasons — the most interesting and revealing document. As part of Goethe's "autobiography," *Dichtung und Wahrheit* (Poetry and Truth, 1811–22), it provides the reader with a detailed description of the Frankfurt ghetto and the impression it made on the young Goethe; at the same time, it is also a self-reflection of the sixty-year-old author about his relationship to the Jews. Looking back on his experience and reflecting on it, the text reveals a pattern that is typical of Goethe: distance and ambivalence. Goethe never participated in the toleration debate of the eighteenth century in any substantial way ("To tolerate is to offend" is one of his famous aphorisms, "for toleration can only be a transitional phase that has to lead to acceptance"[6]), and he was only marginally interested in the emancipation of the Jews, to which he objected. Yet, his concept of Bildung, as he developed it in his educational novel *Wilhelm Meisters Lehrjahre* (Wilhelm Meister's Apprenticeship, 1795), became a model for the cultural assimilation of the Jewish elite. The first sign of this osmosis can be detected in Berlin's Jewish salon culture (1780–1806).

Part Two deals with the encounter of German and Jewish culture in the nineteenth century. Jewish intellectuals began to adapt ideas and values of the dominant German culture, which was at that time one of the richest in Europe, and they transformed those ideas into a Jewish subculture. The German concept of Bildung, developed during the Enlightenment by Moses Mendelssohn and refined by representatives of German Idealism such as Wilhelm von Humboldt, Friedrich Schiller, Johann Wolfgang Goethe, and Georg Wilhelm Friedrich Hegel, became both an educational ideal and part of a new identity for the Jews. This acculturation led to far-reaching social transformations, which resulted in the integration of many Jews into the German *Bildungsbür-gertum* [the cultured middle class] during the nineteenth century.[7]

The third part highlights the Jewish contributions to Goethe's fame and to Goethe philology since the nineteenth century. While the Jewish salon culture at the end of the eighteenth century to around 1830 had already established a Jewish community of Goethe enthusiasts in Berlin and Vienna, the following decades saw this admiration of the greatest national poet translated by Jewish scholars into institutionalized forms of fame. Michael Bernays and Ludwig Geiger started a critical Goethe philology, and Geiger edited the influential *Goethe-Jahrbuch* for more than thirty years; Eduard von Simson was the first president of the Goethe Society; and the bulk of all Goethe biographies were written by Jewish authors, such as Geiger, Albert Bielschowsky, Michael R. Meyer, Emil Ludwig, Georg Simmel, Friedrich Gundolf, Richard Friedenthal, and Hans Mayer. This is, indeed, a much neglected aspect of Goethe research.[8]

The final part commemorates the exodus of many Jewish authors, scholars, and *Bildungsbürger* after 1933. They took their beloved Goethe into exile. Be it in England, France, the United States, Palestine, or other parts of the world, they clung to their belief in the humanitarian promises of Goethe's works. They could not understand the paradox that Germany, the country of so many great philosophers, poets, composers, and scholars, would also be inscribed in the annals of history as the land in which the Holocaust took place. A few survivors returned to Germany after 1945, but the country had lost Goethe's most devoted audience, the German Jews.

When the cultural historian George L. Mosse received the Goethe Medal in Munich in 1991, he ended his acceptance speech with the words: "Hitler destroyed the Jews of Germany, but not their cultural heritage."[9] Mosse himself contributed to this tradition in many books and articles, especially in his *German Jews beyond Judaism* (1985). In it he argued that the German concept of Bildung became part of a new German-Jewish identity, if not an *Ersatzreligion* for a Jewish elite. This thesis became the subtext of our discussions during the thirty-first Wisconsin Workshop, which was held at the University of Wisconsin-Madison from 28 to 30 October 1999.

Time and again, the discussions of the symposium returned to the question whether Goethe's concept of Bildung was really as important for the cultural integration of German Jews as Mosse had declared it to be. The Goethe cult was certainly part of the Jewish salon culture, and the aim of its sociability had been to foster Bildung. But was it really

part of a new German-Jewish identity for Jewish intellectuals at the beginning or middle of the nineteenth century? Or did this turn toward
integration into the German *Bildungsbürgertum* come much later —
say, after the *Reichsgründung* [the founding of the Second Empire] in
1871? Can one speak of an emancipation through Bildung when the
German Jews, even after their emancipation in Prussia (1812), were still
second-class citizens? Or did this concept lead to the slippery road of
assimilation? Jewish scholars certainly contributed greatly to Goethe's
fame, but did their work of love for a national icon really make them
part of the German nation? Or did it reinforce resentments against
Jewish intellectuals who dared to understand and interpret Germany's
greatest poet? And this still leaves the bigger and thornier question unanswered: What is German-Jewish culture? Is it really an integral part of
German culture, to which many Jewish artists, writers, and scholars
contributed so much, or is it a Jewish subculture within German culture? Our workshop touched on those questions but left many of them
unanswered, which should surprise nobody who works with the complex issues of national-identity formation and cultural symbolism. Besides, workshops are not designed to solve all problems; they fulfill a
useful function if they merely raise new questions and lead to fruitful
discussions. The symposium did demonstrate, however, the influence
Goethe's works had on a Jewish elite in Germany and how much that
elite contributed to Goethe's fame. Many German Jews became the
proudest Germans and the best *Bildungsbürger* — until the bitter end,
which they could not have foreseen or expected.

The Goethe Conference was organized by the Center for German
and European Studies in cooperation with the Department of German
and the Center for Jewish Studies. Conferences such as this one would
not be possible without the financial and intellectual support of our institution, both of which we have had in abundance. We would like to
thank the University of Wisconsin-Madison, which supported the
workshop with a generous grant from its Anonymous Fund; the
Goethe Institute in Chicago; and the Deutsche Forschungsgemein-
schaft, which also contributed substantially to our conference. A
DAAD Study Visit to Weimar in preparation for the conference is also
gratefully acknowledged. We also received valuable advice and criticism
from our colleagues and friends the late George L. Mosse and David
Sorkin. Last but not least, we would like to thank Matthew Lange, who
spent many hours in preparation of the manuscript at the keyboard of
his computer, and especially Joan Leffler, the administrator of the

German Department, who handled the many organizational details of the workshop with efficiency and grace.

Klaus L. Berghahn and Jost Hermand
Madison, Fall 2000

Notes

[1] Léon Poliakov, *The History of Anti-Semitism,* 3 vols. (New York: Vanguard, 1975), and Paul L. Rose, *Revolutionary Anti-Semitism in Germany from Kant to Wagner* (Princeton: Princeton UP, 1990).

[2] Adolf Hitler, *Mein Kampf* (Munich: Franz Eher, 1942) 341. Léon Poliakov, *The History of Anti-Semitism,* III, 162 and 175.

[3] Alfred D. Low, *Jews in the Eyes of the Germans* (Philadelphia: Institute for the Study of Human Issues, 1979) 67–86.

[4] Although the word *Bildung* can hardly be translated into English without losing its meaning, we find that "cultural self-cultivation" fits best.

[5] Günter Hartung, "Goethe und die Juden," *Weimarer Beiträge* 40.3 (1994): 398–416.

[6] *Goethes Werke,* ed. Erich Trunz (Hamburg: Wegner, 1950) XII: 385.

[7] George L. Mosse, *German Jews beyond Judaism* (Bloomington: Indiana UP, 1985).

[8] Wilfried Barner is one of the few whose research contributed substantially to this aspect of the Goethe reception. See his "Jüdische Goethe-Verehrung vor 1933," in *Juden in der deutschen Literatur,* ed. Stépane Moses and Albrecht Schöne (Frankfurt/Main: Suhrkamp, 1986) 127–51, and *Von Rahel Varnhagen bis Friedrich Gundolf: Juden als deutsche Goethe-Verehrer* (Göttingen: Wallstein 1992).

[9] Mosse, "Gedanken zum deutsch-jüdischen Dialog," *Chronik der Maximilian Universität München* (1982/83): 58.

I. Goethe and the Jews

Patterns of Childhood: Goethe and the Jews[1]

Klaus L. Berghahn
University of Wisconsin-Madison

"TO TOLERATE IS TO OFFEND," reads Goethe's oft-quoted 151st aphorism. Oft-quoted, yet incompletely so: the related reflection that gives the maxim its practical, and political spice is generally overlooked: "Tolerance should actually just be a transitory form of thinking: it must lead to acceptance."[2] One could almost understand this aphorism as a characterization of Goethe's own relationship to the Jews of his day, if only he had followed it himself.

In the context of the extensive tolerance debate of the eighteenth century, Goethe's aphorism is a provocation. His pointed commentary fits neither into the gentle, benevolent "tolerance of the heart," which tolerates the foreign in a rather condescending manner, nor into the harsh, authoritarian variation, which forces the acceptance of the minority through an edict from above. Goethe understood tolerance as a temporary way of thinking that would necessarily lead to mutual acceptance. As a secondary virtue, it would merely become a condescending gesture and, thus, an insult to those being tolerated. But it should be more than that: it must become a considered, voluntary action, which recognizes otherness in its specificity and its foreignness, accepts it as such, and eventually makes tolerance obsolete. It might well originate in simple forbearance, consideration, and social convention; yet, this sort of passive, gentle tolerance is not sufficient and can hardly be called tolerance. Considered tolerance is a double negation: it grapples with the foreign in order to understand it and in order to overcome prejudice and intolerance. Its ideal would be the abrogation of differences — a utopia of a community of heterogeneous members. Then tolerance would be replaced by "mutual acceptance" and, thus, become superfluous.

As is often the case in Goethe's writing, though, this idea — loftily conceived and sharply formulated — does not correspond entirely to his actual conduct. This contradiction between benevolent theory and

half-hearted practice is nowhere clearer than in his relationship to contemporary Jews. Certainly, Goethe was friends with many Jews and on
friendly terms with many more, but they were only those who aroused
his interest or who were useful to him. Otherwise, he remained aloof
from them. Thus, he praised the "industrious Jew" Jacob Elkan in
Weimar; he thought highly of the philosophy of Baruch Spinoza,
whose treatise on ethics, which he read repeatedly, influenced his own
philosophy of life; he invited the painter Moritz Oppenheim to his
house on the Frauenplan [a street in Weimar] and exhibited his works
there; and, above all, he loved the *Wunderkind* [child prodigy] Felix
Mendelssohn, the grandson of the famous Moses Mendelssohn, who
had been his frequent and favorite guest between 1820 and 1830. And
then there are the Jewish women, who had fascinated him as a boy in
Frankfurt. They were not just pretty, clever, and charming; they also
had the right taste — namely, for Goethe's works. In the salons of
Henriette Herz, Rahel Levin, and the sisters Sara and Marianne Meyer
his works counted as the catechism of true Bildung. They read and admired him; from 1795 onward he often met them at the Bohemian
spas; and in true Goethe style, he fell in love with Marianne von Eybenberg, née Meyer. Only with great difficulty was she able to pare his
passion back to a friendship. Rahel Levin — later Friederike Varnhagen
von Ense — surpassed all of his other female admirers, introducing the
Goethe cult in both of her Berlin salons. She and her husband saw to it
that Goethe's renown did not pale even in hard times. It would not
have occurred to Goethe to refer to them as *Jewish* acquaintances or
friends, except for the "industrious Jew" Jacob Elkan, the court Jew.[3]

Goethe's relationship to Judaism and to the emancipation of the Jews
is more complex, although typical of his time. Like most representatives
of the Enlightenment, he venerated the people of the Covenant. He had
been familiar with the five books of the Old Testament since his childhood, and he loved their stories. He requested lessons in Hebrew and
Yiddish from his father simply out of personal interest; and in Stras-
bourg, Herder called his attention to the beauty of Hebrew poetry. Like
most of his contemporaries, Goethe admired the Jews of the Old Testament, he translated Psalms and the Song of Songs, and he repeatedly occupied himself with biblical subjects, all of which, however, he discarded,
because the German public — despite Lessing's Nathan — rejected Jewish heroes.[4] Goethe, as well as many others during the Enlightenment,
regarded the mission of Moses, the introduction of monotheism, and the
Ten Commandments as decisive steps in the development of mankind —
indeed, as the very beginning of the Enlightenment.

Yet, Goethe's admiration for individual prominent Jews and the cultural achievements of Judaism did not prevent him from ignoring many contemporary Jews and objecting to their emancipation. He had no use for those Jews who led a miserable life as peddlers at the fairs or as junk handlers or beggars in the ghettos or on the highways. They were a disturbing element that did not fit into his picture of the world, and thus he simply forgot about them. He saw them but did not look at them. In this respect, he was similar to most middle-class people during the Enlightenment, who found it easier to praise the accomplishments of the old Hebrews from a historical-philosophical perspective than to occupy themselves with the legal and social position of the Jews living among them. An "Amelioration for the Civil Status of the Jews," as suggested by the Prussian civil servant Christian Dohm in 1781, never entered Goethe's mind.

Thus, it comes as no surprise that Goethe did not participate in the general tolerance and incipient emancipation debates, which after 1780 occupied the best minds of the Enlightenment. Only twice did he express an opinion on this subject in private letters and conversations — more out of curiosity or irritation than out of actual interest in the situation of the Jews. As a former citizen of Frankfurt he was interested in the social and political development of the city, particularly under Napoleon. Grand Duke Karl von Dalberg, installed by Napoleon, issued a new city ordinance for the Jews on 20 November 1807, which improved their situation somewhat in comparison with the old edict of 1616, and which corresponded roughly to the Toleration Edict of Joseph II. Goethe heard about this ordinance from his mother, who regularly provided him with news of Frankfurt, and also from Bettina Brentano. A philo-Semite by conviction, Brentano pressed him to comment on the new ordinance. Goethe, however, was less interested in the new laws for the Jews than in the discussion surrounding them by the "philanthropic Christians and Jews," as he mockingly referred to them. In the letters to his "dear little friend" he made fun of the "Humanitätssalbader" [sanctimonious representatives of humanity] among the pamphleteers and took sides with the opponents of emancipation.[5]

Thus, it was only logical that Goethe also rejected the "new Jewish law" issued fifteen years later by Duke Karl August of Saxe-Weimar, which Goethe had had no part in writing. In his diary the date 23 September 1823 has only a brief note: "Spent the evening with Kanzler von Müller; spoke about Christian and Jewish marriages, unpleasant conversation."[6] We know from the records of Kanzler von Müller that this conversation was about the new Jewish Edict in the grand duchy.

As he reported, Goethe expressed "his passionate anger over our new Jewish law."[7] One has to remember that Weimar did not even have a Jewish community in 1775, when Goethe moved there. The previously mentioned Jacob Elkan was the first protected Jew at the court, and even in 1808 there were only thirty-six Jews in Weimar. It was only after the Vienna Congress, when Weimar-Saxony became a grand duchy, that the Jewish population increased dramatically to 1,300, so that for the first time an edict for the Jews had to be enacted. The new edict for the Jews was a "Zwitter"[8] [hybrid] of old restrictions and new reforms. At any rate, it could not be compared with the Prussian Emancipation Edict of 1812.

Why such a surge of emotion, and to what is Goethe giving vent here? His anger was specifically directed against granting permission for mixed marriages between Christians and Jews, a point to which we will return later. Yet there was more behind it; namely, his fundamental rejection of emancipation, be it for the bourgeoisie, the nation, or the Jews. Goethe was, as is generally known, an opponent of the French Revolution; he distanced himself from the national pathos of the Wars of Liberation; and the emancipation of the Jews contradicted his class-oriented, patriarchal conception of society. In addition, the emancipation of the Jews was considered an idea of the French Revolution, thus something that originated outside Germany, and was also something that was implemented by edict against the will of the people. Both aspects displeased the *Geheimrat* [privy councilor].[9] Already in his letters to Bettina Brentano he expressed his hope that in the new city ordinance the "modern Israelites" would still be treated as "former imperial *Kammerknechte*," that is, as foreigners outside the traditional classes of society who should be put under the protection of the emperor. That attitude was, by 1807, anachronistic and is reminiscent of the medieval Jewish ordinances. Only individuals could emancipate themselves — through Bildung. The first people in Germany to understand that fact were a few Jewish intellectuals.

Here the story becomes problematic. It is not enough to record Goethe's indifference toward the Jews, his silence regarding the tolerance debate, and his rejection of Jewish emancipation; one must also consider those comments that are evidence of an anti-Jewish tendency. At least, that was the view not just of anti-Semites from Theodor Fritsch to Adolf Hitler, who made the greatest German poet into a witness for their ideology, but also, after 1945, the researchers of anti-Semitism from Léon Poliakov to Daniel Goldhagen, who see a consistent development of anti-Semitism in Germany from Luther's pamphlet

"Gegen die Juden und ihre Lügen" (Against the Lies of the Jews) to Hitler's "final solution." Goethe, they argue, belongs in this line-up as well.[10] Thus cornered, it is no surprise that even educated Goethe admirers believe that Goethe was "no friend of the Jews."[11] It is worthwhile to examine this issue more closely.

"Even Goethe is disgusted by the thought that, in the future, marriages of Christians and Jews should no longer be forbidden by law. Yet Goethe was by no means a reactionary or indeed a fanatic; what spoke through him was nothing other than the voice of blood and of reason."[12] Thus Hitler in *Mein Kampf,* using Goethe as a principal witness for his racial ideology. Goethe was, in fact, against the new edict of 1823 for the grand duchy of Weimar-Saxony, which permitted mixed marriages between Christians and Jews, and he called it "scandalous."[13] He later mentioned in conversation that he found the "new Jewish law" abhorrent, as any disrespect of religious beliefs would cause nothing but distress, "but I do not hate the Jews."[14] Goethe is hardly in agreement with Hitler, as he neither hates the Jews nor is thinking about a "voice of blood." He is simply against mixed marriages, like many of his contemporaries — including Jews — because they offend the religious beliefs of both parties and lead to religious conflicts between spouses. In addition, one should not forget that Christian church law still demanded that the Jewish spouse convert before the wedding and that the children be raised as Christians. These requirements were also part of the new Jewish law of 1823. The thoroughly conservative Goethe respected religious differences and insisted on rules that contributed to order and harmony in the state.[15] One can thus not classify him as a racist, and he was never an anti-Semite.

Léon Poliakov, though, has discovered in Goethe's writings evidence to the contrary.[16] He found a passage in *Wilhelm Meisters Wanderjahre* (Wilhelm Meister's Years of Travel, 1821–28) in which Jews are explicitly excluded from an emigration society. In the eleventh chapter of the third book Wilhelm has the philosophy of the *Auswandererbund* [emigration society] and the "American Utopia" explained to him by Friedrich. It is to be a Christian community that will not tolerate any Jews. "In this sense, which may perhaps be termed pedantic, but must be recognized as logical, we do not allow any Jew among us; for how are we to grant him participation in the highest culture, the origin and descent of which he denies?"[17] It is always dangerous to confuse literature and real life, and even more so here, where Poliakov uses fiction to judge reality in order to insinuate that Goethe was an anti-Semite. Poliakov does not even bother to prove his reproach with further research. One excerpt from Goethe's work suffices for him, as he assumes to know exactly who is an anti-Semite. Goethe is.[18] Yet this passage is an important marker in Goethe's works for the "denied emancipation of the Jews" (H. Mayer). Moses and Felix Mendelssohn, Rahel Levin, all the women who admired Goethe — indeed, all of the prominent Jews whom Goethe met in the course of his life — seem to be forgotten here. Goethe's social utopia of the *Years of Travel* is supposed to be a community of the most outstanding people joined together for the welfare of humanity, yet the most outstanding Jews of his time are to be shut out of this community, and that at a time when they — drawn by Goethe's works — were already assimilating themselves into the educated upper middle classes. That is indeed pedantic, if not inhumane, and denies the spirit of the Enlightenment.

Poliakov, however, did not read the *Years of Travel* thoroughly enough, or else he would have noticed another, more ambivalent passage. In the *Pädagogische Provinz* [pedagogical province] Wilhelm is led into a gallery in which the contents of "the holy books of the Israelites" are depicted. Wilhelm is surprised that the "Israelite people are shown the honor" of being the model for this portrayal of religious history. In reply, the elder informs him:

> The Jewish nation has never been worth much, as it has been a thousand times reproached by its leaders, judges, principal men and prophets; it possesses few of the virtues and most of the faults of other nations but on independence, firmness, bravery, and if all that is not of real value, we must look for its equal in tenacity. It is the most persistent nation in the world; it is, it was, and it will be for the glorification of the name of Jehovah through all times. We have, therefore, set it forth as a model, as a principal picture for which the others only serve as frames.[19]

Here we see the aforementioned historical-philosophical perspective, which allowed Goethe to praise the people of the Covenant as exemplary and to simultaneously attest that they "have never been worth much." However, he admires the "tenacity" of this people, that not only was but will be — up to and during Goethe's era. In the *Pädagogische Provinz*, that ideal temple of tolerance, the Jews are transfigured into a "model," whereas they are later excluded from the American utopia. This is just one of the many contradictions in Goethe's relationship to the Jews that needs to be considered. This passage, though, does not fit Poliakov's picture of Goethe the anti-Semite.

These and similar excerpts do not suffice, however, to explain Goethe's ambivalent relationship to the Jews of his time. The roots of Goethe's anti-Jewish sentiments go much deeper, belong, indeed, to Goethe's early childhood experiences. One needs to consider Goethe's autobiography, *Dichtung and Wahrheit* (Poetry and Truth, 1811–22). Goethe's famous description of the Frankfurt ghetto achieves its particular fascination by virtue of being a memory of the then over sixty-year-old author. There is a recognizable tension between the remembered childhood experience and the remembering *I* of the autobiography. From a remembered experience springs a harmonizing description:

> Among the things which aroused the forebodings of the boy and even of the youth was especially the Jewish quarter of the city, properly called the Jewish street, as it consisted of little more than one single street, which in earlier times may have been hemmed in between the walls and trenches of the town, as in a prison. The narrowness, the dust, the crowd, the accent of an unpleasing speech, altogether made a most disagreeable impression, if one only looked in on passing by the gate. It was a long time before I ventured in alone, and I did not readily return again when I had once escaped the importunities of so many men never tired of demanding money and offering to traffic. At the same time, there hovered gloomily before my young spirit the old legends of the cruelty of the Jews to Christian children, which we had seen horribly depicted in Gottfried's chronicles. Although in modern times they were thought better of, the large caricatures, still to be seen to their disgrace on an arched wall under the bridge tower, still bore witness against them extraordinarily, for it had been made, not through private ill-will, but by public order.[20]

This is possibly the most interesting passage about Jews in Goethe's works. It depicts the first meeting of the boy with a world completely foreign to him, which is "hemmed in" on the edge of his familiar hometown "between the walls and trenches of the town." The opposites of bourgeois security and ghetto chaos collide with each other here, and the ghetto wall (here, the gate) marks the visible border between bourgeoisie and ghetto society, between Enlightenment and Middle Ages. This foreign and incomprehensible world is perceived at first from outside, "passing by the gate." What the boy sees is solely "the narrowness, the dust, the crowd" of the dark, overcrowded ghetto; what he hears is "the accent of an unpleasing speech," the incomprehensible "Jewish German," as Goethe later called it. "Altogether [it] made a most disagreeable impression." The fear of this foreign and baffling neighborhood, which was so close to his own safe and secure home, transforms itself into an aversion to the Jews. It only gets worse when he dares to enter the grim *Judengasse* [Jewish street] with its obtrusive, haggling figures. The terrifying impression of this foreign world, so incommensurable with his own, leads to the resolution "not to readily return again."

The anti-Jewish reflex, experienced physically, is then overtaken by the imagination and its dreadful images, which the boy knows from Gottfried's *Historische Chronica:* "At the same time, there hovered gloomily before my young spirit the old legends of the cruelty of the Jews to Christian children." Goethe is referring here to a picture in the *Historische Chronica* that shows the Jews engaged in a ritual murder of a young boy whom they have tied to a cross.[21] The anxiety in the face of the frightening transforms itself into an aversion to the Jews, explained here by the popular hatred of the Jews in medieval times. This passage makes shockingly clear how much the Christian environment had already shaped Goethe before he discovered for himself who the Jews actually were. The vignette is completed by the mention of the "Spott- und Schandgemälde" [large murals on the wall of the bridge tower that pilloried the Jews] that "had been made by public order," thus legitimizing the boy's displeasure. Mark Waldman has identified the picture as the work of a painter named Sebold from the middle of the seventeenth century, and as the source he cites Schudt's *Jüdische Merkwürdigkeiten*[22] [Jewish Peculiarities]. It is a double image: on the upper edge is, again, a reference to the horror story of Jewish ritual murder, and under that is a variation on the common motif of a so-called Jewish sow. Grouped around it are four Jewish men and a Jewish woman, all of whom are engaged with the sow in a most disgusting manner, one sucking on her teats, another eating her excrement, and a third riding on her back. A fourth is depicted with horns, identifying him as a Jewish devil. That this public painting of medieval anti-Jewish propaganda should have made such a deep impression on the boy, so that he did not dare venture into the Jewish street for a long time, is not particularly surprising. Yet the author now distances himself from this anti-Jewish propaganda by referring to it as a "caricature."

"Although in modern times they were thought better of," Goethe continues, the free imperial city of Frankfurt was still hostile to Jews in the second half of the eighteenth century, and this hostility sublimated itself in the mind of the young Goethe. This is, in fact, how Goethe saw it when he discussed with the Prague banker Simon von Lämel in Karlsbad in 1811 what he had recently recorded in *Poetry and Truth* about his earliest impressions of his youth in Frankfurt. Here, though, he adds to the earlier observation a psycho-sociological explanation that compels one to take notice: "that aversion to the Jews which stirred in me in my early youth was more a nervousness in the face of the enigmatic and the unsightly. The contempt that certainly arose in me was more the reflex of the Christian men and women surrounding me."[23] Not young Goethe but the Frankfurt society was of an anti-Jewish mindset, which rubbed off on him. This, in any case, is how he would like to depict himself in conversation with a Jew. However one reads this self-interpretation, it makes clear that his memories were fossilized historical deposits in his subconscious and that they formed Goethe's image of the Jews.

In keeping with the style of Goethe's autobiography, he primarily observes, describes, and depicts, but rarely analyzes. The remembering *I* encounters the world from a distance, reconstructs its surroundings, and examines through description. This is also the case in this passage, which at first glance hardly seems to be hostile to the Jews. For him, the Jewish ghetto is, in the distance of memory, primarily an aesthetic experience. He perceives it with all of his senses and is disgusted by the dirt, the crowds, and the unintelligibility, all of which contradict his sense of order and his need for harmony. His anxiety in the face of the foreign and the mysterious changes into an aversion to Jews, yet without judging them, for he could only do so if he reflected on his own sensory impressions. Like a veil, the aesthetic experience covers the unsightly. Thus, it remains entirely the other, the enigmatic and the incommensurable. But Goethe, being who he is, immediately followed his first, negative memory with another, followed dislike with admiration. Here is the continuation of the quoted passage:

> Meanwhile, they, nevertheless, remained the chosen people of God, and passed, however it came about, as a memorial of the most ancient times. Besides, they were human beings too; as men they were active and affable, and he could not deny respect to the tenacity with which they clung to their customs. Furthermore, the girls were pretty, and were quite pleased if a Christian lad showed himself friendly and attentive to them on the Sabbath in the Fischerfeld. I was therefore extremely curious to get to know about their ceremonies. I did not rest till I had often visited their synagogue, attended a circumcision and a wedding, and had formed a picture to myself of the Feast of Tabernacles. Everywhere I was well received, excellently entertained and invited to come again, for they were persons of influence who had either introduced or recommended me.[24]

Here the self-reflection of the author begins, and he amends his memory and his hostile impulses. The chain of qualifying conjunctions meant to adjust the negative image is itself interesting. "Meanwhile," the Jews "remained the chosen people," who remind us of the "most ancient times," which contributed to their esteem since the Enlightenment. "Besides," the Jews are "human beings, too" a simple statement that belonged to the Enlightenment's basic demand for tolerance and led to the discussion about human rights of the Jews. "Furthermore, the girls were pretty," a conclusion made with shy admiration. The pretty Jewish girls here, however, are also the desired object of a forbidden passion. In the end, he wants to understand the mystery of the Jews by "learning about their ceremonies." The Jews as people do not interest him, but their religious customs do. And on top of that, they are good hosts. But they are, of course, also protected Jews of Frankfurt, on whom Goethe can impose, "persons of influence who had either introduced or recommended me." Protection and power are bound together here, so that Goethe can inform himself about Jewish customs and about Judaism without himself being infringed upon. That is the feat of Goethe's ethnological curiosity: he approaches the foreign without needing or wanting to integrate it.[25]

This text can be seen as symptomatic of Goethe's attitude to the Jews, as it combines in the fiction of autobiography the remembered *I* of his Frankfurt youth with the reflection of a sixty-year-old. In between are many observations of Goethe's, partly literary, partly personal, almost all of which are evidence of the same ambivalence. The Jewish masses as he had experienced them in the Frankfurt ghetto remained foreign to him at best and an object of contempt at worst. Thus, it can hardly come as a surprise that Goethe was not interested in the emancipation of the Jews and basically rejected it. His early dislike of the Jews, which still stood under the influence of his Christian upbringing, was perhaps transformed into respect when he later "met many intellectually gifted, sensitive men of this tribe."[26] Yet his admiration for individual prominent Jews and for the cultural achievements of Judaism did not prevent him from scorning the masses of Jews and rejecting the idea of their emancipation. This ambivalent stance does not make him an anti-Semite. Chauvinism and hate toward other nations were foreign to Goethe; he decried religious intolerance and mockery of the Jews; and he knew no racism. But his indifference, which was so typical of many of his contemporaries, also contributed nothing toward the improvement of the Jews' situation nor toward their acceptance in society. In contrast, Lessing made Nathan into a spokesman for religious tolerance, Dohm developed practical reform suggestions to achieve a "Civil Amelioration for the Jews," Mendelssohn struggled for basic human rights for the Jews, and Wilhelm von Humboldt spoke out in favor of the unrestricted emancipation of the Jews, which (temporarily) became a reality in Prussia in 1812. Goethe, however, remained silent on all of this, as well as during the "Hep-Hep" pogroms in 1819. This silence of Goethe is perhaps more significant than much of what he wrote about the Jews.

Translated by Sara B. Young

Notes

[1] The topic of Goethe and the Jews has been thoroughly researched, and one can hardly expect to still be making new discoveries. A brief overview of the research undertaken thus far is offered by Norbert Oellers, "Goethe and Schiller in ihrem Verhältnis zum Judentum," *Conditio Judaica* I, ed. Otto Horch and Horst Denkler (Tübingen: Niemeyer, 1988) 110–13. The best collections of material can be found in Ludwig Geiger, *Deutsche Literatur und die Juden* (Berlin: Reimer, 1910) 81–101; Alfred D. Low, *Jews in the Eyes of the Germans* (Philadelphia: Institute for the Study of Human Issues, 1979) 67–86; and Günter Hartung, "Goethe and die Juden," *Weimarer Beiträge* 40.3 (1994): 398–416; abbreviated version in *Goethe Handbuch*, ed. Bernd Witte et al. (Stuttgart: Metzler, 1988) 4: 581–89. The most comprehensive apology is Mark Waldman's *Goethe and the Jews: A Challenge to Hitlerism* (New York: G. P. Putnam's Sons, 1934). Almost all of these representations, however, suffer from an apologetic tone, which will be countered here with a more critical approach.

[2] Goethe, "Maximen und Reflexionen Nr. 151," *Goethes Werke*, ed. Erich Trunz (Hamburg: Wegner, 1950) 12: 385.

[3] A list of all the Jews with whom Goethe associated over the course of his life can be found in Alfred D. Low, *Jews in the Eyes of the Germans* 79–84.

[4] *Briefwechsel zwischen Goethe and Zelter* (Berlin: Duncker & Humblodt, 1834) 2: 21 (19 May 1812).

[5] Goethe's letters to Bettina Brentano, 24 February and 3 and 20 April 1808. Compare this with Bettina's completely different perspective in her book *Goethes Briefwechsel mit einem Kinde* (Berlin: Dümmler, 1835). The new city ordinance was rescinded by the Frankfurt City Council after 1815.

[6] *Weimarer Ausgabe* 3.9: 120.

[7] Conversation with Friedrich von Müller on 23 September 1823, in Goethe, *Die letzten Jahre: Briefe, Tagebücher and Gespräche von 1823 bis zu Goethes Tod* (Frankfurt: Deutscher Klassikerverlag, 1993) 1: 112 ff.

[8] Eva Schmidt, *Jüdische Familien im Weimar der Klassik and Nachklassik* (Weimar: Stadtmuseum, 1993) 7–12.

[9] Particularly harsh is Goethe's comment to Müller that "foreign countries obviously believed in bribery" and that he suspected "that the omnipotent Rothschild was behind it" (see note 7). More than ten years after the Prussian Emancipation Edict and many similar laws, Goethe suspected Jewish forces at work behind the new law, which did not even fully emancipate the Jews living in the grand duchy.

[10] Mark Waldman and Alfred Low took it upon themselves to collect all the passages in Goethe's works, letters, and conversations in which Jews are mentioned, in an attempt to free Germany's greatest poet from the stranglehold of the anti-Semites. Their convincing apologies would be effective if they had not whitewashed Goethe's ambivalent relationship to the Jews.

[11] Oellers (n. 1) 121.

[12] Adolf Hitler, *Mein Kampf* (Munich: Franz Eher, 1942) 341.

[13] Goethe's conversation with Kanzler Fr. v. Müller on 23 September 1823. Goethe (n. 7) 113.

[14] Wolfgang Bode, *Goethe: Meine Religion, mein politischer Glaube* (Berlin: Mittler, 1899) 69.

[15] Obviously, Goethe did not oppose the mixed marriages of the Meyer sisters or Rahel Levin, who were also nobilitated, but only after being baptized. Goethe, who was fundamentally against mixed marriages and conversion, made exceptions here — one of his many inconsistencies.

[16] Léon Poliakov, *The History of Anti-Semitism* (New York: Vanguard Press, 1975) 3: 162.

[17] Goethe, *Goethes Werke,* ed. Erich Trunz, 8: 405. English translation: *Wilhelm Meister's Apprenticeship and Travels,* trans. R. O. Moon (London: Foulis, 1947) 2: 277.

[18] Later, Poliakov states, as if it were self-evident, "Even more than the poets (such as Herder or Goethe), the great philosophers polemicized against the 'Chosen People'" ([n. 16], 183).

[19] Goethe, (n. 17) 8: 159–60. English: Moon (n. 17) 2: 114.

[20] Goethe (n. 17) 9: 149–50. English: *Poetry and Truth: From My Own Life,* trans R. O. Moon (Washington, D.C.: Public Affairs Press, 1949) 125.

[21] Joh. Ludov. Gottfridi, *Historische Chronica oder Beschreibung der fürnehmsten Geschichten so sich von Anfang der Welt bis auf das Jahr Christi 1619*

zugetragen (Frankfurt: Matthaeum Merianum, 1710) 689. This chronicle was part of the library of Goethe's father, along with other anti-Jewish publications, such as Johann Andreas Eisenmenger, *Entdecktes Judenthum* (1711) and Johann Jacob Schudt, *Jüdische Merkwürdigkeiten samt einer vollständigen Franckfurter Juden-Chronick* (1717).

[22] Waldman (n. 1) 52–53.

[23] Goethe, *Gedenkausgabe der Werke: Briefe and Gespräche,* ed. Ernst Beutler (Zurich: Artemis Verlag, 1948–54) 22: 875. See also Heinrich Teweles, *Goethe und die Juden* (Hamburg: Gente, 1925) 88–92.

[24] Goethe (n. 17) 9: 150. English: Moon (n. 20) 125–26.

[25] Generally, the Goethe apologists cite a different passage from Goethe's *Dichtung und Wahrheit* to demonstrate how active and unbiased Goethe was in his support for the Jews. They use the episode of the fire in the Frankfurt ghetto (1774), when the young Goethe organized the firefighting operations and protected the fleeing Jews from the ridicule of "malicious boys" (Goethe [n. 17], 10: 83 ff.). For Teweles it is an example of Goethe's motto, "Man is honorable, helpful, and good" ([n. 23] 57–58). Low sees it as conclusive proof of Goethe's attitude towards the Jews of his day ([n. 1] 86). Yet one should not place too much value on this small heroic deed of the young Goethe, as it actually belongs to the numerous heroic stylizations of his autobiography. Rather, it indicates a different personality trait of Goethe's, that he did not tolerate derision or injustice.

[26] Bode (n. 14) 6.

Goethe and the Concept of Bildung in Jewish Emancipation

Ehrhard Bahr
University of California-Los Angeles

ONE OF THE COMMONPLACES of German-Jewish history is the assumption that Goethe's concept of Bildung effected Jewish emancipation from the eighteenth to the twentieth centuries. The *locus classicus* of this assumption is George L. Mosse's statement in his *German Jews beyond Judaism* of 1985, where he says that for German Jews

> Goethe fulfilled an . . . important function. His . . . emphasis on individual freedom, his ambivalence towards all forms of nationalism, and, finally his belief in Bildung seemed to foster Jewish assimilation. More important, . . . Goethe was the embodiment of the ideal *Bildungsbürger* of the period of Jewish emancipation.[1]

Bildung, as Mosse puts it, "transcended all differences of nationality and religion through the unfolding of the individual personality."[2] It was, therefore, "an ideal," as Steven Aschheim has commented, "perfectly suited to the requirements of Jewish integration and acculturation . . . rendering it the animating ideal of modern German Jewry."[3] This may be true for German Jews since 1870, when Goethe's concept of Bildung was promulgated by Wilhelm Dilthey, who introduced the term Bildungsroman; by Albert Bielschowsky in his Goethe biography; and by a surge in public opinion establishing Goethe as a national figure next to Bismarck. On the last pages of his highly popular Goethe biography Bielschowsky declared: "Without Goethe no Bismarck! Without Goethe no German Reich!"[4] During this time Goethe scholarship was established as a national enterprise. A German Goethe Society was founded in 1885, Goethe's house in Weimar was opened to the public as the Goethe National Museum in 1886, the Goethe-Schiller Archives were completed in 1896, and the first volumes of the edition of Goethe's collected works, authorized by Grand Duchess Sophia of Saxe-Weimar, appeared in 1885. Jewish scholars participated in great numbers in these ventures. Three of the most successful Goethe biographies between 1896 and 1916 were by Jewish authors: Albert Bielschowsky, Georg Simmel, and Friedrich Gundolf. This is well documented by previous research[5] and forms the basis of Mosse's paradigm. But the Goethe admiration of these years cannot be applied to the period before 1870.

Although there were the beginnings of a Goethe cult, initiated by Rahel Levin,[6] and although there was appreciation of Goethe by Jewish authors, such as Berthold Auerbach, there is not enough evidence to support Mosse's thesis. Except for the period after 1870 and for the Weimar Republic, when the connection between Bildung and Jewishness was especially strong, Mosse's paradigm needs to be revised. Only few historians have challenged it, such as Steven Aschheim, Paul Mendes-Flohr, and Shulamit Volkov, but most have supported Mosse's point of view as "essentially valid."[7]

My counterarguments are, first, Goethe's ambivalent stance toward Jews and Jewish emancipation, and, second, the use of the term Bildung in the writings of Moses Mendelssohn and the *maskilim*. Instead of tying Bildung, as it effected Jewish emancipation, to Goethe, Schiller, and Wilhelm von Humboldt, the concept needs to be related to Mendelssohn's Enlightenment essay of 1784 and to the tradition that it formed. Scholarship has neglected to notice that the term Bildung pervaded Mendelssohn's essay and that there was an educational-reform movement in its wake that founded schools that educated Jewish students to become members of the dominant culture in terms of Bildung. The most important were the Freyschule [Free School] in Berlin and the Marks-Haindorf-School in Münster in Westphalia, but there were others. These schools were designed to teach Jewish students a kind of Bildung that trained them for employment and prepared them for citizenship in the states of Germany. Bildung in this context had a much more pragmatic connotation but probably did more for Jewish emancipation than the Goethean concept of Bildung.

There is perhaps no better way to pay homage to George Mosse than to challenge one of the basic tenets of his scholarship, and perhaps no better place to do so than here at the University of Wisconsin, where he taught. I was particularly moved by a recent obituary by Walter Laqueur, who said that Mosse was "one of the greatest teachers, perhaps the best known internationally and certainly one of the most beloved,"[8] and I am happy to dedicate my contribution to his memory.

To return to my first argument: Goethe's ambivalent attitude to Jews. He loved and cherished the Jews of the Bible. Its patriarchs, prophets, and kings provided the protagonists for his plays from the puppet theater to his *Faust* drama. Job and Moses served as models for Faust. Goethe's autobiography, *Dichtung und Wahrheit* (Poetry and Truth, 1811–22), contains a long passage in which he retells the story of the Bible from Abraham to Joseph. He justified this exercise by calling the Bible his refuge from daily events and from his overactive imagination:

> I would steep myself in the first books of Moses, and there, amidst the widespread tribes of herdsmen, find myself both in greatest solitude and greatest company. (SE 4: 113)[9]

> [Ich versenkte mich in die ersten Bücher Moses und fand mich dort unter den ausgebreiteten Hirtenstämmen zugleich in der größten Einsamkeit und in der größten Gesellschaft.] (HA 9: 140)[10]

The Old Testament in Luther's translation was not only his refuge but also the treasure house for his imagination, as well as for his style. He quoted twice as much from the Old Testament as he did from the New Testament.

But in his contacts with the population of the Frankfurt ghetto Goethe displayed a clearly ethnocentric attitude, as we can see from his autobiography. His description included all the clichés of eighteenth-century anti-Judaism, including blood libel:

> [The ghetto's] narrowness, filth, the swarms of people, the disagreeable sound of their accent — all of it together made the most unpleasant impression, even if one only looked in at the gate while passing by. It was a long time before I ventured to go in alone and, once I had escaped the importunities of all those people persistently demanding or offering something to haggle over, I was not eager to return. Also some old tales hovered darkly before my young mind about the Jews' cruelty to Christian children. (SE 4: 119)

> [Die Enge, der Schmutz, das Gewimmel, der Akzent einer unerfreulichen Sprache, alles zusammen machte den unangenehmen Eindruck, wenn man auch nur am Tore vorbeigehend hineinsah. Es dauerte lange, bis allein ich mich hineinwagte, und ich kehrte nicht leicht wieder dahin zurück, wenn ich einmal den Zudringlichkeiten so vieler, etwas zu schachern, unermüdet fordernder oder anbietender Menschen entgangen war. Dabei schwebten die alten Märchen von Grausamkeit der Juden gegen die Christenkinder düster vor dem jungen Gemüt.] (HA 9: 149–50)

Although Goethe conceded in the same paragraph that they were "God's chosen people" and paid his respect to their observance of old customs, his gaze at pretty young girls on the Sabbath reveals an attitude that we would call "colonial" today. He addressed himself as "a Christian boy" whose "friendly attention" to the Jewish girls was well received. The young Goethe attended some of the Jewish religious ceremonies and holiday celebrations, but his perspective was at best that of an Orientalist visiting a region of his study.

His relationship to Jews during the rest of his life was distant, if not cool, with the exception of Felix Mendelssohn-Bartholdy, Rahel Levin, and some of his rich admirers in the Bohemian spas. As an administrator in Saxe-Weimar he was reluctant to support Jewish emancipation if not downright opposed to it. When the city of Frankfurt passed legislation to grant some civil rights to the Jews in 1807, Goethe reacted with sarcastic remarks in his letters to Bettina Brentano in 1808. In 1816 he expressed his support of an old Jena regulation that did not allow Jews to spend the night in the city, although this opinion was not voiced in a public document but, again, in a private letter, this one addressed to Sulpiz Boisserée (24 June 1816). In 1823, when Goethe was informed of the passage of a law that allowed marriages between Jews and Christians, he asked Chancellor von Müller whether Saxe-Weimar should "take the lead in such absurd [innovations] and be the first to test every grotesque [new regulation]" [Wollen wird denn überall im *Absurden* vorausgehen, alles Fratzenhafte zuerst probieren?] (23 September 1823).

Avi Primor, Israel's ambassador to Germany until 1999, was more than generous in his appraisal of Goethe's attitude when he suggested before the members of the Goethe Society in Weimar that Goethe perhaps wanted the Jews first to become a people in their own right before they could be recognized as such, thus making Goethe virtually a forerunner of Theodor Herzl. He may have had in mind Goethe's early review in the *Frankfurter Gelehrte Anzeigen* of the German poems of a Polish Jew of 1772 that he found rather conventional. But the review contains a message in its final sentence that may be read in the sense of Zionism *avant le lettre*. "We hope to meet him again," Goethe wrote, expressing the hope that he might find in the Polish Jew at a later date a "more spiritual [state of mind] on the paths on which we seek to find our ideal" (WA I 37: 225). But such a reading is perhaps too generous to be true. To be sure, Goethe was not the anti-Semite that Houston Stewart Chamberlain made him out to be in his biography of 1912, but it would not be historically accurate to call him a champion of Jewish emancipation. As far as the affairs of state of Saxe-Weimar were concerned, Goethe was a pragmatic conservative who probably wanted to wait and see how the emancipation of Jews was going to work out in other German states before it was introduced at home.

Looking at Goethe's works, the most contradictory evidence comes from his last novel, *Wilhelm Meisters Wanderjahre* (*Wilhelm Meister's Journeyman Years*) of 1829. On the one hand, there is the sanctuary in the Pedagogic Province, which contains paintings of scenes from the Old Testament. The reason for their inclusion, as explained by one of the guides, consists, however, of some backhanded compliments, such as the following:

> The people of Israel were never worth much, as it was thousand times admonished by its leaders, judges, chiefs, and prophets. It possesses few virtues and most of the faults of other peoples. But in self-reliance, constancy, bravery, and . . . in tenacity, it has no equal. It is the most persistent people on earth; it is, it was, and it shall be, that it may glorify the name of Jehovah through the ages. That is why we have presented it here as a model, as the central subject, which the others only serve to frame. (SE 10: 207)

But for the speaker of the Pedagogic Province, Judaism is a "pagan religion," and what he admires most about it is its "tenacity" [*Zäheit*]. The other paintings mentioned in the novel present scenes from Jewish history after the destruction of the Temple and from the miracles and parables of Jesus. The innermost part of the sanctuary is dedicated to the crucifixion of Christ, but this part is not accessible to the students or the protagonist. Although the hierarchy of images is clearly Christian, the relegation of the crucifixion to a closed-off area of the sanctuary is contrary to Christian practice and is consistent only with the philosophy of religion of the Enlightenment.

On the other hand, there is the American Utopia in *Wilhelm Meisters Wanderjahre,* a blueprint for a settlement in America that expressly excludes Jews with special reference to their opposition to Christianity: "We tolerate no Jews among us. How can we grant them participation in the higher culture when they repudiate its origin and source?" (SE 10: 378). Although the text is clearly marked as unreliable within the novel and cannot be identified with Goethe's personal opinion, it nevertheless reflects the opposition to Jewish emancipation during the 1820s. It raises the question why Goethe chose to include this text in his "archival novel" without any explanation. This question has engendered a heated debate in Goethe scholarship in recent years.[11]

In conclusion, neither Goethe's life nor his works offered enough clear examples to reassure Jewish readers. Schiller was more popular among them than Goethe. In spite of his enthusiastic acceptance after 1870, we have to acknowledge that Goethe's stance was ambiguous at best, although some of the most recent research tends to be defensive or apologetic (Günter Hartung, Norbert Oellers).

Our second counterargument concerns the Berlin Enlightenment and its vision of Jewish emancipation, as expressed by Christian Wilhelm Dohm and by Moses Mendelssohn in his famous essay on enlightenment. Dohm's historic treatise *Über die bürgerliche Verbesserung der Juden* (On the Civic Improvement of the Jews, 1781) introduced the idea of Jewish emancipation to Germany.[12] Based on a memorandum written by Dohm in French at the request of the Alsatian Jewry, it established the basis of the emancipation discourse in Germany. The Alsatian Jews had first approached Mendelssohn to argue their case; but he turned this request over to Dohm, whom he advised regarding the basic conception of the memorandum. The significance of the German treatise for our argument is the fact that we find the term *Bildung* used here synonymously with "education." In his postscript to the second edition Dohm wrote that he

> would consider [himself] happy, if [his] treatise should contribute even within the next fifty years to the improvement of the misery of an unfortunate people as well as to the kind of Bildung of new and useful citizens that is beneficial to all states. [no pagination]

> [Glücklich werde [er sich] schätzen, wenn auch erst nach einem halben Jahrhundert [seine] Schrift zur Erleichterung des Elends eines unglücklichen Volks und zu der für alle Staaten wohlthätigen Bildung neuer und nützlicher Bürger mitwirken sollte.]

Dohm talked about the "moral Bildung" of the Jews who took care of their own poor so that nowhere had they become a burden to the state (103, cf. 115). Again and again he repeated that the goal of his treatise was "to educate the Jews [who had been corrupted by the conditions of trade] to become better human beings and useful citizens" [die Juden zu bessern Menschen und nützlichen Bürgern zu bilden] (117). The word he used was *bilden*, the verb corresponding to the noun *Bildung*. Dohm recommended that all the arts and sciences be open to the individual Jew, so that "he could train [*ausbilden*] his intellect as far as he could" [auch muß er seinen Geist, so weit er vermag, ausbilden] (126). Here the verb takes the meaning "to train." Dohm made it the special business of wise government "to take care of the moral Bildung and enlightenment of the Jews" [ein besondres angelegnes Geschäft einer weisen Regierung ... für die sittliche Bildung und Aufklärung der Juden zu sorgen] (128).

Mendelssohn's essay "Über die Frage: Was ist Aufklärung?" (On the Question: What Is Enlightenment?), appeared in the *Berlinische Monatsschrift* of September 1784. It was written in response to the rhetorical question about the meaning of enlightenment raised in a footnote by Johann Friedrich Zöllner, a Protestant minister writing against the institution of civil marriage in the *Berlinische Monatsschrift* of December 1783. Surprisingly, Mendelssohn introduced Bildung as his central concept, while he relegated "enlightenment" and "culture" to the status of subcategories. "Bildung is composed of culture and enlightenment" [Bildung zerfällt in Kultur und Aufklärung], he said. Defining the subcategories, he declared:

> Culture appears to be more oriented toward *practical matters*: (objectively) toward goodness, refinement, and beauty in the arts and social mores; (subjectively) toward facility, diligence, and dexterity in the arts and inclinations, dispositions and habits in social mores. . . . *Enlightenment,* in contrast, seems to be more related to *theoretical matters:* to (objective) rational knowledge and to (subjective) facility in rational reflection about matters of human life, according to their importance and influence on the destiny of man.[13]

> [*Jene* (Kultur) scheint mehr auf das *Praktische* zu gehen: auf Güte, Feinheit und Schönheit in Handwerken, Künsten und Geselligkeiten (objektive); auf Fertigkeit, Fleiß in jenen, Neigungen, Triebe und Gewohnheiten in diesen (subjektive). . . . *Aufklärung* hingegen scheinet sich mehr auf das *Theoretische* zu beziehen. Auf vernünftige Erkenntnis (objekt.) und Fertigkeit (subj.) zum vernünftigen Nachdenken über Dinge des menschlichen Lebens nach Maßgebung ihrer Wichtigkeit und ihres Einflusses in die Bestimmung des Menschen.[14]]

Relating "enlightenment" teleologically to the destiny of man, Mendelssohn put the main emphasis within the subcategories on "enlightenment" and not on "culture." "Man as *human being* needs no culture, but he needs *enlightenment,*" Mendelssohn declared, arguing that the enlightenment that is concerned with man as a human being is "universal, without distinction of status."[15] He fully realized that the "universal enlightenment" of man could come into conflict with his enlightenment as citizen but felt confident that it was possible to develop rules and regulations to avoid such conflicts and make exceptions.

At the end of the article Mendelssohn returned to Bildung that is achieved when "enlightenment and culture go forward hand in hand."

He considered the "Bildung of a nation" the highest goal to be achieved.

Since the concept of nation was still in flux during the late eighteenth century and was applied to any group with a common origin, we may conclude that Bildung as culture as well as enlightenment was a central concept for Jewish emancipation during that period, which saw the beginning of Jewish secular education. Jewish elementary, vocational, and secondary schools founded in the late eighteenth and early nineteenth centuries were most important in applying Bildung in its practical as well as theoretical aspects. For the sake of our argument, I identify this as the Mendelssohnian concept of Bildung, as opposed to the Goethean, and define it as a combination of the practical aspects, i.e., culture, with the theoretical, i.e., enlightenment. While Alexander Altmann, the dean of Mendelssohn scholarship, saw Mendelssohn's concept of Bildung later refined by Herder and Goethe,[16] I prefer to identify it as a separate tradition, effective during the nineteenth century and basically untouched by the Herderian or Goethean concepts of Bildung until the 1870s.

The first school, based on Mendelssohn's concept of Bildung, was the Freyschule in Berlin, established by Isaak Daniel Itzig and David Friedländer in 1778. As the name indicated, it offered free tuition. Its educational goals were to train the poor in skills to gain employment — bookkeeping, for example — and to teach them, in addition to Hebrew, German and French, as the current languages of the dominant society. Friedländer wrote a textbook *Lesebuch für Jüdische Kinder — Zum Besten der jüdischen Freyschule* (Reader for Jewish Children — For the Benefit of the Jewish Free School, 1779), which contained material provided by Mendelssohn (Shavit 107–20).[17] Breslau followed the Berlin example with the Wilhelm School in 1791, Dessau with the Franz School in 1799, Seesen with the Jacobson School in 1801, Frankfurt/ Main with the Philanthropin in 1804, and Wolfenbüttel with the Sampson School in 1807.[18] Finally, there was the Marks-Haindorf School of 1825 in Münster. All of these schools were founded by *maskilim* and propagated Bildung in its practical and theoretical aspects, ranging from vocational training to preparing students for the university. David Sorkin devoted a chapter to this movement in his *The Transformation of German Jewry, 1780–1840* (1987).[19] Julia Prestel followed with a book on the Jewish schools and Jewish educational system in Bavaria from 1804 to 1933 in 1989, and in 1997 Susanne Freund published her monograph on the Marks-Haindorf-Foundation in Münster. Alexander Haindorf, a Jewish doctor, founded the Marks-

Haindorf School in Westphalia in 1825 as a vocational school to train students for a craft, but later it also included an elementary school and a teachers' training college. The school's educational philosophy was based on the concepts of the reform school developed by Mendelssohn and his followers. The elementary school had a curriculum similar to that of the Freyschule. Haindorf believed in Bildung as the proper tool to achieve acceptance by the dominant society and called this process "amalgamation." He was confident that his final goal would be reached "on the opportune path of Bildung."[20] Opposed to total assimilation, Haindorf saw Jewish tradition complementing the dominant culture:

> If diverse culture is desirable for the Bildung of individuals, then it is also necessary for nations, insofar as their development takes the same course through space and time. Therefore, it should not be unprofitable to replant foreign culture on domestic soil and to enlarge the sum of the domestic culture by the foreign [culture].[21]

> [Ist vielseitige Cultur für die Bildung der Individuen Bedürfnis und Drang; so ist sie es auch für Nationen, in so fern diese im grössern Raum- und Zeitverhältnissen dieselbe Bahn der Entwickelung zu durchlaufen haben. Immer dürfte es daher nicht unverdienstlich seyn, auswärtige Cultur auf vaterländischen Boden zu verpflanzen, und die Summe des Einheimischen durch das Fremde zu vermehren.]

The language of the educational programs of these schools usually contained the concept of Bildung in the Mendelssohnian sense. It remains for future research to do a systematic study of the educational philosophy of these institutions. In my opinion, the achievement of these schools in terms of Bildung and its impact on Jewish emancipation cannot be overestimated, but I believe that this education was guided by the Mendelssohnian concept of Bildung, not the Goethean, and that "Mendelssohn's understanding of Bildung," as David Sorkin declared, formed "the basis" of the Jewish "claim to emancipation."[22] I am in full agreement with Sorkin on this point.

Statistics are available to confirm the success of Mendelssohnian Bildung. By attending schools and universities, Jewish men made use of "the alliance of the intelligentsia and the state through the university."[23] In this respect, one could argue that Mendelssohn's and Wilhelm von Humboldt's concepts converged. The result was, as Marion Kaplan observed, that

> by the 1840s Jewish men were twice as heavily represented in the universities as their proportion of the population. The Jewish student population grew rapidly. By 1886, Jews in Prussia were eight times as

heavily represented as their proportion of the population and made up 10 percent of all students.[24]

In this context it is not surprising that George L. Mosse does not quote either Mendelssohn or Dohm. Both of their names are absent from his *German Jews beyond Judaism*. As he said,

> Jews were emancipated at a time in German history when what we might call "high culture" was becoming an integral part of both German citizenship and the Enlightenment. The word *Bildung* combines the meaning carried by the English word "education" with notions of character formation and moral education. Man must grow like a plant, as Herder put it, toward the unfolding of his personality until he becomes an harmonious, autonomous individual exemplifying both the continuing quest for knowledge and the moral imperative. Goethe's *Wilhelm Meister's Apprenticeship* summed up this ideal in one phrase — "the cultivation of my individual self just as I am" [*"mich selbst, ganz wie ich bin, auszubilden"*]. Such self-education was an inward process of development through which the inherent abilities of the individual were developed and realized.[25]

Today we read Wilhelm Meister's words differently as the ironic self-delusion of a protagonist who does not achieve what he proclaims as his goal at this stage. But the majority of Goethe's contemporary readers, including Christian Gottfried Körner, Schiller, and Wilhelm von Humboldt, interpreted this phrase in terms of a program of Bildung that Wilhelm achieved in the end. We cannot blame Mosse for reading this passage in the same vein, as did hundreds of German-Jewish readers who were inspired by these words and saw their place in the dominant culture defined by this concept of Goethean Bildung. In this respect, Mosse was part of the problem that he sought to define. He fell for the fetishized concept of Goethean Bildung, as did generations before him. The tragic endnote to this cult of Bildung we find in Victor Klemperer's diaries of 1942 to 1945, when he described the attitude of a woman from the Jewish community in Dresden as expressly non-Zionist and Goethe-German and quoted her as saying: "We shall save Goethe [from the Nazis]!" [Wir werden Goethe retten!].[26]

This stance is no longer prevalent, as is indicated by an article on Goethe and Judaism by Frederick R. Lachman in the New York German-Jewish immigrant paper *Aufbau* of March 1992. There Goethe is compared to Lessing and found wanting. Following Ludwig Börne's example, Lachman quotes several lines from Goethe's well-known poem "Prometheus," each ending with a question mark: "I honor you?

Why? / Did you ever allay the agony that burdened me? / Did you ever dry my terrified tears?" Lachman's laconic answer in reference to Goethe is "No!"[27]

For us, it remains to redefine Goethe's concept of Bildung, not in terms of his Wilhelm Meister novels but in terms of his educational projects and autobiography, and to make room for Mendelssohn's concept of Bildung that has been neglected for far too long and deserves acknowledgment in the history of philosophy and education. Goethe's concept of Bildung was still in flux when he wrote *Wilhelm Meister's Apprenticeship*, and it referred as much to education as it did to nature, as his scientific writings show. We get a better idea of Goethe's concept of Bildung when we look at his drafts for a textbook for the Bavarian schools of 1808, the so-called Niethammer project, and review his autobiography in terms of self-fashioning.[28] The Goethean concept of Bildung has been unnecessarily mystified, as can be seen from the innumerable assertions that the term cannot be translated into English. As for Mendelssohn, the time has come to reestablish his position in the history of Bildung, as he defined and applied it to Jewish emancipation: the so-called German Jewish romance with Bildung began with Mendelssohn in 1784 and not with Rahel Levin in 1812.[29]

Notes

[1] George L. Mosse, *German Jews beyond Judaism* (Bloomington: Indiana UP, 1985) 44–45.

[2] *ibid.* 14.

[3] Steven E. Aschheim, *Culture and Catastrophe: German and Jewish Confrontation with National Socialism and Other Crises* (New York: New York UP, 1996) 32.

[4] Albert Bielschowsky, *Goethe: Sein Leben und seine Werke*, 29th ed., 2 vols. (Munich: Beck, 1914) 2: 683.

[5] Wilfried Barner, *Von Rahel Varnhagen bis Friedrich Gundolf: Juden als deutsche Goethe-Verehrer*, Kleine Schriften zur Aufklärung 3 (Göttingen: Wallstein, 1992) 8–9.

[6] Karl Robert Mandelkow, *Goethe in Deutschland: Rezeptionsgeschichte eines Klassikers*, 2 vols. (Munich: Beck, 1980–89) 1: 71–74.

[7] Aschheim 33: 151.

[8] Walter Laqueur, "In Memoriam," *Los Angeles Times Book Review*, 11 July 1999: 12.

[9] *Goethe's Collected Works*, Suhrkamp Edition, ed. Victor Lange et al., 12 vols. (New York: Suhrkamp, 1983–89; reprint, Princeton: Princeton UP, 1994 ff.). Cited as SE

[10] *Goethes Werke*, Hamburg Edition, 14 vols. (Hamburg: Wegner, 1948 ff.). Cited as HA

[11] Ehrhard Bahr, *The Novel as Archive: The Genesis, Reception, and Criticism of Goethe's* Wilhelm Meisters Wanderjahre (Columbia SC: Camden House, 1998) 87.

[12] References are made to Christian Wilhelm Dohm, *Über die bürgerliche Verbesserung der Juden*, 2nd rev. ed. (Berlin/Stettin: Nicolai, 1783) [1st ed. 1781].

[13] *What is Enlightenment? Eighteenth-Century Answers and Twentieth-Century Questions*, ed. James Schmidt (Berkeley/Los Angeles: U of California P, 1996) 53–54.

[14] *Was ist Aufklärung? Thesen und Definitionen*, ed. Ehrhard Bahr (Stuttgart: Reclam, 1996) 4.

[15] Schmidt 55.

[16] Alexander Altman, "Aufklärung und Kultur: Zur geistigen Gestalt Moses Mendelssohns," *Die trostvolle Aufklärung: Studien zur Metaphysik und politischen Theorie Moses Mendelssohns* (Stuttgart-Bad Cannstatt: fromann-holzboog, 1982) 277.

[17] Alexander Altmann, *Moses Mendelssohn: A Biographical Study* (Montgomery: U of Alabama P, 1973) 352.

[18] David Sorkin, *The Transformation of German Jewry, 1780–1840* (New York/ Oxford: Oxford UP, 1987) 126.

[19] See also Michael Graetz, "Jüdische Aufklärung und Erziehung," in Barkai 1: 333–50, and Michael A. Meyer, "Die Umgestaltung der jüdischen Erziehung," in Barkai 2: 118–25.

[20] Susanne Freund, *Jüdische Bildungsgeschichte zwischen Emanzipation und Ausgrenzung: Das Beispiel der Marks-Haindorf-Stiftung in Münster (1825–1942)*, Forschungen zur Regionalgeschichte 23 (Paderborn: Schöningh, 1997) 30.

[21] *Ibid.* 109.

[22] Sorkin, *Transformation* 73.

[23] Sorkin, "Wilhelm von Humboldt: The Theory and Practice of Self-Formation (*Bildung*), 1791–1810," *Journal of the History of Ideas* 44 (1983): 57.

[24] Marion Kaplan, "1812: The German Romance with *Bildung* Begins with the Publication of Rahel Levin's Correspondence about Goethe," *Jewish Writing and Thought in German Culture, 1096–1996,* ed. Sander L. Gilman and Jack Zipes (New Haven/London: Yale UP, 1997) 125.

[25] Mosse 3.

[26] Victor Klemperer, *Ich will Zeugnis ablegen: Bis zum Letzten: Tagebücher 1942–1945,* eds. Walter Nowojski and Hadwig Klemperer, 2 vols. (Berlin: Aufbau, 1995) 2: 135.

[27] Frederick R. Lachman, "Goethe und das Judentum," *Zeitzeuge Aufbau: Texte aus sechs Jahrzehnten,* ed. Will Schaber (Gerlingen: Bleicher, 1994) 104.

[28] Fotis Jannidis, *Das Individuum und sein Jahrhundert: Eine Komponenten- und Funktionsanalyse des Begriffs "Bildung" am Beispiel von Goethes "Dichtung und Wahrheit"* (Tübingen: Niemeyer, 1996) 37–207.

[29] Cf. Kaplan 124.

II. Goethe Cult and Criticism during the Nineteenth Century

Demarcations and Projections:
Goethe in the Berlin Salons

Barbara Hahn
Princeton University

THE REVERBERATIONS COULD BE HEARD throughout the end of the nineteenth century. For Goethe to be established as *the* true German poet, he had to be rescued repeatedly from the clutches of false worshippers. It seemed wrong that his texts had played such an important role in the Berlin salons around 1800. It seemed wrong that their significance was first recognized and propagated there. In order to save Goethe's name, its connection to a false name had to be dissolved. A Jewish name, and a woman's. That of Rahel — *tout court,* as she has been called far into the twentieth century. Heinrich von Treitschke set the tone for distancing Rahel's name from Goethe's. He called Rahel "a gushing high priestess . . . who prophesies untiringly from her tripod the praise of the deified one." Her worship of Goethe sprang from an "immeasurable vanity, that reveled in its own self through admiration of the first German poet."[1]

Friedrich Nietzsche took a different stance. "We know the fate of Goethe in a Germany sour with morals and spinsterlike," he writes in *Der Fall Wagner* (The Wagner Case, 1888), "he was always offensive to the Germans, he had true admirers only among Jewesses."[2] If the term *Jewesses* is translated into single names, then a specific name intervenes here for Nietzsche, as well, and again, one finds the gesture of distancing. In his *Nachgelassene Fragmente* (Fragmentary Literary Remains) of June/July 1885 he writes: "The women in Europe, totally aside from their normal activities ['Kinder zu legen'] are useful for many good things . . . among the Jewish women there are the lovely gossiping women: the paragon of them, all wrapped up in the lace of Goethe and smugness, was Rahel."[3]

Rahel. There she stands, dressed up in "smugness," shrouded in something that leaves her exposed, laid open to criticism. Wrapped up in lace, which everyone knows does not keep one warm. Her "poor name," of which she had once spoken, no longer protects her. Only a hidden name can offer protection, a name she says is "as comfortable to me as a dark dress that one imagines would keep warm; were it light, I'd be freezing, I couldn't wrap myself up in it anymore."[4] During her lifetime she could wrap herself in this "dark dress" by not exposing her name in public. In the letter just cited, written to an editor of a magazine, she designates herself with the abbreviation R., which, instead of disclosing meaning, only alludes to it. But posterity snatches this protection away from her. Bound to Goethe's name, her name carries the sign of a deficit that cannot be made good. In Goethe's shadow her name signalizes nothing more than a lack. A lack of "self." Her "self" appears as an unattainable goal.

But she does have something on her side. She has something to say, and precisely about the resonance of her poor name with Goethe's. Something that Nietzsche hints at, though he does not make it more precise. Once again in his *Nachgelassene Fragmente* Nietzsche writes that "another element of Goethe achieved its perfection only in Rahel!"[5]

Obviously, there was something in Goethe's texts that others were unable to read, something that needed a certain recipient in order to come into being. One might even say this recipient brings Goethe's text to completion. Taking both of Nietzsche's allusions together, one can risk a supposition. Goethe's texts offered Jewesses the possibility of escaping what is fatally ascribed to them. His name became a shibboleth with which a boundary could be marked as it was overstepped. It was a question of whether a space for negotiation existed between poles that had established themselves in 1800 as inimical and mutually exclusive. In other words: was there a possibility of being both Jewish and German? Was there a possibility of evading these two poles that always from the outset presumed exclusivity? In the following fourfold approach to these questions, the enemies of the Berlin salons and the carping and exclusionary letters they sent to Weimar will not be given voice. Rather, those will speak who, in fact, were engaged in this social, political, intellectual, and communicative experiment called the Berlin salons.

Who understands Goethe's *Wilhelm Meister*?

On 4 October 1803 a letter from Berlin set off to the author of the epoch in Weimar. It was written by the Swedish diplomat Karl Gustav von Brinckmann, who was a close friend of all the Berlin salonnieres and frequented their houses daily. But something seemed to be missing from this intense social and communicative life. "Since my stay in Weimar, I keep longing, indeed, to be back in that promised land, like the old covenant people longed for Jerusalem"[6] — that is what this letter claims. The implication is unambiguous, but compared with his first letter to Goethe, whose acquaintance Brinckmann had made in the spring of 1798, this letter revealed a slight but most significant shift. A few years earlier he had designated the "old covenant people" differently. He turned his "face toward Weimar, as the Jews toward Jerusalem,"[7] Brinckmann had written as a memoir of his first visit to Goethe. In the second letter one no longer hears of Jews but of battles for the faith, battles that Christians carry out among themselves: "True Goethianism (and I only consider the Unitarians orthodox) is propagating itself here gradually, like an invisible church" — "I am at least this lucky, that I only live in intimate connection with fellow believers and I cannot imagine that you are more intimately loved, and (why not?) devoutly worshipped anywhere (else)." These fellow believers are not by any chance the Jewish women in whose houses Brinckmann has regularly appeared for years and with whom he corresponds intimately. Instead, the countesses Caroline von Berg and Luise von Voss, with whom he supposedly has a "truly religious connection," are mentioned. "Of course, like all orthodox believers, we are probably sometimes more intolerant precisely toward the sects that are in closest proximity to us, than we are toward downright nonbelievers, and on the estate of the countess last winter in front of your bust there was held a proper auto-da-fé of all sorts of heretics who it seemed to us had misused the name of Goethe."[8] The "nonbelievers" are clearly identified in the letter: they are August von Kotzebue and Garlieb Merkel, who had criticized Goethe on account of the Berlin performance of his *Natürliche Tochter* (Natural Daughter) in the summer of 1803. The "sects in closest proximity," however, remain unidentified. They are obviously not "baptized in the spirit of your [Goethe's] writing": Brinckmann's friends Rahel Levin, Henriette Herz, Sara Levy, Sara and Marianne Meyer, Dorothea Veit Schlegel, Henriette Mendelssohn, Sophie Fränkel, Lea Salomon, and Hitzel Fliess. The Swedish diplomat carried on correspondence with all of these women, and with at least one of them he discussed Goethe's drama that had been criticized in Berlin.[9]

The underlying denunciation to be read here applies to a social and communicative constellation that has gone into history under the name "Berlin salons." It applies to the hostesses of the houses mentioned, who were all Jewish. So in the salons heresy was being carried on; the

name of Goethe was being misused. And, once again, it is a small semantic shift that establishes a boundary. In the Ten Commandments,
which the monotheistic religions Judaism and Christianity have in
common, it is forbidden to take the name of God in vain, to misuse it.
In the shift from God to Goethe (that Herder had already made), this
commonality is suspended. The secular god Goethe does not correspond to the categories Christian and Jewish. The opposition is struc-
tured in a completely different way, as an opposition of German and
Jewish. This shift has far-reaching consequences.

For centuries, Christian European culture had anchored its superiority in its distinction from the "Jewish." Now this opposition was na-
tionalized: *Jewish* means, first and foremost, "not German." By
ensconcing Goethe in the role of author of the epoch in the terminol-
ogy of the fight for the Christian faith, Brinckmann establishes exactly
this recoding. His letter reclaims a cultural space in the secular world
that is not to be accessible to Jews. The only ones who find a place
there, besides diplomats raised in the tradition of Herrenhut pietism,
are countesses who are bound to the courts in Berlin as well as Weimar.

Consider a second letter from Brinckmann. It bears a double address, as its first recipient immediately recognized. 11 December 1795.
Marianne Meyer, daughter of a Berlin banker, later to contract a mor-
ganatic marriage with Prince Reuss, the Austrian envoy in Berlin, writes
to Goethe, with whom she had become acquainted a few months earlier in Karlsbad: Brinckmann, "that fool, has written me a long letter
about the Confessions of a Beautiful Soul,[10] a real chaos from which he
believes true enthusiasm breathes; since I know better, however, I was
embarrassed when he spoke to me about it. He would certainly have
held it against me if I had said plainly what I thought about it. On top
of that I believe he wrote with the intention that you might see it; if
you want, I'll send it to you."[11]

Goethe's early letters to his Berlin correspondent have not been preserved, but from Marianne's next letter it is easy to conclude that
Goethe certainly did want to know how his *Wilhelm Meister* had been
received in Berlin. On 2 February 1796 she writes: "I'll send you
Brinckmann's letter shortly. I have to look for it among many other
papers that are in a cabinet in an unheated room into which I daren't
go now."[12] Despite the chilly quarters, it evidently was soon found, and
on it went to Weimar, to Goethe. On 1 April 1796 Marianne writes to
him: "I haven't been as amused for quite some time as I was by what
you say about Brinckmann. With a few words you've characterized the
gangly, touchy little fellow better, more correctly, than all the clever

gentlemen here, who torture themselves daily trying to say something fittingly witty about him. It's as if you had seen him."[13]

We do not know whether Goethe's remarks about Brinckmann were passed along or not. In any case, Brinckmann asked Marianne to return this letter to him. But what was in this letter that amused Goethe and called up a decisive rejection on the part of Marianne Meyer?

> Wednesday morning. I have finally finished reading the third Meister, and I've been transported by it into a mood that I cannot represent to you at all, that is so strange, however, that it forces me, completely unexpectedly, out of all present contexts. Precisely that portion of the volume, which I hear is incomprehensible to most and seems by far the most uninteresting, has moved me so powerfully that my feelings are still perturbed. The mighty echo in *Bekenntnisse einer schönen Seele* [Confessions of a Beautiful Soul] of those long faded but so deeply felt tones has roused a magical memory in me; so suddenly that you will hardly understand when I say that I set the book down with real trepidation, and indeed spent a sleepless night over it.[14]

This vehement effect of reading has a simple cause. Brinckmann understands Goethe's text, because it brings back to him an experience that is autobiographically grounded:

> You know that I was educated in Herrenhut pietism, but you can have no idea . . . how seldom such wonderful cheerfulness that seems to be the element of Goethe's friend [the beautiful soul] refreshed me, but how I too in these beautiful moments feel everything, everything that is hinted at in Meister. — How I then understand all of this indisputably even better than Goethe himself. —

If Goethe himself does not adequately understand the sixth book of *Wilhelm Meister,* the book elevated as the kernel of his work, how much less will Brinckmann's addressee be able to do so? She is incapable of taking the step of true "Kunstgenuss" [aesthetic appreciation], a step that, according to Brinckmann, can be achieved only through "such unfeigned self-denial, and a quiet, incorporeal capacity for endurance" as he himself obtained in the "celestial regions" of pietism.

Brinckmann's programmatic letter establishes two exclusions at once. Marianne Meyer, in whose house the Swedish diplomat regularly made his appearance at tea time, lacks the decisive religious experience to read Goethe. The fact that she knows the great author and corresponds with him regularly shifts her even further away from his work. The true texts go right through her hands — as through the hands of a merchant. Thus, in many different ways she is suddenly constituted as a Jewess.

How could one possibly answer that? Marianne Meyer does not answer Brinckmann in the witty distanced tone she used with Goethe. She develops, instead, a way of writing that appropriates Brinckmann's positioning of her and thereby displaces it.

> Haven't I told you long ago that I don't have much judgment or understanding, nevertheless I won't take back my judgment entirely . . . my taste certainly still needs amendment . . . by the way, you might even convince me by the tone in which you speak that your triumph must be great, to have found something against me; and it could easily make me proud to have brought about such a thing with such fervor; because I didn't think I was that important — but you can't humiliate me, either, because I can say to myself in good conscience that if I hadn't judged Meister as you wanted . . . then you wouldn't have read it so carefully, so I've helped it to attain this honor.[15]

In that Marianne Meyer stages herself, ironically, as a dilettante — privy to Goethe, she knows better than Brinckmann how to read Goethe's texts — she gains space in which she can dismiss Brinckmann's assumptions. She would rather perfect her skills in careful readings of Goethe and in letter exchanges with the poet himself than in debates with her Berlin friend. Goethe makes space for various readings, for various kinds of knowledge, whereas Brinckmann excludes his correspondent from Goethe's texts. His humiliation is declined by Marianne Meyer; any further debate is dismissed. Brinckmann's reading of Goethe has set up such a high barrier that henceforth only short notes will be exchanged, marking boundaries in their turn. She knew, of course, wrote Marianne Meyer to Brinckmann, that he was orthodox — and with that, she ends the correspondence.

Baptism — another camouflage?

Another letter. A letter from Berlin to Jena. On 12 October 1795 Wilhelm von Humboldt reports to Friedrich Schiller about a social gathering, perhaps at the Meyer house, or perhaps at Rahel Levin's. Sara and Marianne Meyer have just returned to Prussia's capital from the Bohemian baths, where they made Goethe's acquaintance.

> I'm hearing all sorts of quaint stories about Goethe here, stories that come from two baptized Jewesses that were along in Karlsbad. Further, that he supposedly read aloud to them an astonishing amount, wrote in albums and on fans, corrected their elaborations, one of them, an otherwise very beautiful girl, even says that he told them the

particular circumstances that gave rise to his writing the elegies, namely the verse: And the barbarian rules the Roman bosom and body![16] This suggests Jewish subservience, does it not? And by the way, even if these little stories that are being carried around with much indiscretion give Goethe's image some new characteristics, I find it most reasonable . . . to have chosen these two baptized women, who in fact, much preciousness and affectedness aside, are quite spirited and pleasant. And they will supposedly, as you say, stand as godparents for the expected new little arrival in Weimar.[17]

An astonishing order is established here: Goethe reads aloud to two baptized Jewesses, then writes them fleeting texts that do not find their way into print; and almost in the same breath he corrects their elaborations, which are marked as dilettantish. Humboldt's daring conclusion of an analogy between the Jewish and the feminine characterizes the fatal discursive operation by which Jewish women were distinguished from Jewish men.

If in the first opposition it is a matter of a masculine inhabitant of the north seducing two southern women, then the second half of the passage makes this decisive nuance broader. The "Jewish" shows the same subservience as the Roman woman. It is no longer man and woman, north and south, that stand in opposition to one another but, instead, it is a lopsided opposition, of which one side is the "Jewish." As the argument progresses it becomes clear to what the Jewish is subservient. The exclusive demarcation had already been alluded to once. "Two baptized Jewesses," two women whose identity is equivocal, tell stories in Berlin. Their baptism becomes, in the parallelism to the Roman woman, an act of subservience that grants them no new place in the culture dominated by the Christian. They still represent "the Jewish," set thereafter in opposition to the enlightened men of the Berlin society. And in this opposition, too, they draw the short straw. They remain Jewesses; their baptism is read by their non-Jewish contemporaries as an easily penetrated camouflage. That they appear at the end of the passage as possible godparents for Goethe's illegitimate child fits perfectly into the picture.

Goethe — a Jew?

The meeting in the spa brought Goethe into contact not just with the two Meyer sisters. A third Berlin Jewess had also set out for the south in the summer of 1795: Rahel Levin. That she spoke little in Berlin about this meeting signaled to her contemporaries that she stood in a special relation to Goethe, a relation that differed significantly from that of the Meyer sisters. No correspondence with Goethe has been handed down by Rahel. But in its stead are countless reflections about the texts of the author of the epoch.

The Varnhagen collection has preserved a finished manuscript, one that Rahel Levin, together with her husband, Karl August Varnhagen von Ense, had prepared for publication by 1816. It is Rahel Levin's correspondence with David Veit — a unique project. Unlike the rest of the young Rahel Levin's correspondences, this exchange is an attempt at a programmatic discussion of all the problems that face two young Jews, a woman and a man, when they burst open the door to a new world. And from the beginning all their debates are bound up with Goethe's name.

Straightaway in the first letter, a trip to the author of the epoch is placed on record. In the spring of 1793 David Veit sets out from Berlin to Weimar, where a letter of recommendation from Karl Philipp Moritz opens the house of the privy councilor to him. The visit, which lasts no longer than a quarter of an hour, is translated in the letter into a scene that resembles an initiation. The stairs leading up to the antechamber are described, the furniture, carpets, busts . . . until Goethe steps through the crucial door. "The first thing that I noticed about him and that you desire to know about was his figure." He looked like a Berlin uncle of the writer — thus the astonishing analogy. And then the Weimar privy councilor, described in terms of stature, eye color, facial features, and clothing, is finally completely transformed into a citizen of Prussia's capital: "Everything taken together he could be a minister, a war councilor, a privy councilor, in any case a government official — just not a scholar and certainly not a virtuoso. In Berlin everyone would think he was a local."[18] "I could not believe that Goethe went around dressed so subaltern and antiquated (you see, I don't know the proper word)" — thus the answer from Berlin — "because a person who knows everything also knows this, and why shouldn't he dress himself a bit more tamely, especially since he lives at the court and is in the latest social circles, that would just come naturally by itself, so that I have to think now that he presents himself differently on purpose, and I don't understand that."[19]

The description of Goethe's appearance, both physiognomically and in the staging of his clothing, introduces an amazing play with identities and attributes. Endowed with hooked nose, dark eyes, and dark skin, in terms of his figure similar to the uncle of the writer, Goethe squares in his appearance with the then current cliché of the Jew. Since differences in clothing no longer served as demarcation, the marking of "Jewish" had, as is well known, wandered up to the face. The glances that exclude Jews at that time are reflected back in the description of Goethe. This rebuttal of an identifying gaze remains, therefore, un-commented on in Rahel Levin's remarks — the picture itself is repudi-ated. Her commentary on his clothing, on the other hand, shows that there is space for differences that do not correspond to the demarcation Jew/non-Jew. And so it is worthwhile to question and to interpret. It is worthwhile also because Rahel Levin can refer to herself in one of the following letters as a "Jewish girl,"[20] without it being possible to read this as an identification.

From her equivocal identity as a Jewish girl Rahel Levin creates a whole spectrum of readings that culminate in her reflections on *Wilhelm Meister:* on 2 February 1795 she writes: "Nothing about Meister either. I read it for a long time, instead of divine [*goettlich*] I'll call it Goethe-like [*goethelich*]; crazy — but full of expression."[21] In spite of the promise to say nothing about *Meister,* in the letters that follow she indirectly writes about Goethe's novel. Levin grounds the fact that she does not express herself in a direct and analytically reflec-tive way by claiming that the novel has been inundated in Berlin by a flood of interpretations: "I still have not said a word about it, — I can hardly talk at all any more, — because people are always sticking their interpretations of it into my ears."[22]

What those people saw seems to result from an identificatory read-ing that translates every character in the novel into a real person. Some found similarities between Rahel and Philine; others thought that she was similar to Aurelie; still others thought that Henriette Mendelssohn resembled Aurelie, as well. The letter evades this sort of reading again and again. There is evasion into other Goethe texts — cited here are the poem "Beherzigung" (Take to Heart) as well as *Tasso,* but never *Wilhelm Meister* — and into other genres. A trace in the letter makes clear that the novel of the epoch cannot be translated into a simple un-derstanding. "I am more frenzied within myself than ever, and out-wardly more and more tranquil: apropos de Goethe!" Intimated here is a task that will leave its mark on the next decades. Goethe: a perma-nently assigned reading. So pressing and so inescapable that this trace, left in this early letter, is prepared for publication in 1816.

Together with traces of another sort of text — the diary. To keep the discrepancy between inner frenzy and outer calm from toppling into destructiveness, Rahel Levin writes to her own archive. "If anyone knew how to dissect Goethe's genius, then he would probably be just as great a poet: if Goethe could do so himself, then he would cease to be one. That is one of the funny differences between him and all other people."[23] Thus an entry from the summer of 1799.

"This comforting, gentle bond"

A last step back, back to the beginnings of written traces, a departure toward a different world. In the first pages of a message prepared by the Varnhagens for the world to come, in the never published manuscript for an expanded edition of *Rahel: Ein Buch des Andenkens für ihre Freunde* (Rahel: A Commemoration for Her Friends), is a letter almost completely without context, handed down to us only in a copy made by Levin's husband, Karl August Varnhagen von Ense. It is the first letter we have of the young Rahel to a friend. In the center of the letter is a citation of Goethe.

Rahel Levin is twenty-two years old when she writes to the twenty-five-year-old Henriette Mendelssohn in the spring of 1793:

> Dear Jettchen, you probably don't remember my handwriting or me any more, because it has been so long and it's so outrageous that I still owe you an answer, that it would be no wonder to think me ungrateful — the ugliest vice! because it shows as little understanding as a heart incapable of feeling. But just believe me again — it wasn't completely my fault, that I seemed so: . . . it was for me like Goethe says so truly about the secret: "The tongue is slow to free from bondage, unwilling to release a secret buried so long in ancient silence."[24]

A citation that is not exactly correct. And that can be read symptomatically, because Rahel writes in a letter shortly afterward: "One more thing, par parenthesy: even I know every cited passage, if it's from Goethe: I, who don't know anything."[25] In Goethe's drama Iphigenia does not speak of "bondages" in the plural but of a single bondage that ties her tongue. The sentence comes at a point in the drama at which Thoas offers Iphigenia, the stranger, his hand. He wants to free her from her foreignness by marrying her. Iphigenia really does have only a single secret tying her tongue, a secret that she entrusts to Thoas after initial hesitation. It is the secret of her ancestry: "Hearken! I am from the house of Tantalus." This extraction is the reason she rejects Thoas's proposal. Iphigenia has a choice, and she has a brother with whom she can return to her own country.

Rahel's letter is completely different. Why the Goethe citation is bound so closely to the subject of the letter is not explicated. Yet this letter is also about marriage. Two young women debate about getting married — one of them will never marry, the other will wed more than twenty years later. Where are you from and whose daughter are you? This question is not posed by anyone in the letter. And the other question too, the one connected to it in the drama — Will you marry me? — waits in vain for an answer. So what does the secret — or better yet, what do the secrets, plural — consist of, these secrets that want to be released from various bands?

With respect to Goethe's Iphigenia, one could read marriage as a metaphor for an alliance proposed to strangers, as a metaphor that responds to not-belonging in that it offers a path that leads to community. Since the world is the way it is, so says the letter, there is nothing better than this "comforting, gentle bond of marriage." But perhaps this comforting and gentle bond was an illusion preceding experience. Perhaps the fatal thing was precisely that the descent of these women was a secret to no one. That their tongues had to loose themselves from completely different sorts of bonds. And that in the end they, in contrast to Iphigenia, had no choice.

Out of a whole group of young Jewish women well known to us, Rahel Levin and Henriette Mendelssohn are the only ones who burst out of the traditional world in 1790 without being involved in conflicts with a husband. In doing so they breach their relationship not only to their mothers but also to the tongue of their mothers. A trace of this breach can be read in the names of two other women mentioned in the letter. They are designated by their Yiddish or Hebrew names, Hendel and Recha. Jette, the addressee, and the nameless writer have already lost these names. But they are still a long way from arriving at the world of the other names that scan the text, the names of Goethe and Diderot. And there is no "sanftes Bündnis," no gentle bond, to make the way there any smoother. No brothers to come to pick them up. And so this letter that is actually the beginning of a development ends with a difficult sentence, an onerous sentence about the striven-for alliance with Germans: "Just be afraid — it is a great misfortune."[26]

This sentence takes a rather prophetic perspective on the future development of Jewish acculturation in Germany. The relationship between Germans and Jews could hardly be described in terms of the metaphor of "marriage," this comforting and gentle bond. Quite the contrary.

Translated by Heidi Swanson

Notes

[1] Heinrich von Treitschke, *Deutsche Geschichte im 19. Jahrhundert*, 5 vols. (Leipzig: S. Hirzel, 1879–94) 2: 44.

[2] Friedrich Nietzsche, *Der Fall Wagner*, in his *Sämtliche Werke: Kritische Studienausgabe*, ed. Giorgio Colli and Mazzino Montinari (Munich: Deutscher Taschenbuchverlag, 1988) 6: 18.

[3] Nietzsche, *Sämtliche Werke*, 11: 551.

[4] *Rahel-Bibliothek*, in *Rahel Varnhagen: Gesammelte Werke*, ed. Konrad Feilchenfeldt, Rahel E. Steiner and Uwe Schweikert (Munich: Matthes und Seitz, 1983) 2: 406. (hereafter referred to as *GW*).

[5] Nietzsche, *Sämtliche Werke* 12: 90.

[6] Albert Leitzmann, "Briefwechsel zwischen Brinckmann und Goethe. Nebst einem Briefe Brinckmanns an Karoline von Wolzogen," *Goethe-Jahrbuch* 17 (1896): 35.

[7] Leitzmann, "Briefwechsel" 30.

[8] *Ibid.* 37.

[9] On 16 July 1803 Brinckmann wrote to Rahel Levin: "seit *Eugenia* ist dieses Bedürfnis (Sie zu sprechen) natürl. noch unruhiger geworden. Wie sollte *Göthe*, ich sage nicht das Andenken, sondern recht eigentlich die *Liebe* meiner kleinen genialischen Freundin, nicht ganz frisch wieder aufwecken?" [since Eugenia this need (to talk to you) has of course grown even more urgent. How could Goethe not rekindle completely afresh, I do not say the memory, but really and truly the love of my ingenious little friend?] Brinckmann Collection, Archiv Trolle Ljungby, Sweden. Folder: Rahel Levin.

[10] "Die Bekenntnisse einer schönen Seele"; book 6 of Goethe's *Wilhelm Meister*.

[11] Goethe-Schiller-Archiv, Weimar (hereafter referred to as GSA), Signatur: 28/306/IV.

[12] GSA, Signatur: 28/306/VI.

[13] Ludwig Geiger, "Einundzwanzig Briefe von Marianne von Eybenberg, acht von Sara von Grotthuss, zwanzig von Varnhagen von Ense an Goethe," *Goethe-Jahrbuch* 14 (1893): 30.

[14] Brinckmann Collection, Archiv Trolle Ljungby, Sweden. Folder: Marianne von Eybenberg.

[15] Undated letter, fall 1795. Brinckmann Collection, Archiv Trolle Ljungby, Sweden. Folder: Marianne von Eybenberg.

[16] Humboldt quotes the end of Goethe's second "Römischer Elegie": "Mutter und Tochter erfreuen sich ihres nordischen Gastes, / Und der Barbare beherrscht römischen Busen und Leib." [Mother and daughter take delight in their guest from the north, / And the barbarian rules the Roman bosom and body.]

[17] Friedrich Schiller, *Werke: Nationalausgabe, Briefe an Schiller. 1794–1795,* ed. Günther Schulz and Lieselotte Blumenthal (Weimar: Hermann Boehlaus Nachfolger, 1964) 35: 378.

[18] *GW* VIII/1, 3.

[19] *Ibid.* 11.

[20] *Ibid.* 264.

[21] *GW* VIII/2, 70.

[22] "Noch hab ich kein Wort darüber gesagt, — ich kann nun fast gar nicht mehr reden, — denn die Leute verstehen ihn einem immer in die Ohren hinein." 1 June 1795. *GW* VIII/2, 133.

[23] "Wenn irgend jemand Goethe's Genie zu zerlegen wüßte, der wäre wohl eben so ein großer Dichter: könnte es aber Goethe selbst, so hörte er es auf zu sein. Das ist einer der drolligen Unterschiede zwischen ihm und allen andern Menschen." *GW* I, 57.

[24] Sammlung Varnhagen, Biblioteka Jagiellonska, Cracow, box 207. The English translation of Goethe's "Iphigenia" is quoted from *Iphigenia in Tauris,* trans. John Prudhoe (New York: Barnes and Noble, 1966) 12.

[25] "Noch eins, par parenthese, auch ich weiß jede angeführte Stelle, wenn sie von Goethe ist; ich, die ich *nichts* weiß." *GW* VII/2, 51. Letter to David Veit, 26 December 1794.

[26] "Fürchten Sie sich nur — es ist ein großes Unglück."

A View from Below:
H. Heine's Relationship to
Johann Wolfgang von Goethe

Jost Hermand
University of Wisconsin-Madison

SELDOM HAVE GERMAN WRITERS argued so vehemently among themselves as in the second decade of the nineteenth century. One pasquinade after the other ignited passionate debates in literary circles, from the pamphlet *Wie ward Fritz Stolberg ein Unfreier?* (How Did Fritz Stolberg Become Unfree?, 1819), in which Johann Heinrich Voss accused his former friend, Count Friedrich Leopold zu Stolberg, of having crossed over to the obscurants of reactionary Catholicism, to the exposure of Count August von Platen as a "queer" in H. Heine's *Die Bäder von Lucca* (The Baths of Lucca, 1830).[1] As often noted, these debates were in many respects compensatory outlets for writers who wanted to pursue political issues but felt restricted by the harsh censorship codes set forth in the Karlsbad Decrees of 1819. Barred from polemicizing against anyone who defended the current regime, writers of the period had their field day on the pages of the literary supplements of the larger papers and in small brochures. And here, in order to bring at least a bit of fresh air into the suffocating atmosphere of this era, they perforce focused their attention on aesthetics and relentlessly lashed out against any literary competitor who happened to stand in their way.

The tone of these publications was so provocative, their slanderous rage so hate-filled, that not even the seventy-year-old Goethe was considered off-limits. He was, in fact, a favorite target of authors such as the ultra-right Catholics contributing to the *Historisch-politische Blätter* (Historico-Political Journal), the authors who wrote for Ernst Wilhelm Hengstenberg's *Evangelische Kirchenzeitung* (Protestant Newspaper), and the Lutheran minister Friedrich Wilhelm Pustkuchen in his five volumes of *Wilhelm Meisters Wanderjahre* (Wilhelm Meister's Journeyman Years, 1821–28). These Christian writers accused the great Weimar poet of assuming a heinous, amoral posture and leading German youth away from the straight and narrow "path of piety." Others, such as Wolfgang Menzel of the *Burschenschaft*, the former patriotic student organization, accused Goethe of a cosmopolitan indifference that scornfully dismissed all *teutsch*-inspired ideas. Ludwig Börne, a Jewish convert to Christianity from Frankfurt, entered the fray no less decisively, electing the "warm-hearted" Jean Paul as his model[2] while lambasting the "cold" Goethe as an opportunistic courtier enslaved by his egotism. Those who contrarily, and just as defiantly, stood by Goethe included Georg Wilhelm Friedrich Hegel, Wilhelm von Humboldt, August von Platen, Ludwig Tieck, Karl August Varnhagen von Ense, and Friedrich August Wolf.[3] The controversy that ensued thus involved almost all the authors of this period; in one way or another, they were forced to show their colors.

One of them was the young H. Heine,[4] as he called himself on the title pages of all of his publications, who first appeared on the literary scene in the early 1820s. His very youth and background predestined him to become an anti-Goethean.[5] In contrast to the patrician scion Goethe from Frankfurt, who saw his life in terms of an ever-ripening metamorphosis, Heine regarded his life as standing from the very outset under a bad star. The son of a Jewish textile merchant in Düsseldorf, he had to scrape through as an unpaid business assistant before receiving the financial support of his well-to-do uncle in Hamburg to take up the study of jurisprudence. He was exposed to humiliations and setbacks to which, as an aspiring poet, he reacted with extreme sensitivity. Only a few family members and Jewish friends offered him the human warmth for which he longed. For the Christian girls he met he was hardly a suitable marriage partner.[6] Fellow students in the *Burschenschaft* with whom Heine sought contact in Bonn at the time of his enthusiasm for things German also took offense at his "Jewishness," which ultimately led to his expulsion from the Göttingen *Burschenschaft* in December 1820.[7] When, in March 1821, he continued his studies at the University of Berlin, he made no effort to contact the "Arminia," an organization with equally anti-Semitic views.

But where should he now establish personal and political ties? He had failed in business. He was bored by jurisprudence. As a Jew, he would have secured only a subordinate position as a notary upon completion of his studies. And any hopes for an academic career in Prussia were dashed by the repeal of the philo-Semitic edict of 1812. Thrown back on his Jewishness, Heine joined the Berlin "Society for Jewish Culture and Science," an organization that attempted to steer an ideological course midway between Jewish autonomy and reform-oriented assimilation.[8] In the 1820s he also frequented Rahel Varnhagen's salon, where he met others of his own background, such as Michael Beer and Ludwig Robert.[9] Beyond this he tried to establish himself as an author, writing pain-drenched poems devoted almost exclusively to the theme of unrequited love, as well as critical-ironical reports on social and cultural life in Berlin. Since the Berlin cult of Goethe was centered in Rahel's salon, Heine's early writings also forced him to come to grips with the great Weimarean's overarching role in contemporary German letters.

Thus, when his early *Gedichte* (Poems) appeared in December 1821, Heine immediately — perhaps at Rahel's suggestion — sent them to Goethe, along with an exaggeratedly panegyrical dedication ending with the words: "I kiss the sacred hand that has shown me and the entire German people the path to heaven" (XX, 46).[10] But Goethe responded neither to this gesture nor to the volume *Tragödien, nebst einem lyrischen Intermezzo* (Tragedies, and a Lyrical Intermezzo) that Heine sent him in May 1823 as a "sign of his deepest admiration" (XX, 88). Heine was as embittered about this lack of acknowledgment as he was disturbed by the lack of criticism in the Varnhagen circle's Goethe cult. Hence, in a passage flavored with just a hint of his student-days *Burschenschaft* spirit, Heine wrote in the second of his *Briefe aus Berlin* (Letters from Berlin): "I do not wish to be unjust by failing to mention the respect that is paid here to the name Goethe. . . . But honestly, did not our Goethe's refined, worldly-wise demeanor contribute in large part to assuring that his public position is so radiant and that he enjoys to such a degree the affectations of our upper echelons? Far be it from me to accuse the old gentleman of a petty character. Goethe is a great man in a courtier's silk waistcoat" (VI, 29).

In keeping with this critical perspective, Heine made it a habit to omit Goethe's name whenever he made mention of his literary idols. In 1822 and 1823 "Lessing, Herder, and Schiller" twice appear as his exalted triumvirate (XX, 49 and VI, 65), whereas Goethe is consistently absent from such ancestral galleries. A letter of 24 December 1822 to Karl Immermann includes the startling phrase "Goethe is dead" (XX, 61). In a letter of 26 January 1824 we find a no less derogatory reference to Goethe's "truly Grand Ducal Weimar court prose" (XX, 138). Comments such as these indicate over and over again the young Heine's opinion that Goethe's aristocratic posture made him a blatant reactionary. Though he could not deny the old gentleman's cosmopolitan and anticlerical values, Heine essentially saw Goethe as an outdated representative of that *ancien régime* the World Spirit had long since left behind.

There are several reasons — aside from the one passage in the *Briefe aus Berlin* — for the young Heine's reluctance to voice such views publicly.[11] First of all, he did not want to appear to take sides or become identified with those who attacked Goethe from moralistic-Christian or nationalistic positions. These people damned in Goethe precisely what Heine found quite acceptable in the "old heathen." Strategic literary concerns must also have played a role here. Indeed, at this time almost all of Heine's friends, benefactors, and professors were outspoken Goethe devotees. What might Rudolf Christiani, Georg Sartorius, Gustav Hugo, Hegel, Varnhagen von Ense, and Rahel have said in response to such criticism? So as not to become an absolute loner, Heine had to avoid provoking the circles to which such people belonged.

His relationship to Varnhagen von Ense, one of the few positive reviewers of his early works, was crucial. In this instance Heine was forced to make some concessions, and given his inner sensitivities this undoubtedly entailed certain complications. He must have been especially troubled by Varnhagen's request that he contribute a short, felicitous piece to the volume *Goethe in den Zeugnissen der Mitlebenden* (Goethe as Seen by His Contemporaries), which under Varnhagen's editorship was to appear in the fall of 1823 on the occasion of the bard's seventy-fourth birthday. For a long time Heine hemmed and hawed, and he evidently managed to eke out only a few meaningless phrases. Moreover, he sent off his contribution much too late. In an apologetic cover letter he called this product of his prostituted muse a "wide, hollow jumble of ideas and images" (XX, 94). Unfortunately, this essay is not preserved, either because Varnhagen thought it bad or because it did, in fact, arrive too late. Shortly thereafter there was an open break between Heine and Varnhagen, who had assumed all too vehemently the authoritarian role of Antonio in Goethe's *Torquato Tasso*. But Heine at once made another overture to Varnhagen, since this relationship was important for him. For this reason, mingling genial diplomacy with a barely suppressed irony, he wrote on 27 November 1823 to Rahel's brother in Berlin: "Dear Robert, You will scarcely believe how well behaved I am toward Frau von Varnhagen. Except for a trifle, I have now read all of Goethe!!! I am no longer a blind heathen, but a sighted one" (XX, 125). He expressed himself even more clearly to Christiani, to whom he described his plans for coming to Berlin before long: "I have to court some people on whom my future position depends," he wrote with admirable frankness (XX, 146). And Heine followed through on his intention. During the university Easter break in 1824 he traveled to Berlin and reconciled with both of the Varnhagens.

The same strategy must have occasioned Heine's visit to the sage of Weimar on 2 October 1824, following his hike through the Harz Mountains. The instigation for this visit evidently came from Eduard Wedekind, a fellow student in Göttingen, who had called on Goethe on 17 September 1823 and must have given Heine a detailed account of his visit during the summer semester of 1824.[12] Like almost all visitors seeking an audience with Goethe, Heine sent ahead letters of introduction written by professors in Göttingen. So as not to appear entirely as a stranger, he also referred in his cover letter to the books and dedications he had sent Goethe, as well as to his acquaintance with the Varnhagens and the Berlin classical philologist Friedrich August Wolf (XX, 175). The audience must have been brief. Goethe's diary contains only the words "Heine from Göttingen."[13] The visit seems to have made no further impression on Goethe. Heine was at first laconic about his stopover in Weimar, particularly in his correspondence with Varnhagen. Only in a letter to his close friend Moses Moser do we find the words "I was in Weimar; their roast goose is good, too" and "the beer in Weimar is really good, more about this in person" (XX, 180). Heine's published writings say only that during his visit to Weimar he told Goethe how tasty he found "the plums on the road between Jena and Weimar" (VIII, 163). But in a report to his brother Maximilian he described having stunned Goethe by brashly declaring his intention to write his own *Faust*. Thereupon the old gentleman cut him off with the words: "Have you no further business in Weimar, Herr Heine?"[14]

These are, of course, all half-truths tilted toward mockery, although at the time Heine really did have plans to write a *Faust* (XX, 196). The actual meeting between Goethe and Heine was surely more prosaic. It is possible that they simply exchanged banalities, as was Willibald Alexis's experience during his visit to Goethe five weeks earlier.[15] Goethe preferred not to talk about literature with strangers and on such occasions tended to resort to a "coolly conventional" tone, which had a slightly chilling effect on impressionable young souls.[16] Furthermore, we know that in 1823 Goethe struggled to write his *Marienbader Elegie* (Marienbad Elegy), a work that bespeaks a renunciation of youth and renewal. In other words, at this time Goethe reacted with particular resentment to anything smacking of "young blood."[17]

Whether anti-Semitic affect on Goethe's part was involved is extremely questionable. Heine tended to assume this sort of thing whenever he encountered cool reserve in a person. To be sure, Goethe was somewhat ambivalent on this point. Although he admired the Old Testament and great Jewish personages such as Benedict Spinoza and Moses Mendelssohn, he was hardly an advocate of universal "Jewish emancipation," as is maintained by Fritz Strich.[18] This position is suggested in a remark by Ludwig Börne, who wrote that the privy councilor Goethe, idol of the "ruling party" and himself quite "capable of counsel," was annoyed by the "humanistic twaddle" that dared to grant civil rights to the Jews of Frankfurt.[19] But in his book of 1937 *Goethe und die Juden* (Goethe and the Jews), even such a National Socialist as Franz Koch collected little convincing evidence of anti-Semitic leanings that go beyond such generalities.[20] And more recent studies of this topic, for example by Alfred D. Low, Wilfried Barner, Norbert Oellers, and Günter Hartung,[21] have not come up with much that goes beyond Koch's findings.

One thing is clear: Heine came away from his meeting with Goethe deeply shocked. Whenever he passes over something in silence or cynically frames it with witticisms, genuine disappointment lies underneath. Moreover, Heine's mood was especially volatile at this time: he was facing university exams; he was dissatisfied with his *Rabbi von Bacherach* (Rabbi of Bacherach, 1840); his conversion to Protestantism could no longer be postponed; his professional prospects were worse than ever; and famous writers such as Uhland and Tieck were also failing to respond to the books and letters he had sent them. No wonder he felt unappreciated and misunderstood. He ran into arrogant aristocrats and repulsive anti-Semites wherever he went (XX, 50 and 96), encountered setbacks and disparagement at every turn, and finally had to tolerate having the ennobled Herr von Goethe treat him scornfully like a stupid boy or, at best, a student. A short communiqué by Ludwig Spitta to Adolf Peters indicates how despondent he must have been on his arrival in Göttingen:

> When he [Heine] made the Harz journey he later described, he also visited Goethe in Weimar. Upon his return to Göttingen he allowed himself free rein with the students who came out to meet him, frankly admitting his vexation that His Excellency had actually been excessively cold in receiving him. He felt wounded in his pride as a poet and had expected more.[22]

Small wonder that the nature and human characterizations in *Die Harzreise* (The Harz Journey, 1827), which he wrote soon afterward, read in parts almost like a parody of Goethe's *Werther*.[23] Indeed, *Die Harzreise* concludes with the ironic punch line: "And if you suddenly hear the shot, young lady, have no fear! I have not shot myself" (VI, 137).[24] Yet, one senses throughout this travel sketch how the author — despite all his witticisms — is striving to keep his antipathy toward Goethe from becoming all too obvious. This tactic is evident in a letter of 26 May 1825 to Christiani in which Heine declares himself "at war with Goethe" at that very moment but goes on to say that this state of war would "not be revealed publicly" (XX, 200). A diary entry by Ludwig von Diepenbrock-Grüter, with whom Heine was on friendly terms in Lüneburg in 1825, suggests how Heine would have liked just once not to pull his punches with Goethe: "He, Heine, is burning to speak out against him [Goethe], yet his position in the literary world prevents this. [Heine said that] Goethe would have been well advised to have voiced some of the ideas expressed by Walter Scott."[25]

For the most part, Heine revealed only to his closest friends the comparisons he made between himself and Goethe at this time. Such statements were often accompanied by an obvious feeling of inferiority that sought emotional relief in self-pitying complaints or overstated self-aggrandizement. Around 11 January 1825 he wrote to Moser that as a poet Goethe undoubtedly had unbeatable "talent." This is "no doubt the reason," he continued, "why so many poets fail, for example, I myself!" (XX, 183). Six months later he declared with greater certainty to the same Moser that he and Goethe were "two temperaments" and "in their heterogeneity" must necessarily "repel" each other (XX, 205).

> He is by nature an easy-going man of the world, for whom enjoying life is paramount, who at times feels and senses life for and in the Idea, and expresses it in poetry, but has never deeply grasped, and even less lived it. I, by contrast, am by nature an enthusiast, that is, am impassioned by the Idea to the point of self-sacrifice, and always feel pressed to immerse myself in it.

Heine concluded this train of thought with the emphatic phrase that it was still a "question" of whether even the "enthusiast who is prepared to surrender his life for the Idea does not live more intensely and happily in that moment than does Herr v. Goethe in the course of the entire seventy-six years of his egotistical and coddled life" (XX, 205). Heine was no less frank in the letter to Christiani reporting on his visit to Goethe. There he wrote:

> For the first time I thoroughly understood the contrast between Goethe's nature and mine. For me, all practical things are abhorrent. Fundamentally I despise life, and would recklessly sacrifice it

for the Idea. This is indeed the dichotomy within me. My reason is always at war with my inherent inclination to enthusiasm. Now I know why Goethe's writings always repelled me, although I revered them as poetry" (XX, 200).

These few statements suffice to show that there was more than just wounded vanity behind Heine's aversion to Goethe in these years. Most offensive to him was Goethe's narcissistic self-involvement and the political indifference it entailed, allowing Goethe to circumvent all that had to do with ideals and their attendant social commitment. At the same time, Heine also denounced other writers as pompous parasites who paid homage to life's pleasures while ignoring the momentum of the World Spirit. In these years he considered as significant only those authors who were concerned primarily with issues having a progressive edge. On this point he stuck close to Hegel, who in his *Vorlesungen über die Philosophie der Geschichte* (Lectures on the Philosophy of History, 1833–36) described truly great men as "movers of the World Spirit." "They were not able to enjoy quiet contentment," Hegel wrote, "their entire existence was work and effort, their entire nature solely their passion."[26] Thus, Heine was eager to be a combatant on the main intellectual battlefield of his epoch. All the while the aged Goethe, who might have used his literary prestige to advance progressive political and social programs, instead backed the Metternich restoration in word and deed and thus forfeited Heine's respect.

Accordingly, Heine's irreverent remarks about Goethe only increased in subsequent years.[27] With the success of his *Lyrisches Intermezzo* and the first volume of the *Reisebilder* (Travel Sketches, 1826–31) Heine's self-confidence grew, so that his earlier cautiousness gradually diminished (IV, 240). Moreover, Heine learned in the fall of 1827 that Goethe had responded to the publication of the second volume of his *Travel Sketches* by referring to him as a "Gassenjunge" [guttersnipe — perhaps referring to the term *Judengasse*] (XXIV, 240). On 30 October of the same year Heine wrote angrily to Moser:

> It's only natural that Goethe, the aristocrat, dislikes me. I'm honored by his rebuke, for he praises all weakness. He fears the rising Titans. He has become a weak and decrepit god, peevish because he is no longer able to create. Raumer can attest to the fact that for the past three years now, I have stopped loving him (XX, 303).

Heine now dropped his mask even toward Varnhagen, to whom he wrote on the same day:

I am going to spoil things with the aristocrats even more. Wolfgang Goethe may get away with violating the universal rules of good behavior among writers and intellectuals, but he cannot prevent that in times to come his name will quite often be mentioned together with the name H. Heine (XX, 304).

Because of Goethe's open "violation of the universal rules of good behavior," Heine no longer felt obliged to observe the customary code of literary decency when expressing his emancipatory displeasure at Goethe's arrogant Olympian posture. His positive review of Wolfgang Menzel's history of German literature exemplifies this attitude. Here Menzel, in the spirit of the *Burschenschaft,* accuses Goethe of "lacking" political "principles," of erotic "frivolity," and of "clever epicureanism."[28] The review, which Heine published in 1828,[29] allowed him to state in no uncertain terms: "The mood of brooding that envelops unsatisfied minds is infectious, and the air is getting muggy. The principle of Goethean time, the art-idea, is slipping away. A new time with a new principle is on the horizon, and . . . it begins with the insurrection against Goethe" (X, 247). "The old man," Heine continued, "how nice and polite he has become. How embarrassing to him is all crudeness now, how unpleasant to be reminded of the times when Genius stormed the heavens, or when others, stepping into his old footsteps, give full vent to the youthful Titanism of their high-spirited years." And in closing he rather maliciously compared Goethe to an "aged robber chieftain" who "has put aside his trade, leads an upstanding middle-class life among the local dignitaries of a little provincial town," and "strives to uphold all philistine virtues down to the pettiest detail" (X, 248).

　　To show Goethe that he was truly worthy of the invective "guttersnipe," Heine henceforth employed as many filthy jokes as the subject at hand allowed — as, for example, in his polemic against Platen in *Die Bäder von Lucca* and in his drafts for the *Aus den Memoiren der Herren von Schnabelewopski* (From the Memoirs of Count Schnabelewopski, 1834).[30] It was not a matter, however, of being obscene per se but of giving voice to his revolutionary rebelliousness and closing ranks with those who were in opposition to the ruling "aristocrats." As he tried to assure Varnhagen on 4 January 1830, his attack on Platen was mostly an effort "to divest the title 'count' of its magic" (XX, 384). Compared to a political coup of this nature, he wrote in the same letter, "the *Xenien* campaign, carried on by Schiller and Goethe, was merely a sham battle." That was the "age of art," he continued, "and art, which is only the semblance of life, was at stake, not life itself. Now the highest interests of life are at stake. Revolution is entering literature, and this battle is a much more serious affair." Unfortunately, "Germans are servile by nature, and the cause of the people is not very popular here," he lamented. Yet it was important, Heine continued in a democratic vein, that everyone do "his part" in the impending "battle" (XX, 385).

Soon thereafter, in another letter to Varnhagen he called Goethe a "genius at denying our times" and an aesthete lacking "manliness," that is, a man with neither enthusiasm nor an action-oriented disposition (XX, 389). Here Heine even opined that the old gentleman's disdain for the revolution of 1789 had such an "unfortunate" influence on Schiller that the latter virtually became a "co-aristocrat" (XX, 390). Heine was even sharper on this point after the July Revolution broke out in Paris in 1830, as exemplified in the afterword to the fourth volume of his *Reisebilder*, which he penned on 29 November of the same year:

> My soul quivers and my eyes burn, and this is unfortunate for a writer who should have command of his material and remain nicely objective, as the Classicist School requires, and as Goethe has borne out — this is the way he has advanced to the age of eighty, become a state minister and well-to-do — poor German people! This is your greatest man! (VII, 271).

Heine did not win many friends in Germany by espousing views that placed him ever more firmly on the side of the oppressed, as opposed to those who ruled from above. In May 1831 he moved to Paris to plunge into the revolutionary spirit of the proletariat and the lower middle classes. Unfortunately, the July Revolution did not bring about the general "liberté, égalité et fraternité" of which Heine had dreamed. Even in Paris the upper echelons continued to hold power, although now the older nobility was joined by bankers and industrial magnates in supporting King Louis-Philippe's suppression of all those who were trying to rise from below. In the course of this complex socioeconomic sequence of events Heine became embroiled in a number of contradictions. On the one hand, he continued to sympathize with the broad masses. On the other hand, he tried to uphold a middle-class liberalism that was emphatically subject-oriented.[31] By joining forces with the Saint-Simonians, who held equally emancipatory views and increasingly shifted their attention from socioeconomic to aesthetic and erotic interests, he hoped to find a solution to his ideological dilemma, albeit for a short time.

This new attempt at clarifying his position also colored Heine's relationship to Goethe. In 1831 and 1832 he continued to polemicize against "Goethean egotism" (XII, 46) and the "nonpartisan stance of Goethean school in art" (XII, 254). But in the years that followed, his attitude toward the Weimar poet, who died in 1832, became less abrasive. This change is already evident in his book *Zur Geschichte der neueren schönen Literatur in Deutschland* (Concerning the History of Modern belles lettres in Germany), published in April 1833 by Heideloff and Campe in Paris. On the one hand, Heine renewed his call for the end of the "Goethean Period of Art" (VIII, 125). Again he denounced Goethe's contemptuous manner of praising all the "insignificant nobodies" while deliberately overlooking "any writer with originality" (VIII, 150). Once more he railed against the "rigidity and coldness" of many of Goethe's characters, who were not at all "human, but unfortunate half-breeds of divinity and stone" (VIII, 155). And once again he lambasted Goethe's aversion to all idealistic "enthusiasm" (VIII, 466), which made Goethe an apolitical "indifferentist"[32] who neglected the "loftiest concerns of mankind" and was "occupied only with art toys, anatomy, the theory of color, botany, and observations of clouds" (VIII, 467). Yet, at the same time Heine praised Goethe for his decisive stand against the "hollow Catholic bustling" of the Romantics, who were overcome by delusionary mystical feelings (VIII, 149). Indeed, he went so far as to compare Goethe's essay "Über die christlich-patriotische, neudeutsche Kunst" (Concerning Christian Patriotic Modern German Art), by which Goethe had driven the Schlegels out of the temple of German literature in the manner of the "18th Brumaire of Napoleon Bonaparte" (VIII, 149). Only Goethe, Heine argued, had dared, like a new Greek god, to pillory the unholy alliance of "vermin, garlic, tobacco, and the ✝" (VIII, 155) and in so doing had outraged all those Pietists and churchgoers who during the final decade of Goethe's life — backed by the full force of Metternich's restoration — had hurled one attack after another at him, decrying him as the enemy of all morality. So as not to be lumped together with such bigots and Bible-thumpers, Heine tempered his criticism of Goethe in this book, which he later retitled *Die romantische Schule* (The Romantic School, 1838), and declared with pithy urgency: "Now that Goethe is dead, a strange sadness overwhelms me" (VIII, 125).

In the years that followed Heine became ever more critical of the anti-Goethean Ludwig Börne, who despised all erotic-emancipatory trends. In his essays from this period Heine sided ever more strongly with the naked heathen "Wolfgang Apollo," as he had once dubbed Goethe (VI, 146), a man whose sensualistic pantheism had to be a thorn in the flesh of both Christian-Biedermeier reactionaries and the moralizing champions of neo-Jacobinism. Heine's ever more positive view of Goethe acquired a philosophical underpinning in his 1835 essay *Zur Geschichte der Religion und Philosophie in Deutschland* (Concerning the History of Religion and Philosophy in Germany). Here Goethe is cast as the "great pagan" who nonetheless "strangely modernized" (VII, 100) the old paganism. "His vigorous heathen nature," Heine wrote, "comes to the fore in his clear, unflinching interpretation of all external phenomena, of all forms and colors. But at the same time, Christianity endowed him with a more profound understanding." Thus, Goethe "sympathized just as deeply with the sorrows of a young Werther as with the joys of an ancient Greek god." His pantheism, "different from pagan pantheism," was filled with the same eighteenth-century "spirit that wafts toward us from the writings of Spinoza" (VIII, 100). But the predominantly positive view of Goethe in this essay is attended by ironic asides. At one point he is positioned as a "giant" who remained as quiet in Weimar as the seated Jupiter of Phidias in the temple of Olympia. Had he suddenly jumped to his feet, he "would have shattered the housetop of the state" or even "cracked his skull against it." So he "remained calmly seated," Heine went on, "and simply allowed himself to be worshipped and perfumed with incense" (VIII, 102).

Heine offers an even more positive image of Goethe in *Ludwig Börne: Eine Denkschrift* (Ludwig Börne: A Memorial), which links the opposition between spiritualism and sensualism to the antagonism between Nazarenes and Hellenes. Since Börne had frequently accused both Goethe and Heine of irresponsible epicureanism, Heine was obliged in his own essay to side with Goethe so as to defend the positions of the Saint-Simonians, which "Wolfgang Apollo" surely would have endorsed. The "ascetic, iconoclastic, maniacal-spiritualizing impulses" of the "little Nazarene" Börne, we read here, kept him from grasping the "proudly unfolding, serenely life-affirmative and realistic" views of the "great Greek" of Weimar, just as Börne failed to appreciate the "serenely life-affirmative" Heine (XI, 18). Nazarenes of this ilk, Heine continued, have no access to the "majesty of blissful pleasure." Instead, they feel driven to a republican "martyrdom" that clearly smacks of the "crucifixion-mania of the early Christians" (XI, 19). Seen in this light, all spiritualists are descendants of the old Hebrews. Thus, in his memorial to Börne, Heine characterized even Pustkuchen, Hengstenberg, and Menzel, who rebelled against the "great pagan" Goethe with their "pharisaical screeches," as Nazarene-minded "Jews" (XI, 45).

Such arguments served a dual purpose. On the one hand, Heine emphasized sensualism to remove any suspicion that his polemics against Goethe in the late 1820s sprang from a purely "Jewish" resentment. On the other hand, Heine did not want to be thought of as a neo-Jacobin like Börne, who had emphasized revolution and was obsessed by the idea of mounting the barricades for another storm. Heine's articles in *Lutetia* from these years give ample evidence of how disinterested he was in such fantasies. Again and again he advocated the governmental form of a constitutional monarchy, and based on this outlook he depicted the "citizen king" Louis-Philippe as an altogether acceptable ruler.

Given the internal political tensions of this era, Heine's ideological change of front inevitably came under suspicion as being mere political opportunism. To be sure, during the July Revolution of 1830 in Paris he had made no bones about his revolutionary views and had duly classified Goethe among the "servants of the aristocracy." What, then, were his former supporters among the Young Germans to think of his change in orientation?[33] Well, after 1835 — that is, after the federal parliament's prohibition of their writings — most of them had also made peace with the *juste milieu*. Hence, no criticism of Heine was voiced by the Young Germans. But it was different with a younger literary group, known today as the *Vormärz* [the pre-March period before the 1848 Revolution] writers, who after 1840 appeared on the scene with national-democratic zeal. Among them was a group of anti-Goetheans, but their views on the bard of Weimar lost relevance in the face of the growing crisis in domestic politics signaled by the Silesian weavers' uprising of 1844. In other words, their anti-Goethean polemics were not able to command as much attention as those of the Young Germans in the 1820s. In fact, most of the authors writing between 1840 and 1848 were far more concerned with political action than with the role of art in society. Even those, like Georg Gottfried Gervinus, who continued to admire Goethe's works no longer considered them in terms of any contemporary value but saw them as belonging to a literary heritage that already belonged to the past.[34]

In view of the changed circumstances, Heine also took leave of this topic and the controversies it had once entailed. Certainly we find ever fewer references to Goethe in his writings from this period. It was not until 1847, when Heine adapted the Faust theme for a "dance poem" at the invitation of the London theater director Benjamin Lumley, that he once again drew nearer to Goethe. In the spirit of the desired ballet scenario, he transformed the figure of Mephistopheles into a friskily gamboling Mephistophela. Thus, despite the poem's deliberately kitschy final scene, Heine's approach to the material was almost more Goethean than Goethe's had been. He accomplished this effect by intensifying in a subversive way the life-affirmative, that is to say, the pagan and Saint-Simonian, possibilities of interpretation that resided in the Faust legend.

Hereafter, Heine's preoccupation with Goethe all but ceased. Confined to his sickbed for the last eight years of his life following his collapse in 1848, he could only grieve for the lost utopia based on the concept of a neopagan, Saint-Simonian way of life enraptured by "nectar and ambrosia, purple cloaks, exquisite fragrances, ecstasy and splendor, nymphs dancing in delight, music and comedies," as he had once waxed enthusiastic in his essay *Zur Geschichte der Religion und Philosophie in Deutschland* (VIII, 61). Indeed, increasing physical deterioration turned even him into one of those Nazarenes he had scoffed at only a few years earlier. A short piece dated 15 April 1849 that he wrote for the *Allgemeine Zeitung* (General Newspaper) in Augsburg informed his German readers about the precarious condition of his health:

> In the meantime, I want to admit frankly, a great change has come over me. I am no longer a divine biped. I am no longer the "freest German since Goethe," as Ruge once called me in my healthier days. I am no longer the great pagan No. II who was likened to the vine-crowned Dionysus, while the title of Grand Ducal Weimarean Jupiter was bestowed upon my colleague No. I. I am no longer the joyous and somewhat fleshy Hellene who once cheerfully smiled down upon the melancholy Nazarenes. I am now only a poor, deathly sick Jew, a decrepit picture of misery, an unhappy man! (XV, 1120).

We know what followed: years of inhuman suffering endured with ever greater doses of morphine, years in which he remained at his "lost outpost" to take up the cause of universal liberation for all those who suffered and were oppressed and exploited, years at whose end he even began to sympathize with communism.[35] But the majority of German literary critics in the post-1848 period and the ensuing Bismarck years showed no interest in hearing about pitilessly beaten Negro slaves like the protagonist of Harriet Beecher Stowe's *Uncle Tom's Cabin* or the "poor little grannies" without the "comfort" of coffee and snuff, as Heine described them in his *Geständnisse* (Confessions, 1854; XV, 42) and in the preface to the French edition of *Lutetia* (XIII, 1 167). The literary critics of this time preferred instead to raise on a pedestal the two Weimar classics who were deified as Olympians. While Goethe and Schiller enjoyed apotheosis in the decades following the failed popular uprisings of 1848–49, the heap of invectives attached to Heine's name grew ever thicker.[36] Heine had been the critic of apolitical classicism, a sensualist inspired by the Saint-Simonians, a rebellious Left Hegelian, an advocate of the wretched and the poor. So that he might be eliminated from intellectual life in Germany after his death, he was defamed as a licentious erotomaniac, a francophile who abandoned his fatherland, a Jewish intellectual bent on "distortion." To be sure, the love poems in his *Buch der Lieder* (Book of Songs, 1827), albeit read in a vaguely universal-humanistic sense, as well as the allegedly "humorous" passages in *Die Harzreise*, were still astoundingly popular among middle-class liberals. But the greater part of his other writings — above all, the political and philosophical essays; the polemical writings on Goethe, Platen, August Wilhelm Schlegel, and Börne; as well as the socio-ethical passages in his late works — fell increasingly into oblivion or disrepute.

This development culminated in the years after 1933, when the National Socialists once again elevated the status of the Olympians Goethe and Schiller while they attempted to erase Heine's name permanently from German memory. This process of repression and reversal led Fritz Strich to assert in his 1947 essay "Goethe und Heine" that the "political and social development of the German people" would have been better served by Heine than by Goethe.[37] And this he saw as a great "disadvantage," since it had led to the predominance in Germany of a conservative-authoritarian spirit rather than a liberal-critical one. Such a view may be somewhat exaggerated, as it shifts Goethe too far into the authoritarian camp and, at the same time, overvalues the discourses of high culture in the educational project of Bildung. Yet, Strich's argument should not be dismissed entirely. After all, developmental changes in the intellectual-literary superstructure of a nation sometimes entail consequences that ought not to be underestimated. Among such shifts and changes we can identify those ideological currents that valorized the "spirit of Weimar" after 1848–49, and particularly after 1871 continued to do so in concert with the ruling powers, thus contributing to a societal mindset that became predominantly autocratic.

That this development was extremely advantageous for Goethe's reputation and extremely disadvantageous for Heine's is, unfortunately, an historical fact. One of the main reasons for this disparity was the fundamental difference in the social grounding of their works, a difference that manifests itself even in their liberal middle-class views. At the root of Goethe's Olympian disdain is almost always a selfish, if not altogether aristocratic, feeling of superiority that is characteristic of many of the representatives of the older upper strata. By contrast, even those utterances of Heine's that ring most elitist can always be traced to clearly transparent efforts at overcompensation, efforts by which he tried to raise himself above the basic misery of his existence as a Jewish outsider who longed for assimilation but was not allowed to become integrated into the larger societal structure.[38] And this difference points up disparities that can easily be understood even by those unschooled in ideological criticism.

To conclude: on closer examination Heine can only be understood if, when reading his works, we never forget that "view from below" that he acquired while growing up as a relatively poor Jewish boy and that later, aside from his euphoric Saint-Simonian period in the early 1830s, always stayed with him. Goethe, on the other hand, came from a so-called better background, rose to a well-paid ministerial position in Weimar, and never relinquished that "view from above," a vantage point from which, as already observed by the young Heine, he enjoyed the "affectations of our upper echelons" (VI, 29). For this reason Heine's works have found greater favor and acclaim among restive societal groups, while Goethe's works have appealed more to the privileged. I know that a crude juxtaposition of this sort, like all blanket statements, is inevitably rather trite. And yet, this contrast should not be underestimated nor dismissed outright by anyone who engages in such comparisons and who takes into account their ideological consequences. Literature, after all, to quote the young Heine one last time, is still nothing more than a "nice detail" (XX, 62), while what is political and societal affects our entire life.

Translated by Helen Fehervary

Notes

Translator's Note: Most of the translations of passages from Heine's works and letters are my own. In rendering passages from *The Romantic School* and *Concerning the History of Religion and Philosophy in Germany* I have consulted Helen Mustard's translations in Heinrich Heine, *The Romantic School and Other Essays*, ed. Jost Hermand and Robert C. Holub (New York: Continuum, 1985).

[1] See my article "Heine contra Platen: Zur Anatomie eines Skandals," in *Signaturen: Heinrich Heine und das 19. Jahrhundert*, ed. Rolf Hosfeld (Berlin: Argument, 1986) 108–20.

[2] See Ludwig Börne, "Denkrede auf Jean Paul," in his *Sämtliche Schriften,* ed. Inge and Peter Rippmann (Düsseldorf: Melzer, 1964) 1: 789–97.

[3] See *Goethe im Urteil seiner Kritiker: Dokumente zur Wirkungsgeschichte Goethes in Deutschland,* ed. Karl Robert Mandelkow (Munich: Beck, 1975) 1: 358–488.

[4] On the question of why Heine called himself neither Harry Heine nor Heinrich Heine but preferred the name H. Heine, see my article "Der 'deutsche' Jude H. Heine," in *Dichter und ihre Nation,* ed. Helmut Scheuer (Frankfurt/Main: Suhrkamp, 1993) 257–72.

[5] The following works, among others, indicate how long the legend survived in Germany that Heine held a life-long admiration for Goethe: Walter Robert-Tornow, *Goethe in Heines Werken* (Berlin: Haude & Spener, 1883) 7; Ernst Elster, "Einleitung" to Heine's *Sämtliche Werke,* vol. 1 (Leipzig: Bibliographisches Institut, 1887 ff.) 17 f.; Gustav Karpeles, "Goethe und Heine," in his *Heinrich Heine und seine Zeitgenossen* (Berlin: Lehmann, 1888) 41; Eduard Grisebach, *Das Goethesche Zeitalter der deutschen Dichtung* (Leipzig: Engelmann, 1891) 143; Oskar Kanehl, *Der junge Goethe im Urteil des Jungen Deutschland* (Greifswald: Bamberg, 1913) 73; Erich Loewenthal, *Studien zu Heines "Reisebildern"* (Berlin: Mayer & Mueller, 1922) 85; Heinrich Teweles, *Goethe und die Juden* (Hamburg: Gente, 1925) 98–101; Fritz Strich, "Goethe und Heine," in his *Der Dichter und die Zeit* (Bern: Francke, 1947) 194. A corrective of this image was first undertaken in the following works: Walter Wadepuhl, "Heines Verhältnis zu Goethe," *Jahrbuch der Goethe-Gesellschaft,* Neue Folge 18 (1956) 121–31; Ulrich Maché, "Der junge Heine und Goethe," *Heine-Jahrbuch* (1965) 42–47; Christoph Trilse, "Das Goethe-Bild Heinrich Heines," *Jahrbuch der Goethe-Gesellschaft,* Neue Folge 30 (1968) 154–91; Jost Hermand, "Werthers Harzreise," in his *Von Mainz nach Weimar: Studien zur deutschen Literatur* (Stuttgart: Metzler, 1969) 129–51; Karl Robert Mandelkow's "Einleitung" to his documentation *Goethe im Urteil seiner Kritiker* (see note 3) 1: lxviii–lxxiii; Robert C. Holub, *Heinrich Heine's Reception of German Grecophilia* (Heidelberg: Winter, 1981) 59–86; George F. Peters, *"Der große Heide Nr. 2": Heinrich Heine and the Levels of His Goethe Reception* (New York: Lang, 1989).

[6] See my article "Vom 'Buch der Lieder' zu den 'Verschiedenen': Heines zweimalige Partnerverfehlung," in *Heinrich Heine: Ästhetisch-politische Profile,* ed. Gerhard Höhn (Frankfurt/Main: Suhrkamp, 1991) 214–36.

[7] See Jost Hermand, "Eine Jugend in Deutschland: Heinrich Heine und die Burschenschaft," in *Gegenseitige Einflüsse deutscher und jüdischer Kultur,* ed. Walter Grab (Tel Aviv: Institut für deutsche Geschichte, 1982) 111–33.

[8] See Hartmut Kircher, *Heinrich Heine und das Judentum* (Bonn: Bouvier, 1973) 106–12; Ludwig Rosenthal, *Heinrich Heine als Jude* (Frankfurt/Main:

Ullstein, 1973) 118–45; Edith Lutz, *Der "Verein für Kultur und Wissenschaft der Juden" und sein Mitglied Heine* (Stuttgart: Metzler, 1997).

[9] *Ibid.* 104–6.

[10] Heine's works are quoted from the *Düsseldorfer Ausgabe,* vols. 1–16 (Hamburg: Hoffmann & Campe, 1973 ff.), his letters from the *Weimarer Saekularausgabe,* vols. 20–45 (Berlin: Akademie Verlag, 1970 ff.).

[11] In another passage in the *Briefe aus Berlin* Heine called Goethe the "Ali Pascha of our literature," who was widely considered to be an old, nasty tyrant without scruples. See the *Düsseldorfer Ausgabe,* 6: 49, 466.

[12] See Eduard Wedekind, *Studentenleben in der Biedermeierzeit: Ein Tagebuch aus dem Jahr 1824,* ed. H. H. Houben (Göttingen: Vandenhoeck & Ruprecht, 1927) 86.

[13] Sophienausgabe (Weimar: Boehlau, 1887 ff.), Section 3, 9: 277. On the following see also my commentary on "The Harz Journey" in the *Düsseldorfer Ausgabe,* 6: 518–22.

[14] See H. H. Houben, *Gespräche mit Heine* (Frankfurt/Main: Rütten & Loening, 1926) 90 f.

[15] Published in *Gesamtausgabe von Goethes Gesprächen,* ed. F. von Biedermann (Leipzig, 1910) 3: 128 f.

[16] See Strich 188.

[17] Goethe, *Lyrische Dichtungen in zeitlicher Folge* (Leipzig: Insel, 1961 f.) 21: 294.

[18] Strich 192.

[19] Börne, *Sämtliche Schriften* 2: 857.

[20] Franz Koch, *Goethe und die Juden* (Hamburg 1937) 8, 13, 26.

[21] See Alfred D. Low, *Jews in the Eyes of the Germans* (Philadelphia: Institute for the Study of Human Issues, 1979) 67–76; Wilfried Barner, "Goethe und die Juden," in *Bulletin des Leo Baeck Instituts* 63 (Jerusalem: Bitaon, 1982) 75–82; Norbert Oellers, "Goethe und Schiller in ihrem Verhältnis zum Judentum," in *Conditio Judaica,* ed. Hans Otto Horch and Horst Denkler (Tübingen: Niemeyer, 1988) 108–30; Günter Hartung, "Goethe und die Juden," *Weimarer Beiträge* 40 (1994): 398–416.

[22] Quoted in the introduction to Philipp Spitta, *Psalter und Harfe* (Gotha: Berthes, 1890) ii.

[23] See also my article "Werthers Harzreise" 139–46.

[24] See also Poem 55 in the cycle "Heimkehr" (Homecoming) which ends with the lines: "Don't think I'll shoot myself, / As bad as things now are! / All this, my dearest creature, / Has happened to me before" (1, 269).

[25] See Karl Schulte-Kemminghausen, "Tagebuchaufzeichnungen des westfälischen Freiherrn Ludwig von Diepenbrock-Grüter über Heine," in *Festschrift für Jost Trier* (Meisenheim: Westkulturverlag, 1954) 294.

[26] Hegel, *Jubiläumsausgabe*, 11: 61.

[27] Only vis-à-vis Varnhagen did Heine continue to sidestep the issue: "I was unable to read the passages about Goethe in Menzel's literary history without pain. I would not have written them for any price. What are you thinking of, dear Varnhagen, that I, I would write against Goethe! . . . The present opposition to the Goethean way of thought, namely German national narrow-mindedness and insipid pietism, strike me as the most unfortunate of all. For this reason I must stick with the old pagan, *quand meme* — . . . Even though I count myself among the dissatisfied, I will never cross over to the rebels" (20, 307).

[28] See the commentary in the *Düsseldorfer Ausgabe*, 10: 635.

[29] Shortly before Heine's review appeared, he wrote appeasingly to the Varnhagens on 6 June 1828: "This article will reach you 8 days from now — show mercy — do not write me off" (20, 333).

[30] See Wadepuhl 125–30.

[31] See my article "Tribune of the People or Aristocrat of the Spirit? Heine's Ambivalence toward the Masses," in *Heinrich Heine's Contested Identities*, ed. Jost Hermand and Robert C. Holub (New York: Continuum, 1999) 155–64.

[32] See also Fritz Mende, "'Indifferentismus': Bemerkungen zu Heines ästhetischer Terminologie," *Heine-Jahrbuch* (1976): 11–22.

[33] On the anti-Goethean attitude of the Young Germans, see *Das Junge Deutschland: Texte und Dokumente*, ed. Jost Hermand (Stuttgart: Reclam, 1966) 21–30; Helmut Koopmann, *Das Junge Deutschland: Analyses seines Selbstverständnisses* (Stuttgart: Metzler, 1970) 114–31; Wolfgang Leppmann, *Goethe und die Deutschen* (Bern: Scherz, 1982) 74–76.

[34] See Jost Hermand, *Geschichte der Germanistik* (Reinbek: Rowohlt, 1994) 44–46.

[35] See my article "Die soziale Botschaft der 'Geständnisse,'" *Ich Narr des Glücks: Heinrich Heine 1797–1856*, ed. Joseph A. Kruse (Stuttgart: Metzler, 1997) 313–18.

[36] See Paul Peters, *Heinrich Heine "Dichterjude": Die Geschichte einer Schmähung* (Frankfurt/Main: Anton Hain, 1990).

[37] Strich 195.

[38] See Hans Mayer, *Außenseiter* (Frankfurt/Main: Suhrkamp, 1981) 205–23.

III. Goethe Philology and Jewish Identity

Cultural History as Enlightenment: Remarks on Ludwig Geiger's Experiences of Judaism, Philology, and Goethe

Christoph König
Humboldt-Universität Berlin

IN GERMANY ACADEMICS FEEL INHIBITED in talking about Jewish intellectuals.[1] At first sight, their motivation seems quite unproblematic. No one could wish once again to exclude people who were themselves slow to define their identity according to their status as Jews, or to group them together as an object of study when they had so little in common. No one can forget the Nazis and the way they made so many Germans into Jews. It was, however, just this attitude that Gershom Scholem forcefully attacked when he wrote:

> After they had been murdered as Jews, they are now — in some posthumous triumph — being turned back into Germans, and it suddenly counts as a concession to anti-Semitic theories to wish to stress their status as Jews. What a perversion this is, all in the name of an understanding of progress that does everything possible to avoid confronting realities.[2]

As if there might not have been other difficult forms of Jewish experience than those that the Germans created for them!

The researchers whom Scholem castigates try to argue their way out of their inhibitions. They say: because of the difficulties in defining the Jews, the most that can be done is to define the way in which they were discussed and in which they discussed their own situation. For this purpose, they imply, one can use discourse and system theory, that theories make a convenient distinction between discourses and the people who use them; but in reality the researchers are prepared to recognize the power of the various discourses and are not interested in individuals' resistance to them. The people caught up in these systems are identifiable only when, as a group, they submit to these discourses. The idea of the power of systems is augmented by that of identity, an identity without which the object of study simply does not exist. This means that one can speak of Jews only after anti-Semitism has thoroughly and coherently shaped them. The distinction is, of course, an unreal one; nevertheless, the researchers have to watch their research question creating their object of study and, as critical spirits, they feel that they must prevent this.

Such a distortion of a critical position is possible only when one insists on *identity* and feels that one must protect those people who did not achieve this identity from the attention of historians. But what happens to the suffering of these people and their attempts to escape their fate? I wish to suggest, instead, a dialectical view: the idea that even negativity has a reality. All these Jewish intellectuals living in the Second Empire and in the Weimar Republic were acting within a specific cultural situation in which Jewish traditions were placed against German traditions, and the decisions they reached had a specific quality, too. These decisions do not in themselves justify the use of the phrase "Jewish identity": their *difficulties* give the justification. That is what I mean by the "reality of negativity." Of course, these decisions take highly varied forms, and when one examines them closely — as we did in Marbach in the symposium "Jewish Intellectuals and Literary Study in Germany, 1870–1933" — they come down to a series of different biographies, the biographies of individuals who shared the experience of the problem.

If the historians who refuse to define their theme in this way are historians of science, they believe that they can use a third argument beyond discourse and identity: they argue from the autonomy of science as a system that simply excludes categories such as "Jewish." They argue that it is meaningless in the context of the history of science to talk of Jewish intellectuals, for the personal difficulties of the Jews (to the extent they are prepared to recognize these difficulties at all) influenced neither their scientific methods, nor their style, nor their results. In the halls of academe, they imply, everything is sweetness and light. But we still have to fight off system theory at this point, for system theory — in a way that is simply not understood in France — dominates scholarly writing in Germany. Its weakness lies in its inability to explain the fact that elements of one system can appear within another system and develop their potential there (I am explicitly talking of cultural values and of culture in general). The question I would like to raise and at least provisionally answer in this short paper is: what influence do the difficulties that academics experience, and the decisions that they are forced to take outside the university, have on their activity within the university?

In every period science develops alternatives that have a certain steadiness. In the periods under discussion here there is a polarity between philology in the more restrictive sense of editions, biographical studies, and the like and the broader sense of philology, in which we may include Wilhelm Dilthey and Wilhelm Scherer. They combined factual knowledge with wider philosophical-aesthetic reflections.[3] From that combination developed from 1910 to 1925 what we know as *Geisteswissenschaften*.[4] And the relationship between science and literary criticism contained a whole range of alternatives.[5] There was a tension between the two, for the more intelligent academics knew that there was a methodologically essential link between literary criticism and its values, on the one hand, and philology as a discipline or science, on the other hand. The Jewish philologists, like everybody else, operated in the space between these alternatives (only in rare cases, such as that of Jacob Bernays, did they go beyond the alternatives),[6] but the way in which they chose between the two is invariably related to their biographies. Jean Bollack has shown that it was precisely the Jewish former students of Wilamowitz who made desperate efforts to develop his philological program, while his German former students indulged their genius along the lines of Wilamowitz's much more speculative mode.[7] Such choices, however, have significant consequences for the future history of a particular discipline, even if the options scholars choose lie within the parameters of that discipline.

Ludwig Geiger (1848–1919), to whom the rest of this paper is devoted, ascribed to German culture in general a universalizing force. Everything that is taken up into German culture, Geiger argued, is freed thereby of its prejudices, even of its anti-Semitism. (Incidentally, one finds the same naiveté in Marcel Reich-Ranicki's autobiography *Mein Leben* (My Life, 1999). It is alarming to see how helpless the Jewish *Bildungsbürger* becomes once he has accepted everything that claims to be culture.)[8] Such a culture Geiger sees to be at work in his discipline, and, as a result, he cannot develop a proper dialectic between cultural values and his scientific work. In political terms he belongs to the group Andreas Kilcher calls "the cultural theorists of assimilation."[9] He rejects both the anti-Semites and the Zionists, the latter of whom are, in their own way, also trying to isolate the Jews. His denial of the anti-Semitism in German culture almost makes Geiger a precursor of the discourse theorists, at least as far as his program is concerned. But the limitations of discourse theory are all too clear when one looks at

how his actions go beyond his program. He is forced into these actions
by his object of study, literature itself, which is hardly short of negative
remarks about Jews. Geiger persists in regarding this literature as part
of a universalizing culture, even though — and this is one of his strategies — he has his favorites among German writers: Lessing and Heine,
for instance. Goethe, however, presents more of a problem.

Bearing in mind that Jewish intellectuals, too, operate within certain
scientific options, we may say that Geiger makes explicit use of the
separation between science and public opinion, the area in which crude
anti-Semitism was most at home. More-progressive scholars tried to
overcome this gap, but Geiger holds back in terms of his methodology,
because he has to protect his position — more precisely, he has to protect himself and his own loyalty to the Jewish faith. He achieves this
protection both inside the university and as editor of a scientific peri-
odical, the *Goethe-Jahrbuch* (Goethe Yearbook). I would like to look at
this situation in detail under four headings: his attitude to Judaism; the
"philological triangle" of knowledge, values, and institutions;[10] his
strategies within his discipline; and, finally, his work on Goethe and the
Jews.

Attitude to Judaism

In 1910 Ludwig Geiger published the biography of his father, the celebrated reform rabbi Abraham Geiger, a publication exercise traditionally carried out by the sons of famous scholars. In this biography
Ludwig included the letter written to him by his father in 1866, when
he was seventeen and had just decided to discontinue the study of theology. His father had written:

> Unless I am quite mistaken about your intellectual interests, your
> studies will focus on nothing other than the following: philosophy,
> ancient languages, in particular as they give expression to the most ac-
> tive forms of intellectual life, the history of their literatures, history in
> general, which is to say the development of the human spirit and in
> particular the intellectual movement which Jews and Judaism brought
> to mankind. Ultimately there is no difference between that and Jewish
> theology, regardless of whether it is theoretically acknowledged or
> actually put into practice. In this form you will have got to know it
> and, at least, learned to respect its legitimacy.[11]

The letter goes on to explain that since God's revelation took the preferred form of "great spiritual steps" that built successively on one an-

other, contemporary Jewish theology insisted on an enlightened philosophy of history that — though it was close to German idealism — had its origins in Judaism. It was from Judaism that the idea proceeded of "a spiritual power shaping and guiding the unity of the world."[12] Without this idea of God, every culture would lose its sense of purpose. Abraham speaks of the "monstrosities" that would have to be identified in the Pentateuch if it were thought that Moses were its sole author.[13] For that reason Abraham had little difficulty in giving up old ritual laws — for instance, on diet, circumcision, or prayers such as that calling for a return to Jerusalem.[14] While the father was not forced to separate theoretical and practical theology, his son, as a historian of Judaism and a philologist, would secularize the program. In so doing he was guided less by that process of the rationalization of religion that Max Weber describes and at the end of which all religion is transformed into culture. More important for him is publicly to take away the theological grounds of Jewish rationality[15] but without surrendering its claims to truth. As a defensive strategy the idea of a culture that generates its own enlightenment is preserved — at least in those areas chosen by Ludwig Geiger: literature and a science based on impartial observation. Geiger does not define culture, as his father had, as the expression of a universal idea of God, an idea that comes ever closer to realization through history. Quite explicitly Geiger opposes to "culture" the (political and more protective) idea of "confession."

For times have changed. Geiger's argument is similar to those of the majority of Jewish national-liberal intellectuals in the early years of the Second Reich,[16] and the phrase frequently used by him and others was that they were "German scholars of the Jewish confession."[17] Assimilation, they argued, was a matter for nations and did not concern personal belief. There was no difference between Jews and Germans: if differences existed, then they were between Jews and Christians. As late as 1912, when the pressure on the Jews had become incomparably more acute, Geiger elaborated his opinions in greater detail as he responded to a questionnaire, the answers to which were collected under the title *Judentaufen* (The Baptism of Jews).[18] The questionnaire was a response to the publication in the same year of Werner Sombart's *Die Juden und das Wirtschaftsleben* (The Jews and Economic Life, 1912) and had been sent to scientists and writers of the younger generation. One of the questions was: "What would be the probable consequences — in intellectual, political and economic life (or in just one of these) — of the assimilation of all Jews by means of conversion and intermarriage?"[19]

In his reply Geiger strongly challenged the view that such a state of affairs was desirable. He went on:

> But I wish most energetically to contest the idea that assimilation takes place only by conversion or intermarriage. This is a nonsense and a serious insult to all German Jews who, like their ancestors have done for the last one hundred years, have already become Germans and therefore do not need to become Germans again. If assimilation — and I can attach no other sense to the word — means becoming German in habits, language, behavior and feeling, then it requires neither intermarriage nor baptism.[20]

By taking up the ideas of the reform synagogue, with its clear belief in the enlightened evolution of the human spirit, and then applying these ideas to the German civilization of his time, Geiger was putting himself in an impossible position. He loses the one authority that could identify and condemn the monstrous anti-Semitism of German culture and leaves himself with nothing more than the modest instruments of philology with which to defend himself.

The Philological Triangle

"Separate issues" — this was Geiger's method and the principle according to which he organized his scientific life. He finds himself at a specific stage in the history of German philology, caught in a triangle of knowledge, values, and institutions that, in a consciously subversive way, he must use to his own ends.

The link between academic research and anti-Semitism has often been examined. We might recall two particular approaches: first, sociological studies of institutions have explained which values represented within the university served to block access to these institutions;[21] second, the sociology of knowledge has set out to explain the development of scientific knowledge and has established, at least within the natural sciences, that progress is made by specialization and that the pressure to specialize exists primarily on the periphery of an institution, whether seen geographically or in terms of hierarchy.[22] I wish to examine these approaches in greater detail to show that neither is adequate for the scientific history of Jewish *philologists*. One must bear in mind that in this field the object of study is linguistically and culturally bounded and, therefore, exposed to the value judgments of other interpreters.

1. *Social history.* Monika Richarz's "Zur Sozialgeschichte der jüdischen Intelligenz und der akademischen Judenfeindschaft 1780–1848" (On the Social History of Jewish Intellectuals and Academic Hostility to the Jews, 1780–1848, 1982) analyzes 280 reports prepared by academics from all faculties, giving their opinion on how adequately individual Prussian universities were prepared to implement the legislation on the Jews promulgated that year. "*Privatdozenten,*" "*außerordentliche,*" and "*ordentliche*" Jewish professors could be appointed according to this law, provided that such appointments were permitted by the university's statutes, on grounds of confession. Overall, the professors compiling these reports proved to be more conservative than their governments, and around half of them claimed that even the restricted appointment of Jews was incompatible with the confessional nature of their universities. Their arguments reflect both widely held cultural anxieties (caused by competition within the profession and the low esteem in which it was held) and more general prejudices — for example, the allegation that Jews did not really wish to assimilate. A professor of legal history writes:

> His [the Jew's] nationality is most closely connected with his religion, he cannot be rid of it for as long as he is a Jew. He will not assume German customs [*Volkstümlichkeit*] to any significant extent nor will he make use of the rights which are part of our way of life with the same devotion, love and efficiency as the Germans, nor will he cherish them and be able to teach them.[23]

No less cultural in their implications were the warnings against the subversion of the universities by the atheistic, liberal, and revolutionary ideas of the Jews — these warnings were backed up with reference to the literature of the time. It becomes clear how rigorously the professors wished to control access to the universities. The sociology of institutions can identify this situation, but it has difficulties in describing what these values mean for the life of the universities. For such values do not necessarily regulate research. Germanic philology presents itself to the outside world as a national philology, but within individual teaching seminars it often looks different — less regimented, for instance. Germanic philology does not necessarily identify itself with the supreme goal of national assimilation.

2. *Sociology of knowledge.* The institution creates a space that the individual sciences can use. Shulamit Volkov — her study focuses on the scientific success of the Jews during the Second Empire — bases her work on the idea of the quality of universality that characterizes the

university (or that, as Robert Merton says, represents its highest scientific norm). In this idea she sees the great attraction of the university for the Jews: "Science seemed to exercise particular attraction for those Jews whose fathers had already climbed the heights of success. In its at least apparent universality and in the emphasis it laid on merit and talent, science seemed to promise a community without barriers, in which individual achievement made everything attainable: a community which knew no racial or religious distinctions."[24] Because Volkov restricts her study to individual disciplines in the natural sciences, and because she does not study the research itself or read individual publications, her work relies on a mechanistic reading of an institutional law that we may summarize as follows: The progress of a science is the result of specialization. Specialization takes place only at the periphery, defined either geographically or in relation to the hierarchy of the discipline. Jewish scholars were forced into specialization. They had to stay as "Privatdozenten" for much longer than was normal and, if they were appointed to a chair at all, then seldom were they appointed at a *large* university. At small universities they could continue to cultivate their previous special areas of research without much hindrance.

Once again, one must ask: Is this true of philology? Is specialization the source of institutional success? Is it not rather the case that from 1900 progress in the field depended on the overcoming of philological specialization (positivism) and the introduction of new philosophical or methodological positions? Is it not the case that these innovations did not come from within the university but from the periphery, from those cultural circles that it was no longer considered desirable to exclude from the university? Philology follows its own rules, inasmuch as value judgments — whether or not they are intentional — are relevant to its methodology. In addition, between 1910 and 1925 the history of the discipline is marked by new philosophical positions (for which "progress" is not the appropriate word), whose intention is nothing other than the *overcoming* of specialization.[25] These impulses do, in fact, come from the periphery, but much less from the periphery of the universities than from the cultural-literary area (for instance, from the general philology of Hugo von Hofmannsthal), which was searching for points of contact with the university world.[26]

Philologists hold to the scientific norm in that individual beliefs are not permitted to find their way directly into research. This view comes out in clear mirror image as we read Nietzsche's critique: "Historical culture possesses positive and constructive qualities only in the wake of powerful new life-forces, for instance those of an emergent civilization:

that means only when it is directed under the control of a higher power and does not control and direct itself."[27] A basic distinction is made between facts and their arrangement into systems. Those very values that, in the eyes of the public, are regarded as the justification of the subject and are therefore paraded on ceremonial occasions ("Goethe, the Olympian," for example), are happily deconstructed in philological seminars. What Nietzsche called "life" soon assumed national meaning. Yet, the distinction between the university world and public opinion remains methodologically unsatisfactory, for cultural values are no less present in one area than in the other, and it is inevitable that — despite being discredited within the discipline itself — these cultural values imperceptibly become established within the institutions, at least provided that they are not used directly in selecting the objects of study. In the age of historicism the principal task is to master the diversity of knowledge: Geiger puts his trust in a culture that structures the world according to the values of the Enlightenment, and this is why he fails to recognize the dialectical link between a German culture riddled with prejudices and the scientific methods of philology. He fails to examine his own values not because they are unscientific but because they are the very foundation of his scientific activity.

Where Geiger fights back against anti-Semitic attitudes, he has recourse to philology and its tricks (for instance, establishing a canon) rather than attempting to transcend these attitudes from his awareness of their many theoretical weaknesses. Instead of separating issues, he knows that he ought to mediate. The self-discipline that this mediation requires is nowhere more apparent than in the review that he wrote of Victor Hehn's *Gedanken über Goethe* (Reflections on Goethe, 1887).[28] Geiger distinguishes between what can be said in a specialist journal and what can be said to a wider public. It is only in the nonspecialist journal *Die Nation* (The Nation) that Geiger can respond critically to Hehn's introduction of blatant value judgments into a scientific discussion ("Hehn lashes out at the Jews wherever he can," Geiger writes). He admits that in a scientific journal he would be less forthcoming: "If I praise the work, I am far from agreeing with all its opinions. But the presentation of this conflict is more suited to a specialized journal."

But even in those circles he cannot conduct any argument against the established practices of his discipline. He has only two options if things should turn against him. His positive option is to establish his own canon of texts. In fact, early on Geiger makes a special study of the role of women in literature and thus creates his own canon. His less positive alternative is to catalogue instances of anti-Semitism, as if it were possible from an aristocratic distance to cultivate objects that depended on him for their survival. The philologist as a collector is characterized by his choice of objects and by his blind faith in the many ways in which culture could exercise power in science. For most Germans this "culture" has national implications; for Geiger the connotations are rationalist. Geiger relies on the power of his observing science to transcend prejudices. If science remains full of anti-Semitism, then all that is left to Geiger is a helpless and grieving sense of loss, for he obviously no longer believes in the ability of scientific observation to overcome prejudice. Indeed, he wrote in his review of Hehn's book: "If one reads tirades of this kind in some newspaper article, penned by an anti-Semitic hot-head, one would hardly bother to shrug one's shoulders. When you read them in the book of a man of the importance of Viktor Hehn — a man whom one would wish to respect completely — then one can feel only the deepest grief."[29]

Strategies / Habitus

Geiger's habilitation was as a historian in Berlin: his subject was "Greek and Roman writers in their assessment of Jews and Jewry." He found his way into a university career and into *Germanistik*, in particular, thanks to the explicit support of Wilhelm Scherer, who taught in Berlin from 1877 until 1886 and helped Geiger overcome the two things that made him an outsider: that he was a Jew, and that he came from another subject.[30] In 1880 Scherer ensured that Geiger was appointed extraordinary professor — the highest rank a Jew might expect.[31] In the same year Geiger established himself at the very center of German studies — Goethe scholarship — yet in a position that was both outside Berlin (with the Jewish publisher Rütten & Loening in Frankfurt am Main)[32] and outside the university, the latter by founding the *Goethe-Jahrbuch*.

Five years later, when the Goethe Society was founded, it had little choice but to use the *Jahrbuch* as its house journal.[33] Even though the society had no control over the contents — nevertheless, of course, the Goethe and Schiller Archive regularly used the *Jahrbuch* for publications from its holdings — a considerable subsidy was forthcoming. The Committee of the Goethe Society had few problems with the arrangement, and it was only Erich Schmidt, a pupil of Scherer's and professor of literary history in Berlin, who could not accept such institutionalized powerlessness. In consequence, his attacks on Geiger became more and more virulent over the years: "The Y.book is not in the right hands," he argued in 1894, "Herr Geiger lacks the personality, the authority, the knowledge, the judgment, and the accuracy."[34] Some twenty years later, just before his death in 1913, Schmidt persuaded the Goethe Society to take its *Jahrbuch* away from Geiger.

Schmidt — the modern "Ladies' Professor" — framed his attacks for an anti-Semitic society, even though he himself was probably a bit freer of these prejudices. After Schmidt's death a Jewish colleague, Richard Moritz Meyer, applied for the position and had to hear from Gustav Roethe about Schmidt's aristocratic graces. Roethe explained that the university would rather have a count than a Jew, and — since there was no other Schmidt in sight — Roethe took the job himself. Roethe wrote to Wolfgang von Oettingen on 7 July 1913, just after he had been offered the chair: "I would have preferred them to take Burdach. It is evident that Berlin has to be represented in the executive, but I cannot wish Berlin to be represented by Rich. Meyer, particularly not at this moment — you understand what I mean without having to go into details. So I will get myself elected to the executive." And again on 10 May 1913: "You should not forget that Erich Schmidt had something if not aristocratic then at least something of a man of the world about him, he had that easy grace which comes from those circles and which we scholars generally do not possess." The truth was that Meyer was himself "a man of the world," but as a Jew he had never managed to be professor, thanks to Roethe's continuous obstruction.[35]

The generational conflict between Geiger and Schmidt was, at least in part, a product of anti-Semitism: that is to say, Geiger's defensive weakness came from the need to defend himself against anti-Semitism. Schmidt's urbanity caused him difficulties in more traditional circles, which had taken Geiger under their wing. Schmidt demanded that the *Jahrbuch* be popular and wanted a public figure to be editor. Such a representative literary personality should, he explained, be able to incorporate all aspects of philological knowledge — a standard up to which Schmidt himself never quite lived.[36] Schmidt did not believe that Geiger was such a personality — indeed, Geiger's whole approach was based on a professional concept of truth, rather than on representation — and Schmidt's attacks were personal in character. Geiger tried to make his position impregnable by separating out precisely those qualities that Schmidt wanted to synthesize. This is evident from the *Jahrbuch,* where Geiger kept his two bylines — the general essay and the scholarly critical treatise — quite a bit separate. Geiger was careful to keep his own values out of sight and did not make any general response to the attacks, knowing that it would weaken his position to do so. The documents in Weimar make this clear. Geiger's approach to countering the attacks is unambiguous: to concentrate on the specific situation and individual issue. It is the exact equivalent of his disciplined and defensive personal style in separating out issues, which we observed in his review of Hehn's anti-Semitic book.

Goethe and the Jews[37]

If Geiger wants to talk *personally* about his philological concerns, he turns to the wider public. In *Die Juden in der deutschen Literatur* (Jews in German Literature, 1910) he sets out from a defensive position: "I am not writing here as a Jew, but as a literary historian. As a Jew I am involved in the topic: as a literary historian I have no parti pris."[38] He never expresses his conviction that literature can purify those unformed dark prejudices that are its starting point, even though he hopes that such a general conviction can carry him through the party feuding of the day. Unfortunately, the subject itself kept pulling him down to earth. Two texts in particular make this clear. These are his study of "The Faust Legend and Faust Literature before Goethe," which had appeared in *Westermanns Illustrierte Deutsche Monatshefte* (Westermann's Illustrated German Monthly) in 1889–90[39] and the more recent series of public lectures held in the winter term of 1904–5 at the University of Berlin, whose title we mentioned earlier: "German Literature and the Jews." Of particular interest is the section devoted to Goethe.[40]

Geiger's method is shaped by the idea that the history of culture is a process of enlightenment within which individual writers take their places. Individual works must be placed in a wider context than merely that of the author and his culture, for it is the work alone that can bring to light the pure — that is to say, rational — core of its author and its age. Since Geiger equates literature with reason — at least, within the historical process — it follows that he cannot separate out "literature" (in the sense of a higher power) from the individual works. In any case, he lacks a theory of the individual work and cannot, therefore, distinguish among the various forms in which reason may express itself from one work to the next. As far as the autonomy of the work of art is concerned, Geiger has no option but to regard every remark of the author inside the works as equally valid. Geiger is prevented by his determination to think universally from the recognition he needed: that even aesthetic objects are less individual the closer they come to generally held prejudices — in other words, that aesthetic objects obtain universality only through individual qualities. The step that is distinctive to the aesthetic process is made up of many small steps. It would be a long time in the history of the discipline before there was any understanding of the process by which reason could come to be seen as part of what Theodor W. Adorno (and Peter Szondi) called "the logic of being produced."[41]

The works themselves show little evidence of either rationality or unreason. Geiger is, therefore, forced into elaborate reinterpretations and justifications of difficult works and obscure passages. We now turn to these reinterpretations and justifications.

Reinterpretation. Geiger regards the *Historia von D. Johann Fausten* as a compilation of stories that were in circulation at the time, poorly composed and in a barbaric language. The puppeteers — themselves "actors of the lowest type, people quite without education or intellect"[42] — simply offered the basest section of the population a magnificent theme. The meaning of the theme can be found in the Faustian character of Faust himself, a character that is marked by the quest for knowledge. Geiger reads Goethe's *Faust* texts no differently from Lessing's *Faust* fragment. The downfall of Faust ordained from on high was unthinkable. It was inconceivable in the age of Enlightenment that the desire for knowledge could be punished as hubris. In fact, as we know, Goethe's intentions were quite different from those of Lessing. His natural theology has a considerable influence on *Faust Part Two*. If the diversity of the world increases to a point at which it is unresolvable, then nature intervenes in the form of sleep, unconsciousness, or death. There is a change of scene and the action continues elsewhere. We think, for instance, of the scene in which Phorkyas confronts Helen with the stories that are circulating about her: Helen does not respond by explaining how all these stories hang together; she falls into a swoon. This is an aesthetic action of the author's, which should be interpreted as follows: Goethe fundamentally negates the desire of the Enlightenment to accept and, within the appropriate limits, to know everything.[43] Geiger will not see this, and what he loves in Goethe is his own vision of Lessing.

Justification. In his lecture on Goethe and the Jews Geiger established a number of important facts,[44] among them Goethe's study of Hebrew, his knowledge of the Bible, his occasional Jewish acquaintances, the admiration Jewish women in Berlin bestowed on him, his respect for Spinoza and Mendelssohn. On the other side, no less clearly

Geiger identifies Goethe's support for a far from liberal law concerning the Jews; and he notes Goethe's early "Jewish sermon" and remarks against Judaism, such as those in the *Wanderjahre*. Geiger merely identifies such elements and does not delve more deeply, in an undefined way hoping that Goethe's literary involvement with Judaism would somehow ultimately benefit Judaism. At a more trivial level he does once blame Goethe's ill-humored remarks against Jews on a passing bad mood. Geiger relies on Goethe; and both are wrong, for culture is too weak to defend itself against its own anti-Semitism. In fact, of course, Goethe does differentiate between Jewish culture and the individual Jews whom he happened to meet, whether personally or in his readings in Jewish history:

> These myths are truly great, and they stand at an earnest and dignified distance from us and maintain the devotion we felt for them in our youth. As our heroes step forward into the present, however, we notice that they are Jews, and we feel the contrast between the patriarchs and their descendants — a contrast that confuses and disconcerts us.[45]

The Jewish tradition has been immersed in German culture, and Goethe can accept it in this form. Key concepts are human particularity and cultural universality. When one looks more closely, it is evident that Goethe interprets the Jewish stories within his own Christian culture, mostly according to the oppositions particularity/universality, law/love, and externality/inwardness.[46] This hierarchy is quite unmistakable, for instance, in the "pädagogische Provinz" of the *Wanderjahre* (II/2). Goethe's work is marked by a single construct, one idea that proceeds from particularity in the midst of pluralism. Ideas are universal, yet even if literary works are made from them, life and its prejudices soon find their way in. They are too weak to defend themselves against this invasion. Heteronomous cultural values that are taken up into texts keep much of their old meaning. In his Berlin lectures Geiger's attitude is both defiant and despairing. His basic conviction — that literature separates the poet from the mob — is only partly true of Goethe.

Translated by Hugh Ridley

Notes

[1] These reflections take up some of the critical ideas that led to the preparation of the international Marbach Symposium "Jewish Intellectuals and Literary Study in Germany 1870–1933" (jointly organized by myself in cooperation with a project team from the Marbach Center for the History of Germanistik and held in the Deutsches Literaturarchiv, Marbach, 16–19 June 1999). Similar themes dominated the symposium discussions themselves, as their forthcoming publication (Wilfried Barner and Christoph König, eds.) will demonstrate. The position that I am explicitly contesting at this point is taken up by Jürgen Fohrmann, whose closeness to the ideas of Niklas Luhmann is also shared by Jürgen Kaube ("Jenseits der Identität," *Frankfurter Allgemeine Zeitung*, 30 June 1999). Cf. also Christoph König, "Jüdische Gelehrte und die Philologien," in the publication of the Unit for Research into the History of Germanistik, *Mitteilungen* 9/10 (1996): 10–16.

[2] Gershom Scholem, "Juden und Deutsche," *Judaica II,* ed. Scholem (Frankfurt/Main: Suhrkamp, 1970) 22.

[3] Cf. Wilfried Barner, "Literaturgeschichtsschreibung vor und nach 1945: alt, neu, alt/neu," in *Zeitenwechsel: Germanistische Literaturwissenschaft vor und nach 1945,* ed. Wilfried Barner and Christoph König (Frankfurt/Main: Fischer, 1997) 119–49. Also Nikolaus Wegmann, "Was heißt einen 'klassischen' Text lesen? Philologische Selbstreflexion zwischen Wissenschaft und *Bildung,*" in *Wissenschaftsgeschichte der Germanistik im 19. Jahrhundert,* ed. Jürgen Fohrmann and Wilhelm Voßkamp (Stuttgart, Weimar: Metzler, 1994) 334–450.

[4] *Literaturwissenschaft und Geistesgeschichte 1910 bis 1925,* ed. Christoph König and Eberhard Lämmert (Frankfurt/Main: Fischer, 1993).

[5] Christoph König, "Hofmannsthal unter den Philologen: Zum Verhältnis von Dichtung und Wissenschaft in der Kultur der Moderne." Habilitationsschrift of the Humboldt University in Berlin. (Publication forthcoming.)

[6] Jean Bollack, *Jacob Bernays: Un homme entre deux mondes* (Villeneuve d'Ascq: Presses universitaires du Septentrion, 1998) (Savoir mieux 4).

[7] Cf. Bollack's contribution to the conference (footnote 1) under the title "Die klassische Philologie und die Juden vor 1933."

[8] Marcel Reich-Ranicki, *Mein Leben* (Stuttgart: Deutsche Verlags-Anstalt, 1999).

[9] Andreas Kilcher, "Was ist 'deutsch-jüdische Literatur'? Eine historische Diskursanalyse." (Unpublished manuscript.)

[10] Cf. Christoph König, "Wissen, Werte, Institutionen," in *Zeitenwechsel* (footnote 3).

[11] Ludwig Geiger, *Abraham Geiger: Leben und Lebenswerk. Mit einem Bildnis* (Berlin: Reimer, 1910) 178–79.

[12] Cf. Ludwig Geiger, *Geschichte der Juden in Berlin: Festschrift zur zweiten Säkular-Feier. Anmerkungen, Ausführungen, urkundliche Beilagen* (Berlin: Guttentag, 1871). Guttentag reprinted this with a preface by Hermann Simon and two appendices in 1890. In this work Geiger explicitly commits himself to the scientific study of Judaism and says of Immanuel Wolf: "Judaism, according to Wolf's definition, is marked by the idea of the unity of God, which was alive in ancient times and among the Jewish people, even if it took up influences from other nations and on that basis passed on a message to other peoples. Mosaic law was the body that contained this intellectual content" (177).

[13] *Ibid.* 180.

[14] Ludwig Geiger recalled the second assembly of rabbis in Frankfurt on 21 July 1845, which his father chaired and at which his father distinguished between the eternal moral laws and ritual laws, which were means to a religious end but not an end in themselves (the Will of God). ("Eduard von Bauernfeld und die Frankfurter Rabbinerversammlung," *Allgemeine Zeitung des Judentums*, 1 November 1895) 46–59.

[15] In a public lecture in 1910 he warned against the exaggerated claims being made in Jewish circles, referring, among other things, to the "arrogance about our own, i.e. Jewish achievements" (Ludwig Geiger, *Die deutsche Literatur und die Juden* [Berlin: Reimer, 1910] 7).

[16] Cf. Jacob Toury, *Die politischen Orientierungen der Juden in Deutschland: Von Jena bis Weimar* (Tübingen: Mohr, 1966) 122. The Jews approved — on the basis of his constitutional concessions — of Bismarck's successful foreign policy and could, as a result, share in national feeling.

[17] Cf. for example Geiger, *Die deutsche Literatur und die Juden* 11.

[18] *Judentaufen,* ed. Werner Sombart et al. (Munich: Georg Müller, 1912).

[19] *Loc. cit.* 6.

[20] *Ibid.* 45.

[21] Monika Richarz, "Juden, Wissenschaft und Universitäten: Zur Sozialgeschichte der jüdischen Intelligenz und der akademischen Judenfeindschaft 1780–1848," in *Gegenseitige Einflüsse deutscher und jüdischer Kultur von der Epoche der Aufklärung bis zur Weimarer Republik,* ed. Walter Grab (Tel-Aviv: Nateev Print. and Publ. Enterprises, 1982) 55–73.

[22] Shulamit Volkov, "Soziale Ursachen des Erfolgs in der Wissenschaft. Juden im Kaiserreich," *Historische Zeitschrift* 245 (1987): 315–42.

[23] Richarz, "Juden, Wissenschaft und Universitäten" 70.

[24] Volkov, "Soziale Ursachen" 328–29.

[25] Cf. *Literaturwissenschaft und Geistesgeschichte 1910 bis 1925.*

[26] Cf. Christoph König: "Wahrheitsansprüche: Goethes, Nietzsches und Hofmannsthals Ideen für eine allgemeine Philologie um 1905," in *Konkurrenten in der Fakultät. Kultur, Wissen und Universität um 1900,* ed. Christoph König und Eberhard Lämmert (Frankfurt/Main: Fischer, 1998) 44–58.

[27] Friedrich Nietzsche: *Unzeitgemäße Betrachtungen: Zweites Stück. Vom Nutzen und Nachteil der Historie für das Leben,* in his *Werke. Kritische Gesamtausgabe,* ed. Giorgio Colli and Mazzino Montinari (Berlin, New York: de Gruyter, 1972) 1: 239–330.

[28] The review appeared in *Die Nation* 4.38 (1886–87): 560–70. The quotations are taken from p. 570.

[29] *Loc. cit.*

[30] In 1877 he tried to have Geiger appointed as contributor to the *Zeitschrift für deutsches Altertum und deutsche Literatur,* which was jointly edited by Elias Steinmeyer, Karl Müllenhoff, and himself. He writes on 21 October 1877 to Steinmeyer: "Dr. Ludwig Geiger recently called on me, and I returned the visit. It seems to me important to give him a regular slot for writing on humanist literature in the Anzeiger." On Scherer's critical position during the anti-Semitism conflict see Jürgen Sternsdorff, *Wissenschaftskonstitution und Reichsgründung. Die Entwicklung der Germanistik bei Wilhelm Scherer: Eine Biographie nach unveröffentlichten Quellen* (Frankfurt/Main: Lang, 1979) 215–17.

[31] Geiger recalled nearly forty years later, in 1918: "Scherer's kindness — and, I might add, his estimation of my person and my achievements — were such that, immediately after his move to Berlin, he declared that he wished to ensure that I obtained a professorship. For a man of this transparent integrity, word and deed were one" (*Vossische Zeitung,* 20 June 1918).

[32] Cf. *Deutsch-jüdische Geschichte der Neuzeit,* vol. 2. Also *Emanzipation und Akkulturation 1780–1871,* ed. Michael Brenner, Stefi Jersch-Wenzel, and Michael A. Meyer (Munich: Beck, 1996) 274.

[33] Cf. Norbert Oellers, "Elf Bemerkungen zum Beitrag von Karl Robert Mandelkow (zur Goethe-Gesellschaft in Weimar)," in *Literaturwissenschaft und Geistesgeschichte 1910 bis 1925,* 356–61.

[34] Quoted from a motion proposed by Erich Schmidt to the Goethe Society on 4 April 1894 (Goethe- und Schiller-Archiv Weimar GSA 149/959, p. 313 verso).

[35] Both documents are in GSA 149/968. Cf. also Roland Berbig, "'Poesieprofessor' und 'literarischer Ehrenabschneider': Der Berliner Literaturhistoriker Richard M. Meyer," *Berliner Hefte* 1 (1996): 37–99. Also Hans-Harald Müller's contribution to the Marbach Symposium (footnote 1) under the title "Ich habe nie etwas anderes sein wollen als ein deutscher Philolog aus Scherers Schule: Hinweise auf Richard Moritz Meyer."

[36] Cf. Volker Ufertinger, "Erich Schmidt: Philologie und Repräsentation im Kaiserreich," University of Munich, Magister dissertation, 1995.

[37] Cf. Wilfried Barner, "Jüdische Goethe-Verehrung vor 1933," *Juden in der deutschen Literatur. Ein deutsch-israelisches Symposion,* ed. Stéphane Moses and Albrecht Schöne (Frankfurt/Main: Suhrkamp, 1986) 127–51.

[38] Geiger, *Die deutsche Literatur und die Juden* 81.

[39] Ludwig Geiger, "Faustsage und Faustdichtung vor Goethe," *Westermanns Illustrierte Deutsche Monatshefte* 67 (1889–90) 752–67; cf. also Hans Mayer, "Faust, Aufklärung, Sturm und Drang," *Sinn und Form* 13 (1961): 1, 101–20.

[40] Geiger (footnote 15) 81–101. The chapter is titled "Goethe und die Juden."

[41] Cf. Christoph König, "Loslösungsakte: Zur Vernunft in literarischen Werken," in *Literaturwissenschaft und politische Kultur: Für Eberhard Lämmert zum 75. Geburtstag,* ed. Winfried Menninghaus and Klaus R. Scherpe (Stuttgart, Weimar: Metzler, 1999) 268–73.

[42] Footnote 39.

[43] Cf. Christoph König, "Wissensvorstellungen in Goethes *Faust II,*" *Euphorion* 93.2 (1999): 227–49.

[44] Generally of interest on this issue are Julius Bab, *Goethe und die Juden* (Berlin: Philo-Verlag, 1926) (Die Morgen-Reihe 3); Heinrich Teweles, *Goethe und die Juden* (Hamburg: Gente, 1925); Günter Hartung, "Goethe und die Juden," *Weimarer Beiträge* 40 (1994): 398–416. Cf. also Hartung's "Judentum," *Goethe Handbuch: Personen, Sachen, Begriffe A–K,* vol. 4/1, ed. Hans-Dietrich Dahnke and Regine Otto (Stuttgart, Weimar: Metzler 1998) 581–90. Bab is the first to reject a question forced on the discussion from outside, namely, the isolation of one aspect of Goethe's harmonious personality. But Goethe's life is as exoteric as any extraneous cultural-historical idea.

[45] Letter to Carl Friedrich Zelter of 19 May 1912, in *Goethes Briefe und Briefe an Goethe,* Hamburger Ausgabe in 6 Bänden, ed. Karl Robert Mandelkow,

assisted by Bodo Morawe, 3rd ed. (Munich: Beck 1986–88), vol. 3, *Briefe der Jahre 1805–1821* (1988), no. 961, p. 193.

[46] Cf. Johann Wolfgang Goethe, "Zwo wichtige bisher unerörterte biblische Fragen (1772–73)," in his *Ästhetische Schriften 1771–1805,* ed. Friedmar Apel (Frankfurt/Main: Deutscher Klassiker-Verlag, 1998) (Bibliothek deutscher Klassiker 151) 131–40.

Waiting for Goethe:
Goethe Biographies from
Ludwig Geiger to Friedrich Gundolf

Hope Hague, Brenda Machosky, and Marcel Rotter
University of Wisconsin-Madison

This panel was originally titled "'Ein jüdisches Zeitalter' — Goethe Biographies from Geiger to Gundolf." We realized, however, that the concept of biography (problematic in and of itself) was perhaps not the proper category under which to link the written representations of this figure, "Goethe."[1] In the literal sense of *bio-graphy*, the writing of a life, this may be true. As the paper finally argues, however, biographies are fictions, and like Plato's *Republic*, such fictions reflect an ideal world more than an actual one. Thus, a study of Goethe's "biographers" revealed more about an individual or epochal hope than about either a dead poet or a historical moment. In the original title, Victor Hehn's anti-Semitic description of this period of Goethe-representation as "ein jüdisches Zeitalter" had been appropriated to show its inherent ambiguity and to effect its deconstruction; subsequently, the phrase eliminated itself from the title. Nonetheless, "ein jüdisches Zeitalter" frames a specific period in which Jewish scholars were major players in Goethe scholarship, from the heady times of Jewish assimilation in the nineteenth century to the looming threat of the Final Solution.

TO CONSTRUCT THE "HISTORICAL" NARRATIVE that will render a life meaningful, the biographer does not merely produce body parts from his pockets, like the literary critics indicted by T. S. Eliot, but animates the lifeless tissue of the textual corpus.[2] The biographer's experience is constituted by a dialectical relationship with the written remains of the subject. These remains are molded into a *homunculus*, a perfected totality of appearances that are assumed to reveal the essence of the subject. In a biography that posits itself as social science, Georg Simmel refers to this raw material as the *große Konfession* [great confession] that revealed a *Gesamtdeutung Goethe* [comprehensive interpretation of Goethe]. By a careful study of this material Simmel announces his *telos* to be the revelation of the spiritual sense of the Goethean existence.[3] In each case, the writing of the life seems to reflect a desire to translate a perceived *geistigen Sinn* [intellectual meaning] of Goethe into the *deutschen Geist* [German spirit] for all. For Geiger, Goethe promised a German culture in which being Jewish was an attribute, not an identity. For Geiger's contemporary, Bielschowsky, Goethe stood for the highest potential of humanity, as *Übermensch* [super- or overman]. In the period between the world wars Emil Ludwig described a Goethe not only "menschlich vollendet" [humanly perfect] but "vollendet menschlich" [perfectly human], an image that Friedrich Gundolf elevated to the status of myth. But the final words of Simmel's preface apply to all of Goethe's biographers: "The interpretation of Goethe, who referred to all that he created as a great confession, becomes, intended or not, always also a confession of the interpreter."[4]

Like Samuel Beckett's play about nothing and everything, these biographies stage anticipation and hope, as well as disappointment and hopelessness. While our starry-eyed gaze is directed into the distance, it is revealed that Goethe has always already been here and gone. For Goethe admirers and haters alike, Goethe is present only in his absence.

At the end of the nineteenth century the assimilation of German Jews into German high culture was at its peak. The Jewish-German elite participated in the dominant *Bildungsbürgertum*, the influential literary and cultural scene in Germany. As Peter Gay puts it, the "romance of the Jews with German culture" seemed to be drawing to a happy end.[5] The romance was, indeed, ending, but not with the expected result of Jews and Germans united in harmonious bliss. With historical hindsight, Shulamit Volkov offers an alternative view of this period as one in which certain individuals experienced a sense of integration but in which this feeling of emancipation did not hold for Jews as a group. Rather, as David Sorkin has also argued, the period was marked by the development of an "intimate culture" (or, as Sorkin calls it, a "dual legacy") that formed the basis of a new Jewish-German identity.[6] Schiller's concept of Bildung, the cultural development of an individual that would lead to a better society, was often appreciated in the figure of Goethe and in his works. The concept of Bildung and its perceived realization in Goethe provided a link between Germans and German Jews. Whether Bildung could really sustain this link is highly debatable. Certainly, many *Bildungsbürger*, and most of Goethe's biographers, believed that it could. Friedrich Schiller's *Über die ästhetische Erziehung des Menschen* (On the Aesthetic Education of Man, 1795)

provided the cornerstone for this belief, which, in practice came to resemble a new religion: Aesthetics. In *German Jews beyond Judaism*
George L. Mosse argued that the dialogue between Jews and Germans
(not necessarily as equals) that emerged around the concept of Bildung
was the result of "the search for a personal identity beyond religion and
nationality."[7] Aesthetics offered itself as a nonpartisan, nondenomina-
tional system that would found a new State — Hegel and Kant rolled
into one (and in direct opposition to Plato). In the second letter Schiller urged that we should follow the path of aesthetics, "because it is
only through Beauty that man makes his way to Freedom."[8] For Schiller, the greatest beauty was to be found in art, and the greatest artist
was, of course, his dear friend Goethe.[9]

As Jews gained political and social freedom, they also seemed to
gain credibility among the German cultural elite. The ascendant Jew-
ish-Germans appropriated the doctrine of aesthetics, perhaps almost as
a crusade, and did much to disseminate its practice. And yet, there was
perhaps always an awareness that the Germans were not following quite
the same path toward aesthetic freedom. In 1912 Moritz Goldstein
noted in his essay "Deutsch-jüdischer Parnass" (German-Jewish Parnas-
sus): "We Jews administer the spiritual wealth of a people [the Ger-
mans], which denies us the right and the capacity to do so."[10] Almost a
century later, George L. Mosse agreed that although increasingly involved in cultural and intellectual pursuits, "Jews were continually being cast in the role of outsiders through their engagement with
modernity."[11] The passionate embracing of a "higher culture" widened
the distance between the German people and the *Bildungsbürgertum,*
the cultural elite in which Jewish Germans played a significant role. The
prominence of Jewish Germans in cultural settings contrasted sharply
with the waxing and waning but continuous anti-Semitism among the
masses. Mosse suggests that the history of German Jews is the story of
what happens when "a high culture which was individualistic, humanist, and pacifist" interacted with popular culture. According to Mosse,
the "favorite literary medium" through which to balance these forces
was historical biography, and he speculated that the choice of this genre
reflected "the search for the individual in a Germany whose politics
seemed to shift with the sway of the irrational masses."[12] For many,
Goethe appeared to be that individual, or at least its ideal. Perhaps no
historical figure better demonstrates the tension between an individual
sense of assimilation in scholarship and the public rejection of that individual for his Jewish identity than Ludwig Geiger. That is not to say
that Geiger's sense of integration was self-deceptive, nor is it to say that

the German-Jewish subculture did not play a central role in German culture. A figure such as Geiger illuminates the opacity of the Jewish presence in German culture and the futility of trying to segregate Jewish from German.

Ludwig Geiger's practice of literary history, from his university habilitation in 1873 until his death in 1919, combined the meticulous objectivity of historicism with an ethical and civic pathos derived from the Enlightenment and Reform Judaism.[13] Although he deviated from a religious vocation to become a student of history and literature, his father's example decisively influenced his spiritual and intellectual development, and his secular "German" voice must be understood as originating from within a German-Jewish minority culture.[14] Abraham Geiger founded institutions for educating the religious leadership and the Jewish community, including the College for the Science of Judaism in Berlin, at which Ludwig held a teaching position early in his career. The elder Geiger called on German Jews to master the German language and even to adopt it for prayer.[15] Educated in both rabbinical and university traditions, Ludwig Geiger followed his father in subscribing to the ideal of an identity that could be both German and Jewish.

In the early 1870s, at the college founded by his father, Geiger researched and identified a long history of cultural interdependence between the Jewish minority and the Germans. Later, as a university-trained Renaissance specialist, researcher, and visiting professor at the University of Berlin, he was drawn to study those historic moments when humanist scholarship had served progressive ends or had enhanced the standing of Jewish literature (especially the Hebrew Bible) in the eyes of the Germans. Like his father, he saw "the mind's emancipation from the rule of theology" at work in history, and he identified Humanism, the Enlightenment, and German Classicism as "the three levels of world historical literary development."[16] In this historical continuum the Age of Goethe was the most recent but by no means the ultimate culmination of humanity's historic struggle for intellectual autonomy and civil guarantees that would eventually consolidate the recent civic gains of the Jewish minority.[17] As editor and contributor to the weekly *Allgemeine Zeitung des Judentums* (General Newspaper of German Jewry) from 1912 to 1919 he used his influence to promote and defend cultural assimilation for the Jewish community. He negotiated the boundary between the German and Jewish cultures with unflagging optimism.

At this border, shared by Germans and German Jews, Geiger encountered Goethe, the prophet without honor in his own land. He began his crusade to preserve and interpret Goethe's documentary
remains for the sake of all Germans. By the credo, "der Wahrheit zu
dienen ist mein Beruf" [My vocation is to serve the truth][18] Geiger referred to a carefully researched and documented historical truth, resistant to partisan intention (whether Jewish, nationalist, anti-Semitic,
Zionist, or any other). His emphatic tone, however, can be traced to
unstated intentions related to his German-Jewish identity. First, as a literary historian during the imperial 1870s and after he had to legitimate
his participation as a Jew. Second, as a member of the Jewish elite he
hoped to use "truth" as a bulwark against the irrational and increasingly threatening "*Widergeist*" [hostile spirit] of popular anti-Semitism.
As Wilfried Barner has suggested, "Truth" was a useful "Schutzschild"
[protective shield] which allowed Geiger a certain freedom.[19] Nonetheless, Geiger vehemently denied accusations of *Verjudung* [Jewifica-
tion], insisting that the professional persona of assimilated Jewish
Goethe scholars was completely German: "There is not the slightest
Jewish trace in the work of Bielschowsky or Morris; and likewise, no
critic has ever found any evidence of '*Verjudung*' in the 77 volumes of
the *Goethe-Jahrbuch* (Goethe Yearbook) that I have edited."[20]

Throughout his professional life Geiger was the target of both direct
and indirect anti-Semitic attacks from people he despised, such as the
demagogue Adolf Bartels, and from others he respected, such as the
pioneering scholar Viktor Hehn, who contributed frequently to the
Goethe-Jahrbuch at Geiger's request.[21] During Hehn's Berlin years he
associated with many Jewish *Bildungsbürger,* including Geiger. He even
dubbed one of the literary circles he attended "The Oriental Society"
because all but two members were Jews.[22] As the years passed, and the
aging scholar withdrew into misanthropic solitude, he published an essay excoriating the Jewish character, Jewish journalism, and Jewish influence in public life.[23] In his obituary of Hehn, Conrad Bursian
described the transformation, in Bismarck's Berlin, of the once liberal
"48er": "Exposed to the Berlin air, he gradually turned into a decided
anti-Semite, who painted in the darkest colors what he considered the
dangerous influence of Jews in the press, politics, art and science."[24]

This description of Hehn's racism captures the overall situation of
Jews in the last decades of the nineteenth century. In the insular worlds
of the salons and universities, intellect and culture took precedence. In
the streets, the air was becoming choked with anti-Semitism.[25] Nonetheless, it appears that Hehn's eloquent and intelligent articles on

Goethe mattered more than his anti-Semitic opinions. No doubt, like the great models Reuchlin, Luther, Schiller, and Goethe, Hehn was, for Geiger, a "man of substance" whose contributions admitted him to Geiger's pantheon of *bedeutende Männer* [eminent men]. Geiger focused on the larger contributions of such *Männer* to humanity and to Jewish assimilation, and he ignored the slights of prejudice.

The scholarly interpretation of Goethe was also subject to the anti-Semitic air, even as Geiger insisted that there was no "Jewish question" but only a "völkergeschichtliches Problem" [problem of a people's history].[26] A notable example of competing views of this historical problem was the disagreement between Hehn and Geiger concerning the significance of Goethe's interest in the Hebrew language, his reception of the Hebrew Bible, and his use of biblical language. Hehn argued that Germans had long ago adopted the "Oriental" biblical idiom as their own: the foreign Jewish elements that had entered the German language through Luther's Bible had been appropriated by the Germans through centuries of habitual use in daily speech. Thus, according to Hehn, Goethe's biblical quotations were merely "kernig-deutsch" [unspoiled German].[27] Geiger, who also documented Goethe's use of and respect for the Hebrew Bible, insisted that this biblical language be understood as Jewish in essence as well as in origin, thereby establishing Goethe's admiration for elements of Jewish history and culture.[28] One could find support for this position in *Dichtung und Wahrheit* (Poetry and Truth, 1811–22) where Goethe wrote that the Jews were the walking reminders of the most ancient times.[29] With interpretations of this sort, Geiger (who deeply and personally identified with Goethe) was able to historicize his hero as progressive and to dissociate Goethe from the primitive mentality of the anti-Semites in the streets and beer halls. Geiger's *apologia* for Goethe was undermined on two fronts. First his historicist rhetoric required him to deny any relation between Goethe veneration and Jewish culture. Second, Geiger was also affected by the "Berlin air" and increasingly identified himself as a patriotic German.

The greatest German poet was on the verge of becoming a hero of national literature — not because of what he actually wrote or accomplished but because of the grandiose self-representation the empire required of him. To be placed securely on this pedestal, Goethe had to be removed from that liminal space where the Jewish and German cultures might have come together. Geiger's acquiescence to a nationalist agenda in this early monumentalization of Goethe ran counter to his own lifelong efforts toward a truthful representation of the historical

Goethe, as seen in this troubling remark in *Vorträge und Versuche* (Lectures and Essays): "It has been recently said that we should place Goethe in the service of our times. We accept that, if it means: we want to place our times, ourselves in Goethe's service . . . then we will be able to say: our times will experience their own joyous rebirth through Goethe."[30]

In this spirit of symbiosis with Goethe and of hope for a national rebirth, which were completely at variance with the actual nationalist mania prevailing at the outset of the First World War, and in the same year that the editorship of the *Goethe-Jahrbuch* was wrested from him Geiger presented his biography of Goethe to the German people.

Goethe: Sein Leben und Schaffen (Goethe: His Life and Creation), published in 1913, was a simple narrative dedicated to Geiger's children and subtitled *Dem deutschen Volke erzählt* [told to the German People].[31] Among the rising anti-Semitic tides, Geiger found in the narrative of Goethe a lifeboat in which to preserve German culture for future generations. The simple narrative's "Volkstümlichkeit" [popular tone] reached beyond the *Bildungsbürger* to a wider public.[32] Omitting detailed synopses of Goethe's work (which the public had a duty to read) and abstaining from entertaining anecdotes (which might diminish the seriousness of the subject), Geiger began his defense of "unser Meister" [our teacher] and "unser Held" [our hero] as a desirable national role model. In doubting the "widely held notion" of the public's indifference to Goethe, he was encouraged by the success of Bielschowsky's biography, sales figures for the new inexpensive Goethe editions, and the current popularity of *Faust*.[33] Familiar with every detail of Goethe's life and writings, Geiger cast doubt on the claims that Goethe (unlike Schiller) was not and did not wish to be a writer of and for the people. He asserted that Goethe's apparent lack of interest in the Wars of Liberation was neither elitist nor unpatriotic. Though Goethe was no *Hurraschreier* [super patriot], he did in several instances show *wahres Deutschtum* [true German spirit].[34] In response to the anti-Goethe attacks of nationalists and socialists alike, who suggested that Goethe's life in Weimar was un-German, obsequious, and morally lax, Geiger countered, "This talk of Goethe's servile relationship with the nobility is, at the very least, much exaggerated."[35]

Geiger also stylized Goethe as a writer "for the people," although he admitted that few works could be understood by very young readers, by *züchtige Mädchen* [modest girls], or by those who had not developed through Bildung. Only maturity and experience enabled a reader to understand the moral complexity of *Werther, Wilhelm Meister,* or *Die Wahlverwandtschaften* (Elective Affinities). In Geiger's account, a deep appreciation for Goethe had to be acquired in small steps through a lifetime of persistent dedication, much like a secular religion. Geiger's *Goethe* required an educated public, and yet this devotional intent yielded a contrary reaction. Attending gymnasium at about the same time as Geiger's *Goethe* appeared, Bertolt Brecht later lamented, "these books were ruined for us in school as the world's most boring people praised them in the most boring way . . . the German teachers with their long beards obstructed our access to the only refuge of sensuality in all of German literature."[36]

In hindsight, Geiger the *Bildungsbürger* could be seen as naïve and unrealistic in his exaggerated esteem for German culture and his belief in the power of humanistic literary education. To be fair, the ultimate failure of the assimilative project may not be sufficient reason completely to discredit Geiger's steadfast belief in the goals of Enlightenment thinking. Geiger's life work captures both the hope with which the Jewish-German cultural elite had invested the complex figure of Goethe and the ease with which such hope could be swept away. Walter Benjamin ended his extended essay about Goethe's *Die Wahlverwandtschaften*, an essay about much more than the novel and also an attempt to save German culture from itself, with this sentiment. "Nur um der Hoffnungslosen willen ist uns die Hoffnung gegeben" [Only for the sake of the hopeless ones have we been given hope].[37] For all his literary sensibility, high ideals, and public commitment, it is piteously obvious how far removed Geiger had become from the realities surrounding his education project. As a pillar of the small and dedicated community of highly cultivated *Bildungsbürger* he had become trapped in a fatal and unwanted elite position. The Goethe whom Geiger cultivated with such devotion and skill turned out to be a well-conjured apparition. At the end of his life and his work Geiger was still waiting for Goethe.

If Geiger, arguably the most dedicated and prolific of Jewish-German Goethe scholars, was unable to bring Goethe before the German people, we must seriously question George Mosse's basic assumption that a true dialogue took place between Germans and German Jews by means of historical biography. Albert Bielschowsky's *Goethe: Sein Leben und seine Werke* (Goethe: His Life and His Work) and Emil Ludwig's *Goethe: Geschichte eines Menschen* (Goethe: History of a Man) are works that demonstrate how biographical approaches to Goethe developed and to what extent they were influenced by society's general view of Jews, as well as by the individual personality of a particular author. In general, there are few if any overt signs of "Jewishness" in these works. They do contain, however, clues about the hope for Goethe and his works to serve as a source of Jewish emancipation by means of Bildung. But biographers cannot entirely avoid Goethe's relationship to his Jewish contemporaries or his anti-Semitic comments, even if they appear as a small blot on the immense canvas of his life.

Bielschowsky's biography was immensely popular, being printed in forty-two editions and selling over 80,000 copies from 1895 to 1922. Copies of this work, particularly gilded and leather-bound ones, were popular gifts for bar and bat mitzvahs, as well as for communions and confirmations. We must exercise some caution in assuming that the wide dissemination of the book corresponded to an equally wide readership. Nonetheless, Bielschowsky's *Goethe* made a strong appearance. Like Geiger, Bielschowsky saw himself primarily as a teacher, and, consequently, he enthusiastically subscribed to the concept of Bildung. In fact, his biography comes across like a lecture encouraging young people to follow the example of Goethe. To represent this figure fully, he inundates his reader with nearly 1,200 pages of details about Goethe's life. (Thus the hesitancy in assuming that the book was widely read.) Further to develop the poet as a model, Bielschowsky articulated parallels between figures in Goethe's life and in his works. Unlike Geiger, Bielschowsky summarized Goethe's works.

In Bielschowsky's work the relationship between Goethe and the Jews is most notable for its absence. Bielschowsky avoids anything connected to Jewish life. If he cannot bypass the topic, he plays down its importance. He explains, for example, the exclusion of Jews from Frankfurt's communal life as normal for the time, an argument reminiscent of Geiger's refusal to indict historical figures according to "modern" standards. Bielschowsky attempted literary objectivity, stating facts without raising his voice in commentary. Bielschowsky treated Goethe's Jewish friends and acquaintances as he did all of Goethe's friends and acquaintances, as instruments that allowed the light of Goethe to shine even brighter in comparison. For example, Bielschowsky quotes Heine's comparison of Goethe with Jupiter from *Die romantische Schule* (The Romantic School, 1838) but then goes on to describe Heine as a "half-genius" with "glaring dissonances" in his work, thus using the quote to mark the difference between its author (Heine) and the object of veneration (Goethe).[38]

Bielschowsky placed Goethe on a high pedestal, and his work is lacking in profound criticism. Bielschowsky's *Goethe* borders on the mythic. In his preface he draws Goethe as the "most human of all human beings," even as an "Übermensch." The overwhelming details that inundate the reader are meant to show the superiority and exceptional character of Goethe, but a Goethe of such status could not really exist. The veneration of Goethe, as in Heine's comparison of Goethe to Jupiter, did not foster a dialogue between Jews and Germans; instead, it foreclosed the possibility of such a dialogue. Bielschowsky's biography and its universal acceptance seemed to assert that such a dialogue was no longer necessary because Jews were already sufficiently assimilated to the German *Bildungsbürgertum*. In the figure of Goethe, Bielschowsky seemed to seek the model citizen of the new aesthetic state. As a model, Goethe had to be fully and completely described. It is, of course, not possible to describe a human being, even a dead one, with this level of scrutiny and, at the same time, maintain accuracy, and that is why myth creeps into Bielschowsky's representation of Goethe. With its fancy bindings and blinding praise, Bielschowsky's text may be the most aestheticized conceptualization of Goethe; but again, this Goethe was a concept or a figure, not a person. Even more brazenly, Friedrich Gundolf (Gundelfinger) also framed the image of Goethe in a mythic magnifying glass. For Gundolf, Goethe himself was a work of art, and, consequently, Gundolf subjected both the person and the work to the same lofty judgment. Emil Ludwig and Georg Simmel each offered social-scientific alternatives to the literary Goethe. Despite the gesture to scientific objectivity, neither Ludwig nor Simmel give us anything more than a portrait of the artist.

In the preface to the one-hundredth edition of his biography, Ludwig declared that he did not want to erect a statue "ich will keine Statue meißeln"; rather, he wanted to "let the landscape of [Goethe's] soul appear."[39] Ludwig illuminated Goethe from several perspectives. From a psychoanalytical side Ludwig tried to draw the "history of his soul"[40] and characterized him, for example, as a "volcanic man, driven by passions."[41] From a sociological perspective he explained Goethe's anti-imperial position. Through art criticism he traced Goethe's life by reference to portraits that he included in his biography, with the final image simply titled "Goethe vollendet" [Goethe perfected]. Ludwig claimed to be the first biographer who did not overlook Goethe's ambivalence and struggle in life, and yet, he could not always sufficiently explain such contradictions. In the "History of a Man," as the work is subtitled, Ludwig portrays Goethe as not only *menschlich vollendet* [humanly perfect] but *vollendet menschlich* [perfectly human],[42] an attempt to deflate images like that of Bielschowsky's *Übermensch* to human proportions.

At the time, Ludwig's methodology was new. He attempted to enter the psyche of Goethe, to discover the many facets of Goethe's character that could only be described in polarities such as "wildness and skepticism, chaos of the senses and the soul, morality and cynicism."[43] The best Ludwig could do was to characterize Goethe's soul as having a *Doppelwesen* [double essence]. Although this characterization might encompass all that he has discovered in Goethe's psyche, it amounts to little. Ludwig's Goethe is both everything and nothing — that is perhaps what it is to be humanly perfect and perfectly human. In a speech in Vienna for the one hundredth anniversary of Goethe's death Ludwig explained how he had achieved these insights. He quoted the poet: "One shall not seek anything behind the phenomena. They are the lesson themselves." And he applied this statement to Goethe: "One shall not seek anything behind him. Goethe himself is the lesson."[44] Ludwig equalized works, letters, and conversations, using this material as the basis for his biography and claiming that a quarter of the text is direct quotation. Despite its claims to quasi-scientific scrutiny, however, Ludwig's book not only lacks scholarly references that would support this claim but also weaves fact with fiction, betraying Ludwig's own unfulfilled desire to be a successful fiction writer.[45] It may be that Ludwig's more literary style actually yields a more accurate image of Goethe than is seen in other biographies. Nevertheless, we are still left to question Mosse's assertion that this "historical Goethe" drew Jews and Germans into a dialogic exchange. Ludwig certainly drew readers into this "history transformed into a drama, narrated in breathless intensity."[46] The popular audience to whom the book appealed, however, was composed mostly of men and women who had read few books and likely read this biography more as a detective or adventure story than as history. If Ludwig's goal was to cultivate a sense of Bildung by narrating the history of Germany's "great poet," it was thwarted by the public's desire for entertainment.

The *Doppelwesen* of Ludwig's own life problematizes the idea of a Jewish-German dialogue. His father had advised him to give up the last name Cohen to enhance his career. Ludwig claimed that he grew up without religion; instead, he had been nurtured by "God, Nature, and Goethe."[47] In his autobiography, he distanced himself and his Jewish-German contemporaries from the biblical Jews through whom Geiger had linked Goethe to modern Jews. "Why should one fill the mind of any European child with the history of desert tribes foreign to his very nature?"[48] At one point Ludwig even converted to Christianity; but he left the Church after the murder of Walther Rathenau, claiming to feel "a new attachment to my race, now that it once again suffers persecution in the fatherland."[49] In equating Goethe with the supreme forces of God and Nature, Ludwig indicated that religion did not transcend literature and that morality but was one component of culture and Bildung.

The popularity of these historical biographies in various forms seems, as George Mosse suggested, to lie in the "urge to follow a leader in times of crisis."[50] Ludwig explicitly positions Goethe in this role: "Gab es in der Welt einen willkommeneren Führer?" [Was there ever a more welcomed leader in the world?][51] Ludwig's 1932 speech in Vienna *Goethe: Kämpfer und Führer* (Goethe: Fighter and Leader) projected a Goethe who served as a figure with whom Germans, including Jewish Germans, could identify. In this regard, Ludwig shows his similarity to other biographers. Goethe's biographers, whether chroniclers or psychoanalytic readers, despite their prolific efforts were unable to make a "true Goethe" appear. The universal flaw of these biographies lay in the attempt to produce *a* Goethe, even the definitive Goethe. While recognizing and respecting the importance of this figure for Germany and the German people, the young Walter Benjamin lashed out against the privileges accorded the person and attempted to redirect attention to the work. Rather than write a biographical sketch of Goethe, Benjamin turned his attention to the *Sachgehalt* [real materiality] of Goethe, the language of his texts.

In a posthumously published fragment from 1917 Benjamin brutally criticized one of "Germany's most powerful critical voices," that of Friedrich Gundolf. Benjamin's main work on Goethe is a lengthy and complex essay on *Die Wahlverwandtschaften*. Benjamin opposed both the mythology constructed around Goethe and the facile literary commentary on his work that passed for criticism. Instead, Benjamin centered his admiration on Goethe's language. Benjamin never wrote a biography of Goethe, because he did not believe it was possible to allegorize an individual the way a critic allegorizes a work of art. In treating the historical person as a figure for some value and then subjecting that value to judgment, the biographer exceeds the limits imposed by language. Characters in fiction can never be subject to ethical judgments, and historical persons cannot be treated as characters in fiction. For Benjamin, Gundolf's biography is "morally repugnant" because it is "the falsification of a historical individual . . . into a mythical hero."[52] Benjamin shared Nietzsche's opinion of the modern abuse of history, that Hegelian view in which "a historical phenomenon, completely understood and reduced to an item of knowledge, is, in relation to the man who knows it, dead."[53] The first words of Nietzsche's treatise are from Goethe: "I hate everything that merely instructs me without increasing or directly quickening my activity." Nietzsche declares that Goethe's words preside at the "head of his thoughts on the worth and worthlessness of history." According to Nietzsche, we need history "for life and action, not as a convenient way to avoid [them]."[54] Suspended in a state of absolution from the world, the mythical Goethe is emptied of life and action. Biography does not bring the figure to life; on the contrary, by applying the categories of history in a vacuum it sucks all the life out of the being, leaving only an empty form that can then be filled with arbitrary meaning.

In his criticism of Gundolf, Benjamin confronts us with the question as to whether it is possible to write a biography at all. Biography frames its subject in a moment of being in which all of the moments of becoming are *aufgehoben* [sublated] into a totality in which being and becoming are the same. Only in something divine can they be identical, however. In mortals they are always divided and distinct. In the eleventh letter of *Über die ästhetische Erziehung des Menschen* Schiller carefully differentiates these parts and explains their relation. Although each individual necessarily assumes his own ground by the principle of identity — I am I — the first principle is an assumption and likely a fiction. Nonetheless, the principle is necessary and unchanging: A is always A because the *Person,* which Schiller also calls the "intellectual part," endures. Entirely distinct from this identity is the *Condition,* the becoming of *der Mensch* in time. As eternal and constant the *Person* provides the ground from which time can begin, without itself being subject to time. The succession of phenomenal appearances reveals the eternal part. The perduring and the mutable are thus yoked together in mortal existence. Here we have the makings of biography: a select series of appearances are collated to reveal a particular *Person.* The fallacy of biography lies in the assumption that the *Person* is equal to the phenomenal appearances that reveal it. The temporal condition is ossified into an absolute, but this is tantamount to saying that A is B. The *Person* remains only potential unless it becomes in time, participating through the senses and the will in the phenomenal world. Conversely, the personality is mere material appearance unless it is grounded by the solid matter of the eternal part, through feeling and contemplation. The matter and the material must work together, but they are not the same. They work in a relationship of identity and difference.

Biography, if it is to take a human being as its subject, must respect this relationship of identity and difference, but this proves virtually impossible to do. Geiger, Ludwig, and even Goethe himself (in *Dichtung und Wahrheit,* for example) keep the figure human, but ultimately the *vollendet Goethe* is unavoidable. The division between *Person* and *Condition* collapses, and Goethe is transformed into something divine. Gundolf writes the Gospel of Goethe, treating his life and works as an absolute existence, complete and autonomous, and infusing that existence with meaning. He begins with the assumption that in the representation of Goethe's completed figure the greatest unity of the German spirit has embodied itself.[55] As Benjamin argues, however, the meaning with which Gundolf fills the form of Goethe is arbitrary. For Gundolf, Goethe's works do not reveal the development of an individual but an *ursprüngliches* [originary] life. For Gundolf, Goethe is a *phenomenon* — the sensible appearance of some originary essence. While art qua art is not subject to time, the artist is always subject to time. By assuming that Goethe's life is itself a work of art Gundolf lifts Goethe out of the inartistic world of becoming and into the timeless eternity of art. Goethe becomes the figure for the absolute, and this absolutizing turns him into a suitable object of veneration.

Georg Simmel does not go as far as Gundolf, but he, too, treats Goethe's words and phrases as sacred relics by which to strengthen the faith in the *deutscher Geist* [German spirit] and in Bildung, the dogma and doctrine of Aesthetics. For Simmel, Goethe's genius lay in his ability to empty his subjective life into the objectively valuable productions of art. The works become the mirror of the world, and this reflected world reveals the singular image of Goethe. Simmel argues that Goethe is not subject to envy, because envy requires comparison. Goethe, like Shakespeare and Dante, is incomparable, *not* because of the quality of his writing but because the work itself emerges from a more primordial source. In Simmel, Goethe is not divinity itself but an initiate of its secret. The shibboleth or password to this divine secret is Bildung, the doctrine of aesthetics as the cultivation of reason and the beautiful.

George L. Mosse traced this doctrine back to the emancipation of German Jews at the beginning of the nineteenth century during the "autumn of the Enlightenment," a time when "'high culture' was becoming an integral part of German citizenship."[56] Mosse seems to suggest that the developing Jewish-German identity grew like a grafted plant that did not forsake its Jewish roots — although, perhaps, it forgot them. Mosse cites Berthold Auerbach's claim that although "formerly the religious spirit proceeded from revelation, the present starts with Bildung,"[57] and *this Bildung* begins with Goethe. As Mosse observed, "In his works Goethe appeared to emphasize individual free-

dom, . . . ambivalence toward all forms of nationalism, . . . and a belief
in Bildung" that "seemed to foster Jewish assimilation."[58] More important — and Mosse believed this to be what distinguished Goethe
from other mythic Germans such as Schiller — Goethe embodied the
"ideal *Bildungsbürger* of the period of Jewish emancipation,"[59] an image fostered by Bielschowsky's presentation of Goethe's "genuine humanity," a "total-Man" but human. For these reasons Goethe could be
made to serve as a mediator between Germans and German Jews and to
radiate with the promise of a "personal identity beyond religion and
nationality."[60] In the glow of this promise Simmel is able to absorb
both Judaism and Christianity into the Aesthetic religion. In a Hegelian
worldview, Christianity has sublated Judaism. Simmel argues that
Goethe follows a continuous path from a foundation of immanent divinity, and thus he overcomes the traditional dualisms of Christianity:
the perfection of humanity has progressed from Judaism through
Christianity to Aesthetics. Because it coincides with the time of the
Jewish emancipation and assimilation, the modern era began with
Goethe: the Age of Goethe was a new age. As the ground of time,
Goethe became something divine.

Benjamin offered an alternative to biography and mythology. By
limiting his critique to Goethe's language, Benjamin revealed a Goethe
who tells stories: Goethe as *Erzähler* [narrator], the "figure in which
the righteous man encounters himself."[61] This may explain Benjamin's
praise of Ludwig Strauss's statement that "above all, in a study of
Goethe, one finds one's Jewish substance," a quote favored by Mosse.[62]
In any case, Benjamin characterizes the storyteller as a distant force. He
attributes this distance to the loss in communicable experience that is
most evident in the rise of the novel, the isolation of its writer and its
reader. In contrast, "the storyteller takes what he tells from experience
. . . and in turn makes it the experience of those who are listening to his
tale."[63] As many critics have argued, Goethe was a poet of experience;
the biographies of Goethe, however, cannot tell us *about* this experience, nor about Goethe. Goethe's biographers know how to tell stories, but they do not know Goethe, for, aside from mere biographical
facts, *Goethe does not exist.*

Whether blatantly idolatrous or popularly scientific, all biographies
are fictions. Of interest, then, is the question "What function does this
fiction serve?" In the context of this workshop we have investigated
what these biographies, in particular, might reveal about the fiction of
Jewish *and* German identity. The monumental figure of Goethe is not
a figure of the past but of the future. Do not mistake this for a messi-

anic argument. Goethe may never arrive, but Goethe promises to come. As Jacques Derrida has written: "[Memory] is the name of what for us preserves an essential and necessary relation with the *possibility* of the name, and of what in the name assures preservation." But this is "not preservation as what conserves or maintains the thing named."[64] The name preserves itself as always only the phenomenal appearance of that which it is not. Memory does not synthesize the past with the present but disrupts the very possibility of a relation between them. As Martin Buber recognized, "the traditional concept of Bildung is solely future-oriented," and "a point of departure is as important as a point of arrival."[65] Goethe was not an adequate ground for departure, and the lack of this *truly* absolute ground is what thwarted the harmonious unification of Germans and German Jews by means of the poet. Although he simultaneously insisted on the historical narrative of progress, even Hegel recognized that only the memory that forgets fulfills the Absolute Spirit. But Hegel, too, forgets, and he animates the textual traces of Spirit with the conjuring dialectic of history and phenomenology, of narrative and appearance. Spirit does not develop from the past; it is promised from the future. When Goethe's textual remains are animated by a transfusion of biographical narrative, it is not the past but the future that is remembered. There have been many Goethes, and there will be many more, but there is no Goethe. The participants of this workshop, on the occasion of Goethe's 250th birthday, continue to write in this tradition. Because we are sure Goethe will come, maybe tomorrow.

Notes

[1] In the discussion that followed the paper Barbara Hahn specifically questioned the inclusion of Georg Simmel and Friedrich Gundolf as biographers.

[2] See T. S. Eliot, "The Function of Criticism," in *Selected Prose of T. S. Eliot,* ed. Frank Kermode (New York: Harcourt Brace, 1975) 75. "Comparison and analysis need only the cadavers on the table; but interpretation is always producing parts of the body from its pockets, and fixing them in place."

[3] Georg Simmel, *Goethe* (Leipzig: Klinkhardt & Biermann, 1921) v. "Sondern ich frage: was ist der geistige Sinn der Goetheschen Existenz überhaupt?" It is interesting that Simmel uses *Goethe* as an adjective, as a type of existence, rather than as a noun that would denote the specificity of an individual existence.

[4] *Ibid.* vii. Unless otherwise noted, all translations are by the authors.

[5] Peter Gay, "Begegnungen mit der Moderne: Die deutschen Juden in der Wilhelminischen Kultur," in his *Freud, Juden und andere Deutsche: Herren und Opfer in der modernen Kultur* (Munich: Deutscher Taschenbuch Verlag, 1989) 134.

[6] David Sorkin, *The Spirit of Prussian Jewry: The Dual Legacy of Berlin* (Ramat-Gan, Israel: Bar-Ilan University, 1993).

[7] George L. Mosse, *German Jews beyond Judaism* (Bloomington IN: Hebrew Union College Press, 1985) 2.

[8] Friedrich Schiller, *On the Aesthetic Education of Man, in a Series of Letters* (parallel text) ed. and trans. Elizabeth M. Wilkinson and L. A. Willoughby (Oxford: Clarendon Press, 1967) 6–7 (second letter): "Weil es die Schönheit ist, durch welche man zu der Freiheit wandert."

[9] Cf. the ninth letter and a letter from Schiller to Goethe, dated 20 October 1794: "You will find in these letters a portrait of yourself, beneath which I would gladly have written your name, if I did not hate the idea of forestalling the feelings of thoughtful readers. No one whose judgement you can value will mistake it, for I know that I have conceived it well and drawn it faithfully enough." Cited in *Friedrich Schiller: On the Aesthetic Education of Man*, trans. and ed. Reginald Snell (New York: Continuum, 1990) 55, trans. note 1.

[10] Cited in Hans Schütz, *Juden in der deutschen Literatur* (Munich: Piper, 1980) 112.

[11] Mosse 24.

[12] *Ibid.* 25.

[13] Leopold von Ranke supervised Geiger's habilitation in Berlin. "Geiger, Ludwig Moritz Philipp (eigtl. Lazarus Abraham)," in *Neue Deutsche Biographie*, ed. Historische Kommission bei der Bayerischen Akademie der Wissenschaften (Berlin: Dunker & Humblot, 1953) 144.

[14] In *Die Deutsche Literatur und die Juden* (Berlin: Georg Reimer, 1910) Geiger noted this filiation: "An interest in the literary history of the Jews, instilled in me by my father, preoccupied me from earliest childhood" (vii). Abraham Geiger (1810–1874), rabbi and pioneering reformist, excelled as a religious historian, reform theologian, and Orientalist studying and translating Hebrew literature. Influenced by the philosopher Moses Mendelssohn and other Enlightenment thinkers, Abraham Geiger was devoted to a vision of Judaism consonant with liberal, universalist, and emancipatory trends. He believed that the course of history would inevitably bring religions and peoples into ever closer approximation. This conviction guided his tireless efforts to lessen the perceived gap between Judaism and its (in Geiger's view) derivative religions, Christianity and Islam, by encouraging the Jewish commu-

nity to abandon the anachronistic and separatist national characteristics and practices that had developed during the oppressive centuries of ghetto life. Cf. "Abraham Geiger," in *The Blackwell Companion to Jewish Culture from the Eighteenth Century to the Present,* ed. Glenda Abramson (Oxford: Basil Blackwell, 1989) 258.

[15] *Ibid.* 258.

[16] Ludwig Geiger, "Goethe und die Juden," in his *Vorträge und Versuche: Beiträge zur Litteratur-Geschichte* (Dresden: L. Ehlermann, 1890) 281–82.

[17] *Ibid.*

[18] Geiger, *Die deutsche Literatur und die Juden* 24.

[19] Wilfried Barner, "Jüdische Goethe-Verehrung vor 1933," in *Juden in der deutschen Literatur,* ed. Stéphane Moses and Albrecht Schöne (Frankfurt: Suhrkamp, 1986) 139.

[20] Geiger, *Die deutsche Literatur und die Juden* 10.

[21] *Ibid.* 9.

[22] After retiring from a professorship in Dorpat, Hehn had moved in 1873 to Berlin, where he was a private scholar and respected member of several literary circles. The high esteem Hehn enjoyed is evident in classical scholar Conrad Bursian's informative obituary, "Viktor Hehn," in *Biographisches Jahrbuch für Altherthumskunde* (Berlin: S. Calvary, 1891) 1–62.

[23] Viktor Hehn, "Goethe und das Publikum," in his *Gedanken über Goethe* (Berlin: Borntraeger, 1909) 55–209.

[24] *Biographisches Jahrbuch für Alterthumskunde* 354.

[25] The phenomenon of popular anti-Semitism is seldom addressed in Geiger's scholarly essays. An exception is the introduction to his 1903/04 university lecture series "Juden in der deutschen Literatur," where he characterized with dismissive scorn a flood of contemporary anti-Jewish popular literature and its stereotypes. Aside from this brief polemic before a university audience, the "unscientific rantings" not only of anti-Semitism but also of Zionism, "these two miserable parasitic plants of the waning nineteenth and early twentieth century" were below Geiger's horizon of serious scholarship. Cf. *Vorträge und Versuche* 11. But as Goethe's national significance became more firmly established, instances of his ambivalence toward the Jews could be stylized in public discourse for use against the Jews, and here Geiger certainly hoped his brand of historical research would strengthen the voice of reason.

[26] Geiger, *Die deutsche Literatur und die Juden* 9.

[27] Hehn, "Goethe und die Sprache der Bibel," in his *Gedanken über Goethe* 427–44; first appeared in the *Goethe-Jahrbuch 1885.* See esp. 428–29.

[28] Geiger, *Die deutsche Literatur und die Juden* 82–85.

[29] Book I, part 4.

[30] Geiger, *Vorträge und Versuche* 313.

[31] Ludwig Geiger, *Goethe: Sein Leben und Schaffen* (Berlin/Vienna: Ullstein, 1913).

[32] *Ibid.* 10.

[33] *Ibid.* 11–12.

[34] *Ibid.* 13.

[35] *Ibid.* "Das Gerede von seiner Fürstenknechtschaft ist doch zumindest stark übertrieben."

[36] Cited in Karl Robert Mandelkow, *Goethe in Deutschland,* vol. 1 (Munich: Beck, 1980) 148.

[37] Walter Benjamin, "Goethes Wahlverwandtschaften," in Goethe's *Die Wahlverwandtschaften* (Frankfurt: Insel, 1972) 333. ["Goethe's *Elective Affinities*," in *Walter Benjamin: Selected Writings,* Volume 1: *1913–1926* (Cambridge MA: Harvard UP, 1996) 356.]

[38] Bielschowsky, *Goethe: Sein Leben und seine Werke,* 20th ed., vol. 1 (Munich: Beck, 1910) 369.

[39] Emil Ludwig, "Die Landschaft seiner Seele erscheinen lassen," in his *Goethe: Kämpfer und Führer. Festrede der Goethe-Feier im Deutschen Volkstheater Wien. 20. März 1932.* (Berlin/Vienna/Leipzig: Zsolnay, 1932) 5.

[40] Ludwig, *Goethe: Geschichte eines Menschen* (Berlin/Vienna/Leipzig: Zsolnay, 1931) 23.

[41] *Ibid.* 7.

[42] *Ibid.* 6.

[43] *Ibid.* 24. "Wildheit und Skepsis, sinnliches und seelisches Chaos, Moralität und Cynismus."

[44] Ludwig, *Goethe: Kämpfer und Führer.*

[45] The fiction of biography remains a topic of much debate. At the time of this Workshop (October 1999) Edmund Morris's controversial biography of Ronald Reagan had just appeared. The publication of *Dutch: A Memoir of Ronald Reagan* sparked a fiery if brief media discussion of truth and fiction. Morris admits to inventing a fictional self who has a longer relationship with Reagan than Morris could have had, given his actual age. Although he acknowledges the fiction, Morris simultaneously documents — *with footnotes* — events from this quasi-historical past.

[46] Mosse 28.

[47] Cited in Mosse 26.

[48] *Ibid.*

[49] *Ibid.*

[50] *Ibid.* 27.

[51] Ludwig, *Goethe: Kämpfer und Führer* 7.

[52] Benjamin, "Comments on Gundolf's *Goethe*," in *Walter Benjamin: Selected Writings,* Volume 1, 98.

[53] Friedrich Nietzsche, *The Use and Abuse of History,* trans. Adrian Collins (Indianapolis: Liberal Arts Press, 1957) 11.

[54] *Ibid.* 3.

[55] Friedrich Gundolf, *Goethe* (Berlin: G. Bondi, 1920) 1.

[56] Mosse 3.

[57] *Ibid.* 4.

[58] *Ibid.* 44.

[59] *Ibid.* 45.

[60] *Ibid.* 2.

[61] "Der Erzähler ist die Gestalt in welcher der Gerechte sich selbst begegnet." Walter Benjamin, "Der Erzähler," in his *Ein Lesebuch* (Leipzig: Suhrkamp, 1996) 284. ["The Storyteller," in Benjamin, *Illuminations,* trans. Harry Zohn (New York: Schocken, 1968) 109.

[62] In Mosse 14.

[63] Benjamin, "Erzähler" 262; trans. 87.

[64] Jacques Derrida, *Memoires* [*sic*] *for Paul deMan,* (rev. ed.), trans. Cecile Lindsay, Jonathan Culler et al. (New York: Columbia UP, 1986) 49.

[65] In Mosse 36.

From the Pedestal to the Couch:
Goethe, Freud, and Jewish Assimilation

Robert C. Holub
University of California-Berkeley

O N 29 AUGUST 1930, the day after Sigmund Freud was awarded the fourth annual Goethe Prize on the occasion of the poet's 181st birthday, the *Völkischer Beobachter* printed a short notice that began:

> The Goethe Prize of the city of Frankfurt was presented this year to Professor Sigmund Freud, the celebrated scholar and creator of psychoanalysis — this was trumpeted into the world with all pomp and circumstance in the tenth issue of the Israeli Community Newspaper. The Goethe Prize, the greatest scientific and literary prize in Germany, was given to the distinguished awardee on 28 August, Goethe's birthday, as a part of the festivities in Frankfurt am Main. The award carries with it a 10,000 Mark stipend.

Aside from the reference to the source of this news item, the article to this point remains fairly neutral, relating only the facts. But the last two sentences of this report contain the expected racist invectives: "It is well known that renowned scholars have rejected the psychoanalysis of the Jew Sigmund Freud as highly unscientific drivel and nonsense. The anti-Semite Goethe would turn over in his grave if he knew that a Jew had received a prize that carries his name."[1] The sentiments expressed here are not surprising: Goethe, the pride of German culture and a pure Aryan, was being associated with someone from an inferior race, the Jewish intellectual Sigmund Freud. Moreover, this Jew had scandalized the scientific world by presenting theories that had to do with matters no decent person would mention in public: human sexuality. In calling into question the legitimacy of Freud's work, the *Völkischer Beobachter* more importantly seeks to deny a pseudo-scientific scholar and writer any place in the German community. We know, of course, that Goethe himself often dabbled in scientific arenas that were not always completely accepted by the science of his time or ours, and that an offensive sexuality is part of Goethe's works — and, from the perspective of a moralistic nineteenth century, part of his life as well. We also know that many of Goethe's early champions, and not a small number of his early biographers, were Jews.[2] But Goethe's image, even if he could not always be advanced as a proto-Nazi or even a German nationalist, was for the general public one of a dignified and noble spirit above the common rabble. What did this thoroughly German patron of the highest ideals have to do with a quack Jewish intellectual one generation removed from the ghetto? Was the awarding of the Goethe Prize to Sigmund Freud not a betrayal of its spirit, of its essence?

The National Socialist denunciation of Frankfurt's choice of Freud could not be uttered in polite and liberal circles. But the same questions that the *Völkischer Beobachter* raised in polemical fashion were also part of a discourse that surrounded the entire award and its decision-making process. The public got a hint of the controversy when the Jewish mayor of Frankfurt, Ludwig Landmann, delivered his congratulatory speech in the house in which Goethe was born. In his short talk he mentioned the passionate debate among the members of the selection committee, something that had not occurred on previous occasions. At issue, evidently, was the fact that the prize was again being awarded to a nonliterary person: after Stefan George received the award in 1927, it was given in the following years to Albert Schweitzer and then to the philosopher Leopold Ziegler. But Landmann maintained that Freud had earned the honor because of his enormous impact on the literary world of his time and because of his contributions to the German language, adding that the prize was not conceived solely for literary merit but was meant to acclaim someone whose entire work warrants recognition. Freud had influenced the Zeitgeist, Landmann continued, so that his status as a nonpoet could be overlooked. Although these remarks appear sufficient to justify Freud's selection, the mayor obviously felt compelled to add further clarification concerning the appropriateness of the Freud-Goethe connection: "Many people will think it is inapposite and preposterous that Freud should be associated with Goethe," he declared. Goethe, after all, believed in an ethereal unity of all living creatures; he was more spiritually inclined, more intuitive. Freud, as a natural scientist, relies on strict causality; he believes in natural laws and inclines toward materialism. Landmann also coupled the two men via intellectual history: Fechner, Schopenhauer, and Nietzsche, he claimed, were the nineteenth-century intermediaries between the intuitive worldview of Goethe and the scientific perspective of Freud. Thus, one could construct a bridge between the two men, and Landmann's audience was informed that in the course of intense discussions in committee the inner relationship between Freud, the modern, nonsubjective scientist, and Goethe, the quintessential poet, became increasingly clear.[3]

In contrast to previous years, the name of the awardee had become public well before the ceremony. Although some information about the controversy surrounding Freud's nomination must have surfaced, as well, the exact nature of the discussions in the selection committee became public knowledge only in 1982, when Wolfgang Schivelbusch published an essay that revealed what one might have suspected from Landmann's speech: the provocation that Freud must have represented not only for National Socialists but also for many conservative and furtively anti-Semitic sectors of the German public.[4] Freud was hardly the unanimous choice of the committee, and the mayor was nervous about the controversy that even Freud's supporters anticipated would ensue from his nomination. The sides lined up rather predictably: with the exception of Franz Schultz, the Germanists on the selection committee, who evidently believed themselves self-appointed protectors of German cultural purity, voted against Freud; the government officials from Prussia and Frankfurt, as well as the left-liberal practitioners of culture, Alfred Döblin and Alfons Paquet, promoted Freud's candidacy from the start. Döblin was most articulate in championing Freud and in establishing the connection between Freud and Goethe. Freud's reputation in the world was indisputable, Döblin reasoned, so that the only objection one could raise had to do with his appropriateness. To justify Freud's selection he employed four arguments. The first involved analogy: Goethe sought to overcome the chaotic of the Dionysian with the greatness of the Apollonian, as exemplified in the figures of Orestes and Iphigenie or Tasso and Leonore. One need only replace this opposition with Freud's terms to recognize, according to Döblin, that Goethe and Freud are really working on a common project. Döblin, of course, stacked the deck a bit in providing Goethe's works with a Nietzschean interpretation and in assuming that Freud then covers the Nietzschean bases, but his point was that the two men thought in a similar fashion about human existence. Döblin also noted that Freud was sufficiently literary, having exerted a great influence on contemporary literature: he cited Thomas Mann as an outstanding and eminently acceptable illustration. In a similar vein, Döblin countered the objections of potential detractors of Freud's nomination when he maintained that what really counts is not the identity of their thought but Freud's impact on his own time, which is as great as Goethe's impact in his era. Finally, in his most interesting comment Döblin claimed that Freud merited the prize as an act of *Wiedergutmachung* [compensation] for the relative neglect he had suffered. He pointed out that in German-speaking countries Freud had received no major awards despite his widespread fame, that he had been shunned by the scientific establishment in Germany. Predicting correctly that names such as Einstein and Freud were among the few that would outlive his own epoch, he concluded his plea by stating that "in the name of the nation we have to perform a sort of recompense to Freud."[5]

The conservatives disagreed wholeheartedly with this line of reasoning. The spokesperson for the anti-Freud contingent, the Frankfurt Germanist and future National Socialist Hans Naumann, countered even Döblin's assertion of Freud's fame. Freud was past his prime, Naumann argued; his teachings were in an unstable mode of revision, and it was impossible to say what would remain of them after the dust settled. In any case, his influence did not extend beyond Zurich; he was virtually unknown or disparaged in France and other nations. Naumann continued:

> Of course in America he's alive and known, but we all know that in intellectual matters America is infantile. German scholarship is distanced from Freud. You only need to listen to psychologists, not to mention philosophers. You can ask any religious scholar or any legal expert how distanced we are from Freud and how little is thought of him. I think the entire matter is more of a Russian affair. Freud has had the misfortune to live too long. And for this reason we shouldn't open ourselves up to the reproach of being regressive.

Kurt Riezler, the Frankfurt university trustee who supported the appointment of Max Horkheimer to the directorship of the Institute for Social Research,[6] weighed in on the anti-Freudian side with reasons that appear at first glance less vulgar. For him Goethe and Freud were simply incompatible, no matter how one evaluated Freud's achievements:

> The pregnantly un-Goethean, indeed anti-Goethean, quality lies in the basically causal, mechanical nature of the Freudian world, in its excessively rationalistic structure, in its constructedness, as opposed to any deeply felt universal idea, in its focus on humanity in distressing sickness, in prudery. . . . Whether or not psychoanalysis is correct does not really matter. The confounding of the two names in the awarding of the Goethe Prize will appear to the public, which possesses a very real picture of their respective mental constitutions, as a tasteless mess.

Despite Freud's putatively anti-Goethean mentality and despite the obvious controversy it would cause in the public sphere, the pro-Freudian faction carried the day with a vote of seven to five.

It is not difficult to see that the awarding of the Goethe Prize in 1930 was about, among other things, Jewish assimilation into German culture. Despite its volatile language, the *Völkischer Beobachter* was on the mark, or at least more open than Naumann or Riezler about the actual cultural and political dynamics at play. Although Goethe had not always been regarded as a genuine representative of Germanness — indeed, in his early reception he was frequently upbraided for his failure to support the nationalist cause — by the end of the nineteenth century, at the latest, he had been firmly established as the spiritual pinnacle of the best Germany had to offer. In racist circles around National Socialism his anti-Jewish attitudes and remarks had confirmed his formative role in shaping a German and anti-Semitic agenda, and while these remarks were mitigated somewhat by his humanist reputation and his fervent Jewish admirers, for the Weimar Republic Weimar classicism represented a high point of cultural Germanness.[7] Freud, by contrast, was conceived as an outsider, an interloper. Complicating his alterity were his scientific and methodological presuppositions, as well as his scholarly proclivities. His focus on sexuality and his insistence on a positivist, materialist conception of research — which we now know that he preached more than he practiced — would perhaps have been unwelcome to genuine advocates of German culture no matter who propagated them. But these qualities fit quite well into the stereotype of Jewishness, which had long since developed the motifs of hypersexuality, on the one hand, and a cold, overly rationalist worldview, on the other. Freud's detractors in the public and semi-official discourse do not toss around the vulgar National Socialist slurs; nor do his promoters seek to defend him as a Jew. But the marks of a German-Jewish problem are apparent, nonetheless. Naumann's emphasis on Freud's foreignness from German science and his endeavor to relegate Freud to the land of Jewish capitalism and trivial culture (the United States) or to Bolshevism (Russia) are part of a rapidly forming anti-Semitic mosaic. Similarly, Riezler's emphasis on the overly rationalist and the mechanistic in Freud's thought are part of a larger constellation around Jewish assimilation. And is it entirely coincidental that the Jewish defender of Freud, Alfred Döblin, mentions two Jews, Freud and Einstein, as names that will persevere in the annals of human history, or that he argues the case for Freud's nomination in terms of compensation for someone wronged and neglected?

Was Freud appropriate for the Goethe Prize? Did he have anything in common with classical Weimar and the preeminent features of German culture? Was a twentieth-century Jewish doctor investigating sexuality a good match for a poetic privy councilor from the eighteenth-century Duchy of Weimar? Freud himself certainly thought so, and part of his own endeavor to assimilate himself and his writings into the Austro-German culture surrounding him was his relationship to Goethe. Freud cultivated this relationship consciously and conscientiously in his writings, even claiming that Goethe would have appreciated and perhaps validated his novel conception of the human being. Indeed, Freud repeatedly claimed that Goethe was responsible for his choice of a career in medicine. One of the motifs in Freud's self-fashioning is that Goethe appears at the turning point in his life. In his autobiographical text of 1924 he describes his youth in Vienna, where he was the top student in his class. His father, Freud continues, allowed him to select his own path according to his proclivities, and at that point he was disinclined to study medicine. At first he was more attracted to fields that emphasized relationships between human beings than to areas of knowledge that focused on natural objects. He was swayed in a different direction, however, by two events: one was the general popularity of Darwin and Darwinian thinking; the other was a popular lecture in which Goethe's essay "Nature" was recited.[8] Goethe thus appears as an inspiration at the very start of Freud's scholarly career, and Goethe's thoughts are implicitly brought into association with Freud's later development. If, however, we glance at the essay "Nature," which may not even have been written by Goethe, we find little that could attract Freud. The rhapsodic, hymnic prose in this short piece, the repeated assertion that nature is ever-changing and creative, and the suggestion that nature harbors eternal secrets never to be revealed to mortals — all typical features of an early Storm-and-Stress mentality — seem ill suited to convince anyone to study natural phenomena.[9] It is possible, of course, that the lecture accompanying the oral presentation of the essay, delivered by the comparative anatomist Carl Brühl, was inspirational.[10] But in the various places where Freud reminisces about his youth he never foregrounds Brühl but instead informs his reader of his Goethean beginnings. For Freud the essay and the occasion are less important than the association with greatness. With Goethe rather than his father aiding his career choice, Freud symbolically exits the Jewish ghetto inhabited by Jacob Freud and enters the more respectable world of German letters.

And in subsequent writings Freud makes certain that his readers know that he belongs to this cultivated German world. Since Freud had no qualms about constructing his conceptual framework around borrowings from the literary tradition — witness the Oedipus and Electra complexes; since he believed that creative writing was the consequence of a redirection and channeling of sexual energy; and since, finally, he persistently abstracts from the social and historical conditions in his observations on the psyche, he can feel justified in employing a citation from Goethe to bolster his argument. In a few cases Freud actually uses Goethe in an evidentiary fashion to document psychoanalytic claims. In most instances, however, references to Goethe and his works are superfluous in terms of explicating theoretical insights into human psychology. Their function in Freud's writings lies in their illocutionary force: Freud makes the implicit claim that he and his texts belong to German culture, that the inventor of psychoanalysis is no different from other refined members of society, and that psychoanalysis itself is a universal, and certainly not a merely Jewish, science. Goethe is decorative, a revered writer placed on a pedestal, on display for everyone to admire and to remind the reader that Freud, while posing as an outsider, is really a fully assimilated insider.

Traumdeutung (Interpretation of Dreams, 1900) provides illustrations of the various ways in which Freud showed off his knowledge of Goethe. In his review of dream theories Freud referees Carl Binz's claim that stimuli bombard a sleeping person from every direction (2: 99; 4: 77–78)[11] and compares this hypothesis to Mephisto's plaint (IV; 8: 192)[12] concerning the appearance of ever new seeds in all elements and climates. The allusion to *Faust* at this point in the text has no other function than to demonstrate Freud's knowledge of the literary tradition and to stake his claim for a place in that heritage. At another point Freud seeks an analogy for the mechanism by which dreams hide their real meaning. He finds a similar process at work in social situations, and he cites in this context the compulsion to distortion when he interprets dreams for his reader (2: 158; 4: 142). Again Mephistopheles is allowed to supplement Freud's argument, this time with two lines from his conversation with Faust concerning his teaching practice:

> The best of what you hope to know
> Is something that you cannot tell the youngsters[13]

It is easy to understand why this quotation was one of Freud's favorites: it speaks of the prohibition on direct expression that is the rule for unacceptable urges. Although, again, the function of this citation is as much display as substance, Freud is here able to locate in Mephisto's directness a proclamation of the necessity for indirectness. On other occasions, however, Freud's citations of Goethe appear completely arbitrary and only tangentially related to the line of reasoning: in the analysis of a dream he relates the story of a painter who wanted to make a portrait of a man because of his unusual features. The man responded crudely that the painter would prefer a piece of the behind of a young woman to his whole face. Freud supplies the following puzzling gloss in a footnote:

> Cf. The phrase "sitting for one's portrait" and Goethe's lines:
>
> > And if he hasn't a behind,
> > How can his Lordship sit? (2: 163; 4: 147)[14]

The citation is from an epigram titled "Totalität" (Totality), published in 1815 (1: 469); but the connection with the dream analysis is obscure, and one suspects that Freud included it more for his own amusement than for its relevance to any scientific point — amusement and, of course, as a sign of his belonging to the civilized world in which educated people are expected to cite prominent German authors as aids and embellishments for their thoughts.

One other passage in the *Traumdeutung* merits our attention. It is significant because it contains a dream in which Goethe is mentioned, and because Freud refers to this dream and its analysis on three separate occasions. His most complete description occurs under the rubric of absurd dreams. In the preface to the section Freud states that he will present examples in which the absurdity of the dream disappears when the deeper meaning is explicated; he further claims that the dreams deal with a dead father (2: 413; 4: 426). Freud relates two dreams about his own father — Jacob Freud had died in 1896, a few years prior to the publication of *Traumdeutung* — and about a patient who, like Freud, had recently lost his father. But two additional dreams do not conform to this general description: one in which the viewing of the play *Das neue Ghetto* (The New Ghetto), dealing with the Jewish question, is allegedly translated into an absurd situation with children in Rome, and Freud's dream about his friend, identified only as Mr. M., who was criticized with unjustified vehemence in an essay by none other than Goethe. Mr. M. is naturally devastated by this criticism and complains bitterly about it to his friends; but he never loses his great admiration for Goethe despite the personal attack. Within the dream Freud begins to calculate: since Goethe died in 1832 and must, therefore, have composed this essay earlier than that date, Mr. M. must have been quite a young man. To Freud it seems plausible that he was eighteen years old. Since he is disoriented and not certain of the present year, the entire matter becomes obscure, except that Freud can recall that the attack occurred "in Goethe's well-known essay on 'Nature'" (2: 424–25; 4: 439).

Freud interprets this dream as the reworking of three events from his life. The first is his experience with a patient whose symptoms included psychic paralysis: Freud visited him and found that without any provocation he related embarrassing excesses about his brother's younger years. Freud associates the paralysis of this patient with his own paralysis, when he is unable to recall the correct year. The second source for the dream material is the publication in a medical journal of a review of a recent book by Freud's friend Wilhelm Fliess. The author of the review was young and, according to Freud, incompetent, and Freud broke relations with the journal after he was unable to gain a satisfactory explanation and remedy from the editor — although Freud, like Mr. M. in the dream in regard to Goethe, emphasizes that their personal relationship should not suffer because of this incident. Another patient supplies a third source for the dream's material. Freud relates that a patient informed him that her brother's outbreak of insanity was preceded by his shouting "Nature, Nature," and that this exclamation was ultimately the result of his reading the essay by Goethe and of the exhaustion he suffered in studying natural sciences. The brother was eighteen when he went insane. From these various materials Freud concocts his interpretation, which is less comprehensible than the absurd dream itself. For reasons that remain unclear, Freud claims that in the dream he has placed himself where his friend is. He then asserts that he behaves as if paralyzed, and the dream becomes absurd. He concludes that its content is ironic and can be summarized in two sentences: "Naturally, it's *he* [my friend F.] who is the crazy fool, and it's *you* [the critics] who are the men of genius and know better. Surely it can't by any chance be the *reverse?*" (2: 425; 4: 440). The reversal is indicated in the dream by the absurdity of Goethe attacking the young man, while it is easy for a young man today to attack the immortal Goethe, and by the fact that in the dream Freud calculates from Goethe's date of death, not from the young man's date of birth.

Psychoanalysis is a remarkable exegetical tool. Since it makes no claims to logic or to verifiable results, it has continued to be the darling of literary and cultural criticism long after real scientists have recognized that it is devoid of methodological substance. In writing about

Freud one is tempted to apply his own arbitrary procedures against him. It would, after all, take little imagination to interpret Freud's dream as even more personal than he acknowledges. The cry of "Nature" could be seen as a Goethean rebuke to Freud, who has betrayed the spirit of Goethe's infatuation with nature, and misunderstood the message that he has claimed served him as the inspiration for his studies of the human mind. The distance between Freud and the venerated figure he continues to esteem could be translated as a combination of fatherly reproach, since the first dreams in the section deal with dead fathers, and a still failed Jewish assimilation, which is the putatively real content of the dream Freud next narrates. Or one could ruminate on what it means that Fliess's book panned by the inept young reviewer was most probably the monograph of 1897, "Relationship between the Nose and Female Sexual Organs."[15] Freud never really accounts for the fact that the friend was named Mr. M. rather than Mr. F. So we could speculate that Freud had in (his unconscious) mind the name of John Noland Mackenzie, a Baltimore laryngologist, who had proposed the nasal-sexual connection a decade prior to Fliess.[16] Psychoanalysis continues to be a great machine for cranking out interpretations, which is, unfortunately, increasingly what literary and cultural studies are about, no matter how perverse and absurd these interpretations may be. But the only thing that seems rather certain about this dream is that it indicates how central Goethe was to Freud's psyche: his obsession with his origins as Goethean, his fear of rebuke from Goethe, and, the corollary to these fears and obsessions, his concern with assimilation into a culture in which he desired acceptance but from which he simultaneously sought to distance himself.

Let me turn now to the couch, that is, to the one place in Freud's oeuvre where he offers an extended analysis of Goethe gleaned from one of Goethe's writings: Goethe's essay on memory in *Dichtung und Wahrheit* (Poetry and Truth, 1811–14). In a short piece that originally appeared in *Imago* in 1917, Freud comments on an early passage in Goethe's autobiography in which the author relates how, egged on by some neighborhood boys, he tossed bowls, pots, and other tableware out the window and into the street. Freud points first to the significance of Goethe's including this tale in *Dichtung und Wahrheit* at all: since reminiscences from early childhood are rare, the ones that do remain in one's memory are of particular psychic import, which for Freud means that they contain a deeper psychoanalytic meaning. We are thus compelled by the mere fact that Goethe narrates this recollection to interpret it and consider it a cover for something that Goethe does not want to concede openly. After the usual caveats concerning the difficulty of, in effect, performing psychoanalysis on a person unable to respond in a therapeutic setting, Freud goes on nonetheless to offer a narrative of his own for "solving" the problem posed by this passage. After reading it, recognizing that it must conceal a deeper meaning, and determining that it would be best to let the matter rest, he informs the reader about an anonymous patient who similarly threw tableware out of the window. This action was evidently part of the patient's displaced anger at the birth of a brother when he was four years old, and Freud reasons that Goethe's actions have identical origins: in Goethe's case Freud hypothesizes that his ill feelings were directed toward Hermann Jakob Goethe, who was born on 27 November 1752 and died on 13 January 1759. Similar reports of comparable incidents confirm his opinion: throwing tableware or other items out the window is a symbolic or magical act, by which the child expresses his desire to rid himself of the newly arrived competitor for the affections of the mother. For Freud it is also significant that Goethe never mentions his brother, that he represses Hermann Jakob's existence entirely. For Freud the case is, therefore, clear, and he offers us the following translation of the episode: "I was a child of fortune; destiny preserved my life, although I came into the world as though dead. Even more, destiny removed my brother so that I did not have to share my mother's love with him" (10: 266; 17: 136). Freud concludes by theorizing that being a mother's favorite child results in a feeling of conquest and a confidence in success that often actually leads to success.

What are we to make of Freud's interpretation? At the very least we can point to two errors. Freud's initial claim that childhood memories have a particular significance for one's psychic life may be true, but what Goethe writes in *Poetry and Truth* is not reported as *his* childhood memory. Indeed, Freud begins his reading with the following citation from Goethe, which occurs in the paragraph prior to the episode about the tableware: "If we try to recollect what happened to us in the earliest years of childhood [Goethe actually wrote *Jugend* or "youth," not *Kindheit* or "childhood"], we often find that we confuse what we have heard from others with what we ourselves have witnessed" (10: 257; 17: 147).[17] Goethe's point here is simple: what he is going to relate may or may not have occurred, but it is definitely something that was told to him by others. And Goethe is consistent: before recounting the story of how he threw tableware out the window, he states that his relatives [*Die Meinigen*] were fond of talking about all kinds of mischief to which he was provoked by three brothers named von Ochsenstein, who lived across the street. His tale of the tableware is an illustration of something others remembered and told him. Goethe does not represent the story as part of his memory but as part of familial lore. Obviously, the status of this particular statement is crucial for Freud's interpretation. If it is does not belong to Goethe's memories but merely to the stories conveyed to him by others, then its value for an analysis of Goethe's psyche is questionable. Freud's misreading thus allows him to construct an interpretation to which he is not entirely entitled.

Freud's second error concerns the contention that Goethe never mentions his brother in *Dichtung und Wahrheit*. In fact, Goethe does mention him; if we are inclined to be charitable toward Freud, we could conjecture that initially Freud simply overlooked the passage, which occurs later in the first book. In the passage Goethe says that he wants to recall at this point his brother, who suffered from the childhood illnesses that Wolfgang also contracted. Goethe comments further that Hermann Jakob had a "zarte Natur" [fragile constitution], that he was withdrawn, and that he died as a young child. Thus, Goethe does not suppress the memory of Hermann Jakob at all. By the time Freud got around to publishing this essay for the third time, someone must have alerted him to his mistake. But instead of revising the essay on the basis of this information or withdrawing it from circulation since it was apparently seriously flawed, he simply added a footnote acknowledging his error. Why did Freud not revise his text? We cannot know for certain; we only know that a correction of the main text would have significantly weakened the argument that Goethe's story about the jettisoned tableware was a substitute for something he repressed. Was Freud simply too lazy or too busy to revise his text, or was he again fudging his evidence? Freud's essay on Leonardo can assist us in our evaluation of his scholarly rigor. In a discussion of Leonardo's dream about the vulture, which also turns out to have something to do with a maternal relationship, Freud inserts in the second version of the essay (1919) a footnote devoted to his Goethe analysis in which he refers to "the remarkable absence of any mention whatever of a young brother" (10: 111–12; 11: 85) as the original impetus for undertaking the analysis of the passage from *Dichtung und Wahrheit;* his statement here is consistent with his ignorance of the actual state of affairs at that time. In the 1923 version of the Leonardo essay he modifies the footnote to read: "the absence in this passage of any mention of the young brother"; thus, the circumstance is no longer "merkwürdig" [remarkable], and "überhaupt" [whatever] becomes "an dieser Stelle" [in this

passage]. Freud retains the claim, however, that this circumstance —
now not "remarkable" — caused him to pursue his analysis. He then
includes in parentheses: "This child is in fact mentioned at a later point
in the book, where Goethe dwells on the many illnesses of childhood."
For any reader who has followed Freud's editorial legerdemain the obvious question is: why should Goethe have mentioned his little brother
in recounting a story he is repeating from his relatives concerning how
he — Wolfgang — threw tableware out of the window? The only possible reason Goethe would have to mention his brother at that point
would be if he associated his own destructive act with his brother. But
why should Goethe have made this association, since it is Freud's? But
then how can Freud make this association, which depends at least in
part on a repression of the younger rival, when the younger rival is not
repressed? Freud's evidentiary practice is, stated quite simply, utterly
dishonest. When he believed that Goethe did not mention his brother,
the repression of the brother was a significant piece of evidence. When
he learns that Goethe did mention his brother, he either relegates that
knowledge to a footnote, leaving the text and the main argument un-
altered, or fabricates a new tactic, claiming that it is significant that
Goethe fails to mention his brother "in this passage" when there is no
reason whatsoever for Goethe to do so.

Clearly there is something fraudulent in Freud — I am hardly the
first to have noticed it[18] — something deceptive about psychoanalytic
argumentation. But as curious readers we might ask: what is going on
in Freud's essay on Goethe? If the interpretation does not fit the facts,
even when Freud knows the facts, why does he continue to republish
the Goethe essay in unchanged form and retain the misleading footnote
in the Leonardo essay? Why is Freud's investment in this reading of
Goethe so great? Unlike Freud, I will not claim that the following hy-
potheses are based on science. My interpretation is clearly conjecture,
but in contrast to Freud's procedure, at least mine is based on evidence:
perhaps it is even a persuasive reading, but it belongs to the art of her-
meneutics, not the pseudoscience of psychoanalysis. I start with a simple question: if Goethe does not fit the facts, is there someone else who
does? We do not have to search far for the answer. Freud himself is an
almost perfect match. Little Sigismund Schlomo was particularly attached to his mother; as the forty-year-old doctor reported to his close
friend Wilhelm Fliess, his "libido toward *matrem*" had been aroused on
an overnight railway journey from Leipzig to Vienna when he had the
opportunity "of seeing her *nudam*."[19] It was Freud who displayed jealousy of his little brother, at least as he recollects for Fliess. His self-

analysis revealed that he welcomed the death of Julius, who died as a seven-month-old infant. It is Freud who admits that he harbored "adverse wishes and genuine childish jealousy" toward his putative rival.[20] We have no report of broken dishes, but otherwise Freud, in his analysis of Goethe, could be describing himself. Indeed, the "true meaning" of the tableware incident fits Sigismund, not Wolfgang: "Destiny removed my brother so that I did not have to share my mother's love with him." And, finally, Freud is the person who is overly concerned with success, whose ambition drives him so fiercely that he is willing to ignore and distort evidence to validate his "theoretical" insights. The next question we might want to ask is: why would Freud speak of himself in his Goethe essay? Why does he impute to Goethe feelings and desires that were his own? Again I speculate, but with some evidence and logic behind my conjecture. Quite simply, Freud substitutes himself for Goethe because he wants to identify himself with Goethe, and in that identification lies his aspiration to be accepted, integrated, assimilated into the German world. His passion was to be recognized as a great man, to be not only an assimilated Jew but a Jew whose celebrity was so apparent that he could remain a Jew and still be part of German society. He did not want to compromise — he never considered conversion; and he never abandoned his religious community — he was an atheist who always affirmed his Jewishness.[21] Let me go one step further: is it not possible that the anonymous patient who "solved" the Goethean tableware conundrum, and who is described as someone of a foreign nationality, someone "not acquainted with German Bildung" (10: 260; 17: 150) — in short, an outsider to Germanness, its very antithesis, perhaps — is the symbol for the Jew Freud was, or at least of the prototype of the Jew as seen through German eyes, who comes, through the similar experience of desiring the mother and hating the rival brother, to resemble the greatest of all German writers? Is it possible that the Goethe essay is thus really about Jewish assimilation? Could it be that Freud is saying — and here I, like Freud, will strive to reduce my interpretation to a single thought: "I, Sigmund Freud, want to be recognized by German-speaking society as a great man, as a second Goethe, or at least as Goethe's equal?"

If all of this is more than mere idle speculation, then perhaps, when in 1930 Freud was honored in absentia in Frankfurt, he could feel affirmed in both his identification with the great man whose prize he received and his acceptance in the greater German world. Perhaps he could believe that assimilation, symbolized by the spiritual proximity of Sigismund Schlomo to Johann Wolfgang, had become a modern reality. If Freud did feel that he and his teachings had gained a permanent foothold in German society, that a German-Jewish, or at least an Austro-Jewish, identity could become a lasting reality in the fourth decade of the twentieth century, he would soon find that he was mistaken. The dispute surrounding the awarding of the prize, in particular the National Socialist response, was indicative, as we now know, of the actual state of affairs. Not the outcome, of course, which was controlled by the liberal forces of Frankfurt, but the framework for the debate, which called into question the compatibility of Freud and Goethe, of Jew and German. Ultimately, as Adorno and Horkheimer wrote in *Dialektik der Aufkläung* (Dialectic of Enlightenment), the liberal view of Jewish assimilation was true only as an idea and was opposed by the more palpable naked truth of Nazi racist dogma.[22] To the last moment Freud clung to his native land; he likened his departure from Austria to a soldier's desertion of his post. When he finally and reluctantly left Vienna on 4 June 1938, he left part of himself behind. "One has been told so often that one is not a German," he wrote in London. "And indeed one is glad oneself that one no longer needs to be a German."[23] Nonetheless, in his last sustained piece of writing, Moses, the Jew who is not really a Jew, who belongs, yet does not really belong, is compared in greatness to Goethe (9: 555; 23: 108).

Notes

[1] *Völkischer Beobachter,* 29 August 1930: 2.

[2] See, for example, Wilfried Barner, *Von Rahel Varnhagen bis Friedrich Gundolf: Juden als Deutsche Goethe-Verehrer* (Wolfenbüttel: Wallstein, 1992) and "Jüdischer Goethe-Verehrung vor 1933," in his *Pioniere, Schulen, Pluralismus: Studien zu Geschichte und Thorie der Liteaturwissenschaft* (Tübingen: Niemeyer, 1997) 129–49.

[3] The text of the mayor's speech can be found in the *Frankfurter Zeitung und Handelsblatt,* 29 August 1930: 7.

[4] A more complete review of the committee's proceeding is contained in Hanna Leitgeb, *Der ausgezeichnete Autor: Städtische Literaturpreise und Kulturpolitik in Deutschland 1926–1971* (Berlin: de Gruyter, 1994) 85–104.

[5] Cited from Wolfgang Schivelbusch, "Der Goethe-Preis und Sigmund Freud," in his *Intellektuellendämmerung: Zur Lage der Frankfurter Intelligenz in den zwanziger Jahren* (Frankfurt/Main: Insel, 1982) 77–93; here 84–85.

[6] See Rolf Wiggershaus, *The Frankfurt School: Its History, Theories, and Political Significance,* trans. Michael Robertson (Cambridge: MIT Press, 1995) 129.

[7] See, for example, Houston Stewart Chamberlain, *Goethe* (Munich: Bruckmann, 1912).

[8] Sigmund Freud, "Selbstdarstellung," in his *Gesammelte Werke chronologisch geordnet* (London: Imago, 1948) 14: 34. In English in *The Standard Edition of the Complete Psychological Works of Sigmund Freud,* ed. and trans. James Strachey, 24 vols. (London: Hogarth Press, 1953–74) 20: 8.

[9] Johann Wolfgang Goethe, "Die Natur," *Hamburger Ausgabe* 477–79.

[10] See Uwe Henrik Peters, "Goethe und Freud," *Goethe Jahrbuch* 103 (1986): 86–105; here 96. The English edition of Freud's autobiographical sketch mentions Brühl; the German does not.

[11] First references to Freud in parentheses are from Freud, *Studienausgabe,* 10 vols. (Frankfurt/Main: Fischer, 1982). Second references and citations in English are from *The Standard Edition of the Complete Psychological Works of Sigmund Freud.*

[12] References to Goethe in parentheses are from Johann Wolfgang von Goethe, *Berliner Ausgabe* (Berlin: Aufbau, 1971).

[13] Translation by Peter Salm, from *Faust: Part One* (New York: Bantam, 1962) 113.

[14] The footnote in German is more telegraphic in style:

> Dem Maler sitzen.
> Goethe: "Und wenn er keinen Hintern hat,
> Wie kann der Edle sitzen?" (2: 163)

[15] See Paul Robinson, *Freud and His Critics* (Berkeley: U of California P, 1993) 41.

[16] Frank J. Sulloway, *Freud, Biologist of the Mind* (New York: Basic Books, 1979) 150.

[17] The citation occurs in Goethe's writings in 13: 13.

[18] Among the many works that reveal Freud's diverse errors and dishonest practices I cite only the anthology edited by Frederick Crews, *Unauthorized Freud: Doubters Confront a Legend* (New York: Penguin, 1998), and Malcolm Macmillan, *Freud Evaluated* (Cambridge MA: MIT Press, 1997).

[19] I leave it to the more psychoanalytically inclined to comment on Freud's recourse to the Latin for the words *mother* and *nude.*

[20] *The Complete Letters of Sigmund Freud to Wilhelm Fliess, 1877–1904,* ed. and trans. Jeffrey Moussaieff Masson (Cambridge: Belknap Press, 1985) 268.

[21] "In 1939 he told the London branch of YIVO: 'You no doubt know that I gladly and proudly acknowledge my Jewishness though my attitude toward any religion, including ours, is critically negative.'" In Marsha L. Rozenblit, *The Jews of Vienna 1867–1914: Assimilation and Identity* (Albany: SUNY Press, 1983) 10.

[22] Max Horkheimer and Theodor W. Adorno, *Dialectic of Enlightenment*, trans. John Cumming (New York: Continuum, 1999) 168–70.

[23] Cited in Peter Gay, *Freud: A Life for Our Time* (New York: Norton, 1988) 632.

IV. Goethe in Exile and His Return

Upholding the Ideals of the "Other Germany": German-Jewish Goethe Scholars in U.S. Exile

Gisela Hoecherl-Alden
University of Pittsburgh

D EMANDING "LIGHT FROM GOETHE ON OUR PROBLEMS," as Alexander Hohlfeld did in his presidential address to the Modern Language Association (MLA) in 1913,[1] is not a novel concept for us as American Germanists. In 1999 a comic book about Goethe's life was published and advertised by the American Association of Teachers of German (AATG) in an expressly stated attempt to revitalize waning student interest in German literature.[2] Throughout our discipline's relatively short and turbulent history the nature of the problems we face has constantly changed, and while German classicism in general, and Goethe in particular, were invoked to solve them, they did not succeed. Whenever the professorate lacked an original approach to re-evaluate the shape of American Germanics, Goethe, and to a lesser extent Schiller, have functioned as stand-ins.

By the late nineteenth century universities demanded the inclusion of science, social sciences, and modern languages in the academic curriculum alongside a more scientifically exact focus. Concurrently, the newly founded MLA set out to undermine the dominance of the classics at American universities and thus played a key role in the institutionalization of German as an academic discipline. Despite the MLA's continued efforts, when it came to matters of prestige and recognition, administrative and academic perceptions of the value of studying modern languages and their literatures were slow to change.[3] Germanists not only had to defend the inherent worth of studying a living language but also felt growing pressure to conform to academic standards upheld by the sciences. With the goal of justifying the study of the literary canon, the academic journals contain multiple reassurances that reading Goethe and Schiller safeguards aesthetic education in a classical sense. Some academics even employed sacred imagery and in their articles and essays figuratively embarked on a crusade to educate their American students, culminating in the elevation of Goethe to the "patron saint" of their discipline.[4] Despite the fact that the "idealist" Schiller and the "realist" Goethe had often stood for opposing ideals during their lifetimes, by the end of the nineteenth century the two had merged to become the most revered symbol of German bourgeois culture in American Germanics. Thus, when Harvard's Kuno Francke was invited to lecture at institutions around the country during the "Goethe year" 1899, he chose to promote "Goethe's Message to America" alongside "Schiller's Message to Modern Life."[5] Yet, the discipline's overall line of reasoning essentially remained unsuccessful in changing prevailing institutional and public perceptions.[6] In addition, the First World War and the resulting precipitous decline of German proved the failure of the professorate's experiment in education through Goethe's ideas, mainly because their approach had been both too esoteric and too rooted in German nationalism.

Barely having recovered from the catastrophic decline in German instruction after 1917, American Germanists were presented with a new dilemma by Hitler's ascent to power. Several articles were quick to stress the inherent value of studying German.[7] The *New York Times*, on the other hand, seemed to anticipate the professorate's inward turn toward classicism by exclaiming: "What better challenge to Hitlerism can there be than to get to know Lessing, Schiller, and Goethe!"[8] Afraid of provoking a repetition of First World War Germano-phobia, Germanists remained unobtrusively apolitical to the point of failing to join academics from other fields in voicing public protests against mass dismissals from all Nazi-dominated Central European universities. The prevailing atmosphere in the 1920s and 1930s sheds additional light on their indecision: Germanists were well aware that patriotism unleashed during the First World War had set a precedent for considering teachers' attitudes a threat to national security. Likewise, growing trepidation of communist subversion placed numerous jobs of politically active faculty members at risk.[9] Moreover, in the severe economic crisis, when even U.S.-trained Germanists were hard pressed to find suitable jobs, the onslaught of foreign-trained scholars played directly to xenophobic tendencies within American academe. As the archived correspondence of the German professorate reveals, xenophobia and anti-Semitism indisputably influenced the job market.[10] The complaint that American universities had "become asylums for political irreconcilables and social misfits . . . exiled from their native land for political, usually Communistic, activities or opinions"[11] is indicative of the prevailing fear of subversive activities, a fear that seemed even to outweigh existing anti-Semitism. As common distrust of leftist intellectuals, xenophobia, and the dismal job situation suggest, and as the letters, diaries, autobiographies, and personal essays of several displaced academics have corroborated, the established American Germanists generally did not extend a warm welcome to their exiled colleagues.[12]

Thus, once arrived, the refugee intellectuals had to contend with several factors. For one thing, on the part of the established professorate there existed a general unwillingness to condemn Nazi Germany, despite the regime's well-publicized atrocities. In addition, even though the vast majority of Germanists were national-conservative, there were undeniably Nazi sympathizers among the faculty.[13] Conversely, a low opinion of American cities and of the quality of American universities tinged the cosmopolitan refugees' perceptions. In fact, the consensus among exiles teaching literature seems to have been that of them all, only Karl Viëtor received an appropriate appointment at Harvard.[14] On the whole, the displaced academics found it difficult to reconcile the differences in status and workload[15] with the fact that they also lived in small college towns, far from vibrant cultural centers.[16] In retrospect, it is easy to classify the refugees' adjustment problems as culture shock, and it is, therefore, "somewhat of a tragic paradox that these people who had been forced to leave their homes because they were regarded as non-German, were now too German for America."[17] Yet, open criticism of Nazi Germany, especially when voiced by émigrés, was not welcomed in the academic community. For example, as an exiled student, Werner Vordtriede initially regarded it as his duty to inform the American public about the displaced "other Germany."[18] When he lectured on Nazi Germany at the University of Cincinnati, however, the Ph.D. candidate lost his financial support; and when Brown University, which had offered him an assistantship, reneged, he found out that the FBI had been observing him.[19]

This other Germany, which Thomas Mann, his children, and many of the refugees teaching German perpetuated, was that of bourgeois high culture. It expressly excluded Mann's own brother Heinrich, Bertolt Brecht, Lion Feuchtwanger, and other politically active, leftist intellectuals. Doubtless, their conservative mindset played a role in the way American Germanists reacted to Nazi Germany. In part, however, their hesitation to condemn Nazism outright may also have stemmed from the fact that they had greatly admired some of their more illustrious German colleagues who had become Nazis in 1933.[20] From today's vantage point, this seems the only feasible explanation for the fact that

even a shrewd scholar such as Yale's Hermann Weigand, who actively
supported the incoming refugees, seemed more amused than appalled
by Julius Petersen's *Die Sehnsucht nach dem Dritten Reich in deutscher
Sage und Dichtung* (The Longing for a Third Reich in German Tradition and Literature, 1934).[21] Besides, some of the refugees, while quite
outspoken when it came to condemning the Nazi regime, seemed oddly
hesitant to attack their teachers or former colleagues. Their profound
emotional ambivalence lies partially in the fact that many of the first-
generation exiles perceived themselves as Germans first and foremost
and only secondly, if at all, as Jews.[22] This fact may account for one of
the most puzzling documents to emerge from academic exile: the
obituary written by an exiled Jewish Germanist of his Nazi mentor —
Richard Alewyn's tribute to Julius Petersen. In it Alewyn, whose short
but promising career as Friedrich Gundolf's successor in Heidelberg had
ended in 1933, described Petersen as having been a focal point of German spiritual life, the center of a glowing tradition, and the most influential of Germanists. Alewyn circumvented the question of professional
responsibility by excusing Petersen's Nazi sympathies as a mere error of
judgment.[23] Also, Karl Viëtor, who initially embraced Nazism before he
left his position at the University of Giessen, was not only unwilling to
condemn his teacher Petersen but even tried to organize a Festschrift in
his honor from exile.[24] His Harvard colleague and fellow Goethe scholar
Stuart Atkins termed Viëtor's death in 1951 a great loss for American
academe. Nevertheless, Viëtor, whose work, in Atkins's words, gave "in
polished and lucid German a picture of Goethe's total achievement as
interpreted by a sensitive representative of German humanistic culture,"[25] remained oriented toward Germany. Viëtor's correspondence
reveals that the Germanist continued to feel disdainful of his fellow aca-
demicians in the United States, whom he regarded as relatively unedu-
cated,[26] and complained that he needed to be quite elementary, since
abstract thinking was not one of the strengths of the American mind.[27]
Viëtor's stance is undoubtedly tinged by bitterness at having left behind
an illustrious career and is a trait he shares with displaced Jewish Germanists such as Richard Alewyn, Wolfgang Liepe, and Werner Richter.
There is no doubt that Viëtor's "distinction as a scholar and a writer was
matched by his brilliance as a lecturer and excellence as a teacher."[28] Yet,
the fact that he continued to publish articles almost exclusively in German, which unequivocally position him as a national-conservative advocate of *Geistesgeschichte*, unperturbed by his exile, indicates that he never
saw himself as part of American academe.[29]

Indeed, elements of superiority also color other exiles' perceptions of their roles as educators. There are, nevertheless, subtle differences between Viëtor's and other refugees' views of themselves as proponents of an education through classical ideals. Those intellectuals who had not lost prestigious university positions in Central Europe utilized Goethe's legacy differently. What both the Jewish and non-Jewish exiles have in common, and what also has a demonstrated tradition in American Germanics, is that they all saw themselves as spiritual leaders.[30] The post-Storm-and-Stress Goethe, who had proclaimed a quasi-utopian ideal of the educated man and autonomous art existing outside of political turmoil, greatly appealed to the displaced intellectuals. Like their late-nineteenth-century forerunners they found that even though "none of the great writers of the Western world has more profoundly influenced the convictions and attitudes of his own countrymen than Goethe," the bulk of his later work was virtually unknown in the United States. In fact, to the majority of Americans, who tended to know only *Werther* and the first part of *Faust*, Goethe "was the very prototype of the self-centered romantic . . . who turned too soon into a purveyor of generalized wisdom."[31] Thus, by elevating humanistic education and the autonomy of art to the highest of aesthetic criteria, as the Goethe of Weimar Classicism had done, the exiles could create a new identity for themselves in opposition to the home that had expelled them.

Just how profoundly refugee Germanists perceived of themselves as spiritual leaders and the true representatives of the other Germany can be derived from three of Oskar Seidlin's publications between 1939 and 1943. Born Oskar Koplowitz in Upper Silesia, Seidlin was a Ph.D. student at the University of Frankfurt when Hitler came to power. As a leftist homosexual Jew, the aspiring poet and children's-book author escaped first into Swiss, then American exile. When his Frankfurt mentor, the literary scholar Martin Sommerfeld, died of a heart attack in Vermont in the summer of 1939, Seidlin's rousing obituary lamented Sommerfeld's death as a loss not only for American Germanics but for American education as a whole. He portrayed the exile Sommerfeld as a spiritual leader whose teaching encouraged critical thought; therefore, Sommerfeld's books had what Goethe expected of great books: they guided the readers' self-discovery and enlightenment.[32]

A year later Seidlin elevated Goethe himself to the status of a spiritual leader of the other Germany in exile. In a lecture titled "The Humane and the Poet," which he gave on a hill in Middlebury, Seidlin stated that German literature had found its highest fulfillment in Weimar Classicism. The fact that the Nazis had co-opted Goethe and German Classicism provoked him to exclaim that where the animalistic power of blood drove decisions, spiritual freedom had ceased to exist. Nazi idealism was to Seidlin "sacramentalization of the material," as well as mindless collectivism, tyranny, and racism. His vocabulary and the location he chose for his lecture are reminiscent of a sermon; thus Seidlin took on the role of a high priest of German culture — again a role that had a tradition in American Germanics, only this time it was played in the name of denationalized classicism. Goethe stood here for a "citizen of the world," thus providing Seidlin's weapon against National Socialism. Throughout his lecture Seidlin cautiously avoided any direct mention of the Nazis; yet, his juxtapositions of "blood," "magic," "collectivism," and "global domination" were explicit enough to characterize National Socialism as the absolute antithesis to Weimar Classicism and to the other Germany of which he, as the speaker, was the representative.[33]

Simultaneously, Thomas Mann, more or less the only contemporary exiled author to warrant serious scholarship in American Germanics before the Second World War, increasingly came to be regarded as the rightful heir to German Classicism. Mann himself furthered this development by publishing *Lotte in Weimar*[34] and later *Doktor Faustus*. Thus, three years after he had condemned the Nazi appropriation of the classics, when Seidlin once again invoked German Classicism, the bourgeois-conservative Mann took Goethe's place as the figurehead of the other Germany's fight against Nazi dictatorship and for democracy. Having attained the status of a modern classic, Mann's work could become part of the canon. As such, it seems that it was revered for its superior humanism and artful structure rather than critically analyzed within its contemporary contexts. In Seidlin's Middlebury lecture, "Thomas Mann and Democracy," the Nobel prize laureate increasingly evolved into the pronoun "we," while "Democracy" was replaced by the adverb "now," the lecture thus becoming a call to action in the war against Hitler.[35] Studying and teaching German had instantaneously become synonymous with fighting for democracy, though it is noticeable that this direct appeal was not made until after Seidlin had become an American soldier. Equally conspicuous is the continuing absence of any direct allusion to National Socialism. It seems, then, that even though the Jewish intellectuals felt that a "community of German spirit existed in exile,"[36] Jewish and non-Jewish Germanists alike only proclaimed the other, better Germany after America's entry into the Second World War.[37]

After 1945 those exiles who had become American Germanists but had left prestigious prewar positions were called on to help rebuild German universities. Some of them decided to remain in the United States, together with the far greater number who were not called on to aid in rebuilding Germany, because they had been writers, fledgling Germanists, or had come from other professional fields to American Germanics. Regardless of their decision, though, they turned to German journals almost immediately. Karl Jaspers and Dolf Sternberger's short-lived journal *Die Wandlung* (The Transformation) seemed especially attractive for discussing both the future of Germany and the legacy of Nazism and the Holocaust. The journal explicitly dispensed with set rules for publication, as they smacked too much of totalitarianism,[38] a premise that had to appeal to the Germanists who had called on the constants of Goethe's spiritual and cultural heritage. It was in precisely this sense that Oskar Seidlin interpreted Hermann Hesse's *Glasperlenspiel* (Glass Bead Game, 1943) as depicting "the noblest image of Western culture: man according to Goethe,"[39] and conversely, Sternberger wanted to have Seidlin's essay understood as a political contribution to the rebuilding of Germany.[40]

Yet, by 1949, when Germanists again celebrated Goethe's legacy on both sides of the Atlantic, it is noteworthy that the majority did not allude to the recent past. Seidlin, who before 1942 had lamented the Nazi abuse of Classicism, chose instead to focus on Goethe's work as autonomous art. On the other hand, Richard Alewyn, who had just returned to Germany, maintained in his lecture "Goethe as Alibi" that these uncritical celebrations were not only a "sacrilege" against the writer but also deeply dishonorable. Alewyn reminded his audience that Germany would henceforth have to contend with Goethe and Hitler, the humane and the bestial, and exclaimed: "between us and Weimar lies Buchenwald." Alewyn, who eight years previously had absolved his mentor Petersen of political responsibility, now spoke from the morally superior vantage point of the returned exile. By using the pronouns "we" and "us," however, he also signaled to his audience that he considered himself part of postwar Germany.[41] Thus, the bourgeois other Germany, which Alewyn had represented in the United States, had now been transferred from exile to become a bastion against Soviet totalitarianism.

Meanwhile, in the United States, xenophobia and fear of communist subversion, while already highly problematic during the 1920s and 1930s, became virulent after the Berlin Blockade. Loyalty oaths and blacklists, where they did not already exist, were instituted, and the

House Un-American Activities Committee (HUAC) had the power to deport foreign-born citizens to their countries of origin.[42] Among its victims were women who renounced their traditional roles as wives and mothers;[43] Jews; African-Americans; foreigners; and, as more recent research has shown, a disproportionately high number of gay men and women.[44] Basically, for anyone who did not fit the image of a white, Protestant, heterosexual, conservative male American the mere hint of "otherness" could merit the perilous adjective "un-American." Thus, in the highly charged atmosphere of the so-called McCarthy era, Germanists who had suffered expulsion from their home country in the 1930s needed a safe haven in which to continue their work. Their quest for legitimate research paradigms was rewarded by their fellow exiles' immensely successful theoretical publications. For instance, it is known that Hannah Arendt felt extremely vulnerable in the New York of the late 1940s and 1950s because she was an immigrant, a woman, and Jewish.[45] Her life circumstances undoubtedly colored her theoretical perceptions, and, just as she had in her *Origins of Totalitarianism* (1951), her fellow exiles, at least in public, came to accept the theoretical premise that "brown equals red." For literary scholars, Prague linguist René Wellek and his colleague Austin Warren affirmed their apolitical approach with their *Theory of Literature* (1949). It became one of the most influential books in postwar literary criticism as it provided both the former exiles and those Germanists who had openly admired Nazi Germany and its authors with the theoretical justification to move into the ivory tower in pursuit of classical German Humanism. By studying literature as an autonomous work of art divorced from the historical, social, and political forces that drove its production, both groups considered themselves secure in a world of ever-shifting political alliances. In his book *Goethes Kunstauffassung* (Goethe's Perception of Art, 1957) Mathijs Jolles of the University of Chicago hoped to influence the art of interpreting contemporary literature by illuminating how Goethe had viewed art. Jolles concluded his ahistorical attempt to interpret Goethe by claiming that style alone was the determining factor by which one could measure the quality and worth of literature. Goethe's work here provided the former refugee with a set of permanent criteria for interpreting literature.

In contrast to exiles from Germany, refugees from the former Habsburg Empire began including their Jewish heritage in their research after the war, though they initially did so indirectly. Erich Heller, a former lawyer from the Czech Republic, spent his first fifteen years of exile in England and moved to the United States in 1954. In the introduction to his collection of essays on German literature, *The Disinherited Mind,* he justified his choice of topics as personal preference. As David Suchoff has pointed out, however, including the Jewish authors Karl Kraus and Franz Kafka alongside Goethe after National Socialism in combination with the term "disinherited" clearly conjures up the Holocaust.[46] Though he had acknowledged his membership in the Jewish community and would occasionally continue to analyze Kafka, Heller did not concentrate on Jewish aspects of Kafka's work, as later generations of Jewish Germanists would. Moreover, in his introduction Heller described the responsibilities of the literary scholar as "determined by his own character" and his business as not "the avoidance of objectivity, but its purification."[47] Such open affirmation of ivory-tower Germanics also kept him from positioning his literary analyses into their sociohistorical contexts, for, like his German-born colleagues, Heller resided firmly within the paradigm of New Criticism and made a name for himself as a Goethe scholar. Nevertheless, *The Disinherited Mind* clearly marks the beginning of a widening of the German literary canon in American Germanics.

After the war, unlike their German and American colleagues, former exiles had not only started to stress Goethe's cosmopolitanism but had also begun introducing a comparative focus. They integrated German literature into a global literary context and thereby tore open the nationalistic limitations traditionally afforded the American language and literature departments.[48] For them, Goethe's humane idealism meant "that the deed done for the sake of [man's] own personal redemption harbors in its folds the future destiny of the whole world."[49] From an apolitical but moralistic perspective they had set out to demonstrate that Goethe was "a man of letters in the comprehensive sense" who had, perhaps for the last time, presented "a unified and effective vision of man."[50] Thus, both Jewish and non-Jewish exiles such as Bernhard Blume, Peter Demetz, Erich Heller, Heinrich Henel, Mathijs Jolles, Victor Lange, Heinz Politzer, Oskar Seidlin, and Guy Stern were later honored with the Golden Goethe Medal for their work on German classical literature. The titles of their publications bear witness to their prolific scholarship on German classical literature: Blume's *Thomas Mann und Goethe* (1949), Demetz's *Goethes "Die Aufgeregten"* (1952), Liselotte Dieckmann's *Goethe's "Faust"* (1972), Melitta Gerhard's *Schiller* (1950) and *Leben im Gesetz: Fünf Goethe-Aufsätze* (1966), the Festschrift in Heller's honor titled *Versuche zu Goethe* (1976), Victor Lange's *Goethe* (1968), and Seidlin's *Von Goethe zu Thomas Mann* (1963) and *Klassische und moderne Klassiker: Goethe, Brentano, Eichen-*

dorff, Gerhart Hauptmann, Thomas Mann (1972). Conversely, Fest-schriften compiled in their honor reveal the comparative and cosmo-politan focus of those who had not given up a position in Europe before their exile: *Weimar am Pazifik: Literarische Wege zwischen den Kontinenten* (Weimar on the Pacific: Literary Paths between the Conti-nents, 1985) for Werner Vordtriede and *Exile and Enlightenment: Studies in German and Comparative Literature* (1987) for Guy Stern are examples.

Their eloquence notwithstanding, for many Jewish exiles their heri-tage, often also their former political orientation, and frequently their unorthodox education alone would have precluded their successful in-tegration into prewar German or American academe. During and shortly after the war the majority of the younger exiled Germanists joined their American colleagues in concentrating their energies une-quivocally first on the American war effort, then on rebuilding Western Europe. This circumstance,[51] alongside their thorough humanistic edu-cation and knowledge of Goethe, eventually led to the exiles' becoming part of mainly conservative American German departments. In fact, as Jost Hermand has argued, the former refugees frequently renounced their exile status to become firmly ensconced American Germanists whose European identity was encapsulated in the literature they ana-lyzed and taught.[52] That many of them had been writers rather than academics before they were forced into exile elevated scholarly style in American Germanics to a new, often brilliantly essayistic level. In the end, however, just as it had on the eve of the First World War, the idea of spiritual leadership through Goethe and the classics ultimately had to fail. It is no coincidence that the explosion of language programs after the so-called Sputnik Shock eventually led to the end of New Criticism. First, as members of the younger exile generation such as Peter De-metz, Walter Sokel, and Guy Stern moved into positions of influence in American Germanics, they began to reconcile their Jewish heritage within German literature. Second, as Egon Schwarz recalled in his autobiography, the theoretical premises of New Criticism were neither academically nor personally meaningful to him, for they clashed with his life experience. He had studied with both Blume and Seidlin at Ohio State University. While he gratefully acknowledged his mentors' art of conducting close readings as a valuable tool for literary analysis, their ahistorical view of literature created a gap he eventually sought to bridge by repositioning literature into its sociohistorical context.[53] For the younger exiles a perceived lack of "ethnocentrism" and "national-ism"[54] became a positive way to unite "their multiple professional, national, cultural, and personal identities" and prevented them from becoming politically, nationally, religiously, and academically one-sided.[55]

Simultaneously, American Germanics had begun to absorb a new group of immigrants from Germany who had studied under former Nazis. Among them were Klaus L. Berghahn, Reinhold Grimm, Walter Hinderer, Jost Hermand, Peter Uwe Hohendahl, Anton Kaes, and Frank Trommler. As diverse as they were personally and in their research interests, they found their frustration with the way the profession had been headed mirrored in their younger American colleagues' dissatisfaction. Not only had they begun to take a closer look at the way the National Socialists had co-opted Goethe and the Classics as a whole; they had also begun to use other approaches in analyzing the canon. When Henry J. Schmidt, also a Seidlin student, deplored the professorate's "inner immigration" into the Ivory Tower of humanistic idealism as an unacceptable alternative to political activism,[56] his criticism was voiced from the perspective of an angry young man discontented with the discipline. I concur with Schmidt, in that New Criticism and its premise of ahistorical literary analysis legitimized the silence surrounding the Holocaust in American postwar Germanics. Yet, I also want to argue that the so-called inner immigration into insular scholarship and close readings of classical German literature was, at least for the older Jewish exiles, existentially motivated. Those whose otherness placed them at risk[57] had to accept a new professional persona in order to survive and assimilate, a thesis vindicated, I believe, by the number of name changes undertaken to obscure their Jewish origins.[58]

In fact, it turned out after the war that the universities were anything but a safe haven. Public opinion, prompted by the media, generally considered them un-American hotbeds where foreign professors routinely indoctrinated naïve American youths.[59] Moreover, that two Germanists' jobs were among the first casualties of the Cold War waged on the country's campuses was well publicized.[60] This situation at least partially explains the staunchly conservative and decidedly apolitical stance that well-known and widely respected Germanists such as Oskar Seidlin and Bernhard Blume chose to take. Before their exile both had sympathized with leftist groups. They were foreign and, in Seidlin's case, not only Jewish but also gay.[61] Both taught at the University of Ohio, which was embroiled in the notorious case of an allegedly Communist physics professor.[62] Like every other faculty and staff member, they had to sign a loyalty oath defending "the State of Ohio against all enemies, foreign and domestic" before they were issued paychecks.[63]

Years later, Seidlin thanked the United States for saving his life and
letting him live within his true home, the German language and its literature,[64] and he meant just that! Apparently, not racism, exile, loss of
his entire family in the Holocaust, nor his work for the U.S. army as a
soldier in intelligence units or as a scriptwriter for documentaries on the
death camps destroyed his profound love for the German language and
its literature. As an American Germanist, Seidlin became instrumental
in expanding the German departments at the Universities of Ohio and,
later, Indiana, and by forging connections between German and
American universities earned — among numerous other awards — the
prestigious *Preis für Germanistik im Ausland* [Prize for German Studies in Foreign Countries] in 1968. In his acceptance speech in Darmstadt, Seidlin, conscious of increasing controversy surrounding his
approach to the study of literature, portrayed himself as a moralist. He
justified his adherence to New Criticism by the fact that his American
students, because they were studying literature via a language foreign
to them, were unable to position it within its social, cultural, and historical contexts. Instead of proposing to provide the necessary sociohistorical background, he argued that his students would only accept
what he could demonstrate from the text. By adding that close reading
of literature was also close to his heart, he unequivocally endorsed New
Criticism.[65] How completely Seidlin had come to accept his conservative worldview had already become evident in the deterioration of his
formerly close relationship with Klaus Mann shortly after the end of the
war.[66] Another indication of how ingrained his flight into the ivory
tower had become is his refusal in 1968 to accept a position at the
University of Munich, where he claimed to recognize the rebirth of
"totalitarian" and "radical" movements of the Nazi era in the student
protests.[67]

While the new immigrants from Germany questioned the dichotomy between so-called high and low culture, Jost Hermand suggests
that they were not questioning the canon as such but, rather, re-
evaluating it. The conservative insistence on analyzing literature as
autonomous art in the wake of the civil rights movement and the Viet-
nam War provoked the politicization of literary criticism,[68] which culminated in the notorious second Wisconsin Workshop, titled "Die
Klassik-Legende" [The Legend of German Classicism]. Organized by
Hermand and his colleague Reinhold Grimm, the workshop irrevocably
destroyed the illusion that meaningful literary criticism was possibly divorced from social and historical reality and thus also attacked New
Criticism and its most vocal and prolific proponents. The venom with

which Seidlin, for example, reacted to both the workshop and its organizers revealed a profound dismay that went deeper than mere professional resentment. Grimm, Hermand, and the majority of workshop participants had attacked the core of his being and brought down the foundations of his professional world. The Silesian Jew had, after all, denied his political past, his aspirations as a contemporary writer, and his heritage in order to save himself into a utopian world of German Humanism and Classicism where he could survive during the turbulent years of exile, war, and, later, the Cold War. Investigating the suicides of seemingly well-established Jewish and non-Jewish literary scholars[69] more thoroughly might also lend credence to the theory that the older generation of former exiles felt existentially threatened by getting caught in the crossfire of questions their students and younger colleagues raised about political responsibility and civil action.

In conclusion, the frequency with which questions about "Jewishness" versus "non-Jewishness" intersect when studying this period of American Germanics raises important issues about exile and identity. The mere fact that academics of the older generation were exiled from Germany seemed automatically to signal "Jewishness," whether they perceived themselves as Jewish or not. Thus, Karl Viëtor seems to have been referred to as "one of the greatest Jews of the twentieth century" by merit of his exile status alone.[70] Many members of the younger exile generation, who were from the former Habsburg Empire and had completed their education in the United States, widened the canon during the 1950s to include German-Jewish literature, while their older colleagues, Jewish and non-Jewish alike, excluded authors such as Kafka, Kraus, and Schnitzler. In fact, Walter Sokel's testimony suggests that they turned to Jewish authors in order to explore their own Jewish identity.[71] The further politicization of approaches to the canon undertaken a decade later by the new German immigrants resulted not only in the inclusion of leftist and exile literature but also in the final deconstruction of the painstakingly upheld ideal of "the other Germany."

Notes

[1] Alexander Hohlfeld, "Light from Goethe on our Problems," *PMLA* 29 (1914): lvii-lxxxvi.

[2] See Friedemann Bedürftig (text) and Christoph Kirsch (drawings), *Zum Sehen geboren* (Stuttgart/Munich: Egmont Ehapa Verlag/Goethe Institut, 1999), a comic book about Johann Wolfgang von Goethe's life.

[3] Neil Hamilton, *Zealotry and Academic Freedom: A Legal and Historical Perspective* (New Brunswick, N.J.: Transaction, 1995) 10–11.

[4] Julius Goebel, "A Proposed Curriculum of German Reading," *Modern Language Notes* 2 (1887): 26. "An der ebenso großen als schönen Aufgabe, die deutsche Sprache und Literatur und mit diesen den deutschen Geist nicht nur denen zu erhalten, die sie von ihren Eltern ererbt haben, sondern ihnen ein immer größeres Gebiet zu erobern, wollen wir unentwegt festhalten, in der Überzeugung, dass sie fruchtbringend auf die Entwicklung unserer großen Nation und auf die *Bildung* des Volkscharakters wirken müssen." Max Griebsch, "Was wir wollen," *Die pädagogischen Monatshefte* 1 (1899): 2. "Many of you . . . may be wondering why I should have chosen Goethe as a guide in considering some of the professional problems of the modern language men of this country. . . . To reassure you, however, I can truthfully say that my admiration is not blind. Nor is it ignorant of all that the most determined *advocatus diaboli* could urge against the canonization of my saint." Hohlfeld lvii-lviii. "Ich brauche kaum zu sagen, daß das Goethesche Evangelium der Tat und die Goethesche Forderung der Entsagung, der Gegensatz zwischen Vielseitigkeit und Beschränkung, zwischen stürmischem Streben und beschaulicher Ehrfurcht, zwischen Wirklichkeitsfreude und Versenkung ins Innere, zwischen Volkstum und Weltbürgertum die Hauptpunkte desjenigen waren, was ich aus der Gedankenwelt des deutschen Dichters als besonders bedeutsam für Amerika auswählte." Kuno Francke, *Deutsche Arbeit in Amerika* (Leipzig: Felix Meiner, 1930) 38.

[5] Francke 36–39.

[6] Nearly forty years later the exiled Henry Remak states: "Zu meiner amerikanischen Studentenzeit wurde mir gesagt, ein moderner Fremdsprachenprofessor würde es schwer haben, zum Dekan, geschweige denn zum Präsidenten einer amerikanischen Universität gewählt zu werden, wenn der Gegenkandidat ein klassischer Philologe wäre; und wenn der moderne Fremdsprachler schon in Frage käme, dann hätte wiederum der Sprachphilologe und der Mediävist einen erheblichen Vorsprung vor dem Spezialisten des 18. und sicherlich des 19. Jahrhunderts." Henry H. H. Remak, "Deutsche Emigration und Amerikanische Germanistik," in *Modernisierung oder*

Überfremdung? Zur Wirkung deutscher Exilanten in der Germanistik der Aufnahmeländer, ed. Walter Schmitz (Stuttgart: Metzler, 1994) 176.

[7] See, for example, Carl Baumann, "Why Study Foreign Languages?" *Modern Language Forum* 21 (1936): 33–34. Baumann's argument was that one could understand a country's culture better if one knew the language and could therefore counter the fanaticism that was gripping Germany. Another example is Theodore Huebener's appeal to Germanists to teach their students that the Nazis cannot destroy the German language and German culture: "Lernt Deutsch!" *Monatshefte* 27 (1935): 294–96.

[8] Editorial, *New York Times,* 11 April 1938.

[9] Hamilton 16–18. By 1936, twenty-one states and Washington, D.C., had reinstated the First World War practice of requiring the signing of loyalty oaths by their teachers. During the interwar years Coats cites numerous cases of arbitary dismissals of university and college faculty members. See A. W. Coats, "Economists, the Economics Profession, and Academic Freedom in the United States," *Academic Freedom on Trial: 100 Years of Sifting and Winnowing at the University of Wisconsin,* ed. W. Lee Hanson (Madison: U of Wisconsin P, 1998) 138.

[10] A notice in *Monatshefte* describes the Emergency Committee's efforts to place refugee intellectuals, while emphasizing that "at least 20% are not Jewish." To assuage fears that these émigrés could permanently take away jobs, the report points out that professors placed by the committee had a one-year contract, after which the institution that took them on was under no obligation to keep them. *Monatshefte* 26 (1934): 47. Fear of anti-Semitism was presumably what prompted Richard Alewyn to stress: "I am a protestant by religion, married, and have two children." See Lebenslauf 1938, Richard Alewyn, Alewyn file, German 7/14/2, Box 1, University of Wisconsin Archives.

[11] Karl J. R. Arndt, "Should Americans Teach Foreign Languages?" *School and Society* 27 (July 1935): 130. Arndt goes on to ask: "why not place some of our own American Jews before we establish professorships for Jews exiled from Europe?" The degree to which anti-Semitism existed varied from institution to institution. Hermann Weigand remembered that there was no open anti-Semitism at the University of Michigan, whereas Yale was extremely anti-Semitic during the 1930s. See Henry J. Schmidt, "Interview with Hermann J. Weigand (1892–1985)," in *Teaching German in America: Prolegomena to a History,* ed. David P. Benseler et al. (Madison: U of Wisconsin P, 1988) 288. Compared to other disciplines, the German professorate included considerably more Jews among its ranks. In history, for example, the late George L. Mosse recalled: "In jeder Abteilung, wo ich gelehrt habe, war ich der erste jüdische Historiker." *George Mosse: "Ich bleibe Emigrant," Gespräche mit George L. Mosse,* ed. Erika Runge and Uwe Stelbrink (Berlin: Dietz, 1991) 60.

[12] Werner Vordtriede remembers that the eminent German-American Baroque scholar Harold Jantz, his superior at Princeton, visited his course on modern German literature and discussed his text selections. He admonished Vordtriede for not including Sudermann and Kolbenheyer, both Nazi-sanctioned authors. See Werner Vordtriede, *Das verlassene Haus. Tagebuch aus dem amerikanischen Exil 1938–1947* (Munich: Hanser, 1975) 357. Similarly, Egon Schwarz mentions that exiled Heinrich Schneider, an avid antifascist, ran into problems when he did not attend events his colleagues had planned with Nazi functionaries. See Egon Schwarz, "Die Exilanten und die heutige amerikanische Universität," in *Modernisierung oder Überfremdung?* 122–23.

[13] Heinrich Meyer (Muhlenberg College), Hugo Schnuch (affiliations vary), Anna Schafheitlin (Kent State University), Matthias Smitz (Smith College), Friedrich J. Hauptmann (Rutgers University), and the most notorious of all, Max Otto Koischwitz (Hunter College). While Schafheitlin, Schmitz, Hauptmann, and Koischwitz returned to Germany, Meyer and Schnuch remained in the United States and evidently went on teaching. The belief that there were many Nazis among the German faculty teaching at American universities was also voiced by the leftist exile Stefan Heym, who somewhat rashly concluded that most German books published in the United States were textbooks: "Diese Schulbücher waren leider mehr oder weniger nazi-beeinflußt. Die Redaktion der Schulbücher liegt meist in den Händen der deutschen Departments der Universitäten, und viele dieser deutschen Departments (vor allem das einflußreichste an der Universität Wisconsin) werden von Nazi-Professoren beherrscht." Stefan Heym, "Eine kleine deutsche Chronik. USA," *Das Wort* 3.8 (1938): 145.

[14] In his autobiography Bernhard Blume, who in 1956 was to become Kuno-Francke-Professor himself, wrote that only Viëtor had been awarded a good position — in fact, the best position available in American Germanics. See Bernhard Blume, *Narziß mit Brille: Kapitel einer Autobiographie,* ed. Fritz Martini and Egon Schwarz (Heidelberg: Lambert Schneider, 1985) 238. Blume, however, includes neither philologists nor women in his equation, since the émigrés Konstantin Reichhardt and Hans Sperber already had full professorships at the Universities of Ohio and Minnesota, and the Austrian literary scholar Marianne Thalmann was a full professor at Wellesley College at the same time.

[15] "Meine Klassen habe ich ganz schlecht werden lassen. Ich weiß überhaupt nicht mehr, wie man unterrichtet . . . , bin langweilig, ungeduldig und hilflos bei dieser Spracheinpaukerei." Vordtriede 376. Also: "Die verwünschte Schule läßt mir so gar keine Zeit — Du erinnerst Dich wohl, daß ich ja auch noch an Sonntagen für sie 'malen' muß." Oskar Seidlin's handwritten note on

Dieter Cunz's letter to Herbert Steiner, 5 July 1943, German Literature Archives, Marbach, 74.2863.

[16] Vordtriede refers to a possible job at a college in rural Wisconsin as a "Jack-London-Existenz." Vordtriede 289. Walter Naumann calls Kansas "Fuchsloch" (letter to Herbert Steiner on 24 June 1942, German Literature Archives, Marbach, 74.3969/1), whereas Dieter Cunz complains that he had to decide against moving from Maryland to New York for practical reasons (same letter to Herbert Steiner as quoted above in footnote 15).

[17] See Remak 180.

[18] Vordtriede 14.

[19] *Ibid.* 63–64.

[20] Thus, the philologist Hans Naumann of the University of Frankfurt spent a year in Madison, Wisconsin; see "Umschau der Schriftleitung," *Monatshefte* 20 (1928): 45, 221. Carl Viëtor from Giessen and Wolfgang Liepe from Kiel spent a year at Harvard and Columbia, respectively. In 1933 Julius Petersen's visit to Stanford was announced in the professional journals; see "News and Notes," *German Quarterly* 6 (1933): 144 and "Berichte und Notizen," *Monatshefte* 25 (1933): 79.

[21] Hermann J. Weigand, "Julius Petersen. Die Sehnsucht nach dem Dritten Reich in deutscher Sage und Dichtung," *Modern Language Notes* 50 (1935): 268–71.

[22] On the loss of his position in Heidelberg, Richard Alewyn had written to Julius Petersen: "Schwerer noch freilich als die Vernichtung meiner beruflichen und wirtschaflichen Existenz trifft mich die gleichzeitig damit ausgesprochene Aberkennung meines Deutschtums. . . . Ich habe sogar die feste Überzeugung ein besserer Deutscher zu sein als diejenigen, die mir mein Deutschtum nehmen wollen." Alewyn's letter to Petersen, Heidelberg, 24 August 1933, quoted in *Klassiker in finstren Zeiten, 1933–1945: Eine Ausstellung des deutschen Literaturarchivs im Schiller-Nationalmuseum Marbach am Neckar,* ed. Bernhard Zeller, vol. 1 (Stuttgart: Ernst Klett, 1983) 268. Also, Karl Viëtor lamented the fact that his wife was deprived of her German identity and maintained that she was more German than most so-called Aryans. See Viëtor's letter to Erich Rothacker, 21 January 1934, quoted in Walter Schmitz, "Vorbemerkung," *Modernisierung oder Überfremdung?* ix.

[23] Richard Alewyn, "Julius Petersen," *German Quarterly* 14 (1941): 233–34.

[24] See Karl Viëtor's correspondence with Julius Petersen in the German Literature Archives in Marbach, specifically the letter dated Cambridge, Mass., 16 November 1937, 66.1143/5: "[Sie sind unterrichtet], dass Korff und ich planen, Ihren 60. Geburtstag zu ehren durch eine Festschrift."

[25] Stuart Atkins, "Karl Viëtor. November 29, 1892 — June 7, 1951," *Germanic Review* 26 (1951): 172.

[26] In a letter to Friedrich Beißner of 26 January 1939 he complains that most scholars present had not understood his MLA-talk, "weil er zu abstrakt war und zuviel literatur- und kirchengeschichtliche Kenntnisse voraussetzte." See Carsten Zelle, "Emigrantengespräch: Ein Brief Richard Alewyns an Karl Viëtor," *Euphorion* 84 (1990): 218.

[27] "Das hat es in diesem Land wohl noch nicht gegeben. Natürlich habe ich recht elementar sein müssen: methodisch-abstraktes Denken ist für den angelsächsischen Geist, vor allem in der amerikanischen Spielart, hart." Viëtor's letter to Julius Petersen, 12 February 1939, German Literature Archives, Marbach 66.1143/7.

[28] Atkins 172.

[29] Viëtor, "Deutsche Literaturgeschichte als Geistesgeschichte. Ein Rückblick," *PMLA* 60 (1945): 899–916.

[30] For example, Werner Vordtriede's self-perception as a spiritual leader becomes obvious from his diary. "Es geschah, worauf ich doch im Grunde immer warte, vom ersten Tag meiner Lehrtätigkeit an: daß ein Schüler einfach nicht anders kann, als nach der Stunden vor den Lehrer hinzutreten und zu sagen: 'Hier bin ich. Du hast gerufen und ich habe dich gehört.' Der Soldat D. kam, sehr bewegt, wirklich nach der Stunde und sprach . . . von sich. Wie richtungslos er sei und wie er erst durch meine Worte einige Anleitungen erhalte. Er fühlte sich . . . statt in einem Klassenzimmer, plötzlich 'aux pieds du poëte.'" Vordtriede 232. "Ich selber fühlte [das Harvarder Germanische Museum] als eine Notwendigkeit, wenn das von mir vertretene Fach sich gegenüber dem alles überwiegenden englischen und französischen Einfluß dauernd behaupten sollte. In den dreizehn Jahren meines Harvarder Aufenthaltes hatte ich . . . doch immer aufs neue . . . empfunden, wie fremd . . . dem durchschnittlichen Neuengländer schließlich doch [die deutsche Kunst blieb]. . . . Dieser Voreingenommenheit gegen deutsches Wesen hoffte ich nun durch die Errichtung einer Art von Heiligtum des deutschen Geistes . . . entgegenzuwirken." Francke 41.

[31] Victor Lange, "Introduction," *Goethe: A Collection of Critical Essays*, ed. Victor Lange (Englewood Cliffs, N.J.: Prentice-Hall, 1968) 1–3.

[32] Oskar Seidlin, "Martin Sommerfeld 1894–1939," *Monatshefte* 31 (1939): 355–56.

[33] Seidlin, "Das Humane und der Dichter," *Monatshefte* 31 (1940): 333–38. Instrumentalizing Goethe in opposition to National Socialism was nothing new in American Germanics, but Seidlin's speech was the clearest and most vehement example.

[34] With the help of his close friend Klaus Mann, Seidlin, who is referred to as "Bubi Koplowitz" in Mann's diaries and his correspondence with his father, was given Thomas Mann's manuscript of *Lotte in Weimar* to recopy by hand for twelve dollars. This and similar jobs for the Mann family helped Seidlin survive in his first months in American exile. See Thomas Mann's letter to Oskar Koplowitz, Princeton on 6 November 1938 in *Thomas Mann: Briefe 1937–1947*, ed. Erika Mann (Frankfurt/Main: Fischer, 1963) 63.

[35] Oskar Seidlin, "Thomas Mann und die Demokratie," *Monatshefte* 35 (1943): 438.

[36] Heinz Politzer, who was to become an important Germanist at Berkeley, felt able to deal with the shock of exile because of this sense of community spirit, as he stated in his report to the American Guild, dated Jerusalem, 25 August 1938, after he received a scholarship from the organization; cited in *Deutsche Intellektuelle im Exil: Ihre Akademie und die "American Guild for German Cultural Freedom."* *Eine Ausstellung des Deutschen Exilarchivs 1933–1945 der Deutschen Bibliothek Frankfurt am Main,* ed. Werner Bertold et al. (Munich/New York: K. G. Saur, 1993) 160–61.

[37] See also Ernst Feise, "Chapel Address," *Monatshefte* 35 (1943): 438.

[38] "Wir machen kein Programm. Niemand dürfte es heute wagen, über den Dingen zu stehen, einen Plan des Ganzen zu entwerfen, den einen einzigen weg als den von ihm vermeintlich gewußten anzugeben . . . — Wir glauben nicht an sich ausschließende, 'letzte Standpunkte,' sondern an den gemeinsamen Ursprung des Menschseins." Karl Jaspers, "Geleitwort," *Die Wandlung* 1.1 (1945): 4.

[39] "Das edelste Menschenbild, das die abendländische Kultur sich ersonnen hat, das Bild des Goetheschen Menschen." Oskar Seidlin, "Hermann Hesses 'Glasperlenspiel,'" *Die Wandlung* 3.4 (1948): 308.

[40] "Der gegenwärtige Beitrag wird gleichwohl sinnvoll erscheinen, zumal wenn der nachdenkende Leser ihn zu den übrigen zeitdiagnostischen Beiträgen dieses Heftes in Beziehung setzt. [Europa steht] unvermindert auf dem Spiel. Darum erscheint es nichts weniger als überflüssig, vielmehr dringend nötig, einer bedeutenden literarischen Erscheinung auch politsch — das Wort im weitesten und genausten Sinn verstanden — nachzuspüren." Dolf Sternberger, "Redaktionelle Anmerkungen," *Die Wandlung* 3.4 (1948): 375.

[41] Alewyn, cited in Klaus Garber, "Weimar und Buchenwald: Richard Alewyns Kölner Goethe-Rede aus dem Jahr 1949," in *Wir tragen den Zettelkasten mit den Steckbriefen unserer Freunde: Beiträge jüdischer Autoren zur deutschen Literatur seit 1945,* ed. Jens Stüben and Winfried Woesler in collaboration with Ernst Loewy (Darmstadt: Jürgen Häuser, 1993) 335. Complete text: "Goethe als Alibi," *Hamburger Akademische Rundschau* 3, 1948/50, H. 8–10, (1949): 685–87.

⁴² As Egon Schwarz remembers in *Keine Zeit für Eichendorff: Chronik unfrei-williger Wanderjahre* (Frankfurt/Main: Büchergilde Gutenberg, 1992) 295–96.

⁴³ Women, whom the Second World War and the resulting absence of men had catapulted into the universities and the job market, insisted on higher education and jobs. Especially in conjunction with the GI Bill, conservative politicians frequently equated women's refusal to return to home and hearth with Communist subversion. While there are no cases among the female Germanists that I know of, the Jewish art professor Luella Raab-Mundel was relieved of her position as head of the art department in West Virginia's Fairmont College because her insistence on keeping her job was seen as un-feminine and interpreted as evidence of Communist sympathies. See Charles H. McCormick, *This Nest of Vipers: McCarthyism and Higher Education in the Mundel Affair, 1951–52* (Urbana/Chicago: U of Illinois P, 1989) 30–39, 58–60.

⁴⁴ In fact, sexual orientation played a much more important role in the McCarthy witch hunts than has been assumed. See Robert J. Corber, *In the Name of National Security: Hitchcock, Homophobia, and the Political Construction of Gender in Postwar America* (Durham, N.C.: Duke UP, 1993) 1–55, and Jonathan Neil Katz, *Gay American History: Lesbians and Gay Men in the USA* (New York: Meridian, 1992) 91–109.

⁴⁵ Anthony Heilbut, *Exiled in Paradise: German Refugee Artists and Intellectuals in America from the 1930s to the Present* (New York: Viking Press, 1983) 413–14. Hannah Arendt explains how Jews were often identified as leftists during the McCarthy era simply by virtue of being Jewish. Their social status as immigrants or exiles made them especially vulnerable to the frequent calls for deportation.

⁴⁶ David Suchoff, "Jüdische Kritiker in der amerikanischen Nachkriegsgermanistik," *Weimarer Beiträge* 39 (1993): 395.

⁴⁷ Erich Heller, "Preface to the Original Edition," in his *The Disinherited Mind* (New York: Farrar, Straus, Cudahy, 1957) viii–ix.

⁴⁸ See, for example, Victor Lange's essay "Goethe's Craft of Fiction," where he writes: "If we realize that the main stream of fiction in which Goethe himself shared extends from Boccaccio and Cervantes to Fénélon and Prévost, from Richardson and Sterne to Rousseau and Marmontel, from Cooper and Irving to Scott, Stendhal and Balzac, we cannot expect him to have remained untouched by the varying conventions of that tradition." *Goethe — A Collection of Critical Essays* 66.

⁴⁹ Oskar Seidlin, "Goethe's Iphigenia and the Humane Ideal," in *Goethe — A Collection of Critical Essays*, 64.

[50] Lange 1–3.

[51] Bradley F. Smith, *The Shadow Warriors: O.S.S. and the Origins of the C.I.A.* (New York: Basic Books, 1983) 379. While Smith referred to leftist historians and social scientists working for the OSS, I found his thesis to be applicable also to the Germanists, especially if one keeps in mind Seidlin's, Plant's, and Gerhard Loose's decidedly leftist pasts before they came to the United States.

[52] Jost Hermand, "Das Eigene im Fremden: Die Wirkung der Exilanten und Exilantinnen auf die amerikanische Germanistik," in *Exilforschung: Ein Internationales Jahrbuch*, vol. 16 (Munich: Text + Kritik, 1998) 165.

[53] Schwarz, *Keine Zeit* 265–66.

[54] *Ibid.* 319–23.

[55] As the late George L. Mosse told Jost Hermand. See Jost Hermand, "Deutsche Juden jenseits des Judentums: Der Fall Gerhard / Israel / George L. Mosse," *Jahrbuch für Anti-Semitismusforschung* 3, ed. Wolfgang Benz (Frankurt/Main: Campus Verlag, 1994) 191.

[56] Henry J. Schmidt, "What is Oppositional Criticism? Politics and German Literary Criticism from Fascism to the Cold War," *Monatshefte* 79 (1987) 293–94.

[57] It was not until the late 1970s and 1980s that the former exiles would openly reveal their sexual orientation. Richard Plant's foreword to his *The Pink Triangle: The Nazi War against Homosexuals* (New York: Holt, 1986) is as autobiographical as it is documentary — a coming to terms with his own past, as a German Jew and a homosexual.

[58] Oskar Koplowitz changed his name to Seidlin in American exile, as Richard Plaut changed his to Plant, Paul Albert Kranz to Ernst Erich Noth, and Klaus Hilzheimer to Claude Hill. In his diary Werner Vortriede never refers to his mother, Käthe Blumenthal, by her name. Born into a Jewish merchant family, she was a Social Democratic editor for the Freiburg paper *Volkswacht* and was briefly imprisoned by the Nazis before she was able to leave Germany. See Regina Weber, "Der emigrierte Germanist als 'Führer' zur deutschen Dichtung? Werner Vordtriede im Exil," *Exilforschung: Ein internationales Jahrbuch* 13 (1995): 143–44. In fact, Joseph Strelka, a personal friend, recalled Vordtriede saying that he had left Germany voluntarily because Hitler had taken away his spiritual home. See Joseph P. Strelka, "Werner Vortriede," in *Deutschsprachige Exilliteratur seit 1933*, vol. 2: *New York*, ed. John M. Spalek and Joseph P. Strelka (Bern: Francke, 1989) 976.

[59] McCormick 32; especially those institutions founded by immigrants, such as Black Mountain College in North Carolina, which topped the list of suspicious schools.

[60] Ironically, the first Germanist to find himself on HUAC's blacklist and subsequently lose his job was the Head of New York University's German department, Lyman Bradley. It seems that he attracted HUAC's attention simply because he had been instrumental in placing many refugee intellectuals in American German departments during the Nazi era, and his refusal to disclose personal information about the refugees cost him his job. Simultaneously, the outspoken antifascist Thomas Mann scholar Harry Slochower of Brooklyn College lost his job because of his alleged membership in the Communist Party.

[61] Jürgen Eder, "Mit Eichendorff nach Amerika: Oskar Seidlin," in *Wir tragen den Zettelkasten* 353; Egon Schwarz, "Die Exilanten und die heutige amerikanische Universität," in *Modernisierung und Überfremdung?* 121. The cases of the immigrant anthropologist Franz Boas and the Jewish Germanist Harry Slochower also demonstrate how charisma was wont to attract the HUAC's attention. See Ellen W. Schrecker, *No Ivory Tower: McCarthyism and the Universities* (New York/Oxford: Oxford UP, 1986) 168, 183, 268–69, 283.

[62] See The Byron Darling case in Lionel S. Lewis, *Cold War on Campus: A Study of the Politics of Organizational Control* (New Brunswick, N.J./Oxford: Transaction, 1987) 61–66.

[63] Erving Beauregard, *History of Academic Freedom in Ohio: Case Studies in Higher Education 1808–1976* (New York: Peter Lang, 1988) 88, 197.

[64] See Oskar Seidlin's speech on the occasion of his having been awarded the Culture Prize of Upper Silesia in 1975, cited in Eder 350.

[65] Oskar Seidlin, "Interpretation als eine moralische Veranstaltung betrachtet: Ansprache bei der Verleihung des Preises für Germanistik im Ausland," *Jahrbuch der deutschen Akademie für Sprache und Dichtung* (1968) 32–45.

[66] Eder 351.

[67] Regina Weber, "Der emigrierte Germanist als 'Führer' zur deutschen Dichtung? Werner Vortriede im Exil," in *Exilforschung: Ein Internationales Jahrbuch,* vol. 13 (Munich: Edition Text + Kritik, 1995) 140–41.

[68] Hermand 165–68.

[69] Walter Solmitz (1962), Matthijs Otto Jolles (1968), Robert Ludwig Kahn (1970).

[70] While Viëtor is usually referred to as "Protestant," the Nazis had identified his wife, Alice, as Jewish. Judging from Viëtor's comments, however, she must not have perceived herself as Jewish — like so many other members of the exile community. "[Meine Frau Alice ist], wie sie erst in diesem Jahr zuverlässig erfahren hat, Jüdin, und zwar ohne Milderung." See Viëtor's letter of 21 January 1934 to Erich Rothacker, quoted by Schmitz viii. As for

Viëtor's being called "einer der bedeutendsten Juden des 20. Jahrhunderts," see Walter Tetzlaff, *2000 Kurzbiographien bedeutender deutscher Juden des 20. Jahrhunderts* (Lindhorst: Askania, 1982) 342.

[71] "In Schnitzler I discovered the mythologies of my family, the gossipy stories told in the circle of relatives and acquaintances. . . . My father, all my aunts, my mother's cousins, family, friends and many others disappeared forever. . . . I mention . . . death to emphasize the monstrously personal relevance that the world of Schnitzler and Stefan Zweig assumed because of the circumstances in which I read of it. . . . It was not . . . nostalgia that moved me to study German literature." Walter H. Sokel, "Discovering Austrian Literature in Nazism's Shadows," in *Language and Culture: A Transcending Bond,* ed. Charles Merrill and Susan Cernyak-Spatz (New York: Peter Lang, 1993) 22–24.

"Humanitätssalbader": Goethe's Distaste for Jewish Emancipation, and Jewish Responses

W. Daniel Wilson
University of California-Berkeley

FOR MY PURPOSES the question whether Goethe was anti-Semitic is not irrelevant, but it is secondary to the question of his attitude to political rights of *any* group. If pressed on the issue of Goethe's attitude to Jews, I would say that a thorough examination of all the evidence leads to a paradoxical conclusion: Goethe described in *Dichtung und Wahrheit* (Poetry and Truth, 1811–22) his youthful prejudice against Jews, as it was gleaned from books.[1] This passage would logically make the reader conclude that the Goethe writing his autobiography had by then — the second decade of the nineteenth century, in the second half of a long life — conquered this prejudice from his youth. And Goethe gives the same impression in a well-known conversation with Simon Edler von Laemel in 1812, i.e., that he had earlier "despised" Jews under the influence of Christian men and women around him, but later, when he got to know intelligent and sensitive Jews, he overcame this prejudice.[2] Other sources tell a different story. It was precisely in his early years that Goethe — in the most generous interpretation — could be said to have been more open toward Jews; Norbert Oellers claims that in *Das Jahrmarktsfest zu Plundersweilern* (The Annual Fair at Plundersweilern, 1774) and other pre-Classical works Goethe was not far from openly opposing anti-Semitism.[3] And it was in *later* years — in fact, as soon as the early 1780s — that Goethe's attitudes to Jews were marked not only by what could be called "dictionary anti-Semitism" but by open contempt for Jews in documents ranging from fictional ones like the unpublished "Wilhelm Meisters theatralische Sendung" (Wilhelm Meister's Theatrical Mission) to the published late novel *Wilhelm Meisters Wanderjahre* (Wilhelm Meister's Journeyman Years, 1821–28) and from letters to conversations. His consistent image is of a treacherous, stingy, and untrustworthy people.

The only positive thing he has to say about Jews is that they exist, that is, that they have managed to survive, and he summons up some admiration for the qualities of tenacity that have helped them prevail. Otherwise, he has complimentary things to say only about a few cultivated Jews, who, of course, serve the function of "exceptions," as so often for the prejudiced; Goethe's attitude seems to be: "Some of my best friends are Jews." Besides these cultivated exceptions, Jews are mentioned most often in the company of scoundrels and whores, and even his appreciation of a cultivated Jew could turn on its head; he once wrote of the "jüdische Pfiffen" [Jewish sneakiness] with which Moses Mendelssohn operated.[4] The question arises, then, as to why Goethe claimed in his autobiography that he had overcome these prejudices later in life. As we shall see, at precisely the time he made this claim — i.e., from a position of supposedly newfound tolerance — he was vigorously opposing Jewish emancipation. It seems to me possible that Goethe was simply following a pattern that scholarship has otherwise clearly established, namely, attempting to shape later interpretations of his life and character — in particular, future biographies — by means of his autobiography. But this explanation is not entirely satisfying, since it would presuppose that Goethe saw the error of his anti-Semitism and yet held to it rather openly, hardly attempting to disguise it in letters or other documents that he knew would be published. Another explanation would suggest that Goethe's latent anti-Semitism was only activated when he otherwise found fault with particular Jews. This explanation would account for the remarks about Mendelssohn, whose philosophical position Goethe opposed. And it would explain some of the remarks that I want to look at in more detail on the question of Jewish emancipation: it seems entirely plausible that Goethe, who *never* supported expansion of human rights, opposed Jewish emancipation not *primarily* because of the character of the Jews (though he may have argued this way) but on the fundamental political principle of his opposition to democratic encroachments on princely authority and sovereignty. It is well known that later in his life Goethe was far more conservative on this issue than even his own duke, opposing, most notably, Carl August's introduction of a new "constitution" in Saxe-Weimar in 1816 and particularly its guarantee of freedom of speech. All this does not mean that Goethe was not prejudiced, but his alibi could easily conceal his prejudice until particular Jews aroused his ire. This is not an entirely satisfying explanation for his contradiction, but I am in any case concerned more with the *reception* of his attitude on Jewish *emancipation,* whatever its causes.

An examination of Goethe's position on the legal rights of Jews has to take account of two earlier episodes that I have never seen adequately considered in treatments of Goethe and Jews, and one of them has never even been mentioned in such scholarship. The one that is sometimes mentioned is usually taken out of its governmental context: in 1782 Goethe wrote to his uncle, a powerful official in Frankfurt, asking that the Frankfurt *Schutzjude* [Jew without full rights of a citizen] Reiss be granted permission to leave the ghetto on Sundays and holidays.[5] This incident does not carry the weight in terms of a personal attitude of Goethe's that some interpreters lend to it, since Goethe wrote this letter in his official capacity at the behest of the duke or the Privy Council. Nevertheless, it is remarkable that he wrote the letter despite his prejudice against Jews — he could probably have argued effectively against doing so. The other episode is less well known because it is documented in the least used of all Goethe editions, the *Amtliche Schriften* (Professional Papers); the documents appear in the first volume, published in 1950, and the planned commentary volume to this collection has never been published, so the context is unclear. But we can at least see pretty clearly what happened: in a conflict between Jews traveling through Saxe-Weimar and some ducal officials who apparently insulted them, Goethe and the other members of the Privy Council took the side of the Jews and ordered restitution.[6]

Now, it is important to remember two things in connection with these events. First, both involved financial interests of the duchy: according to Goethe's description, the Jew Reiss was an important creditor for merchants in Eisenach and Apolda; and one of the insulted Jews in the second case was the Weimar court Jew Elkan, who was an important creditor there, including for Goethe personally; furthermore, Goethe mentions in his report that this incident comes at a time when the duchy has to be careful to make the journey through Weimar "safe and pleasant for each and every passenger"[7] — referring to the efforts to transform Weimar's roads into regional arteries so that the duchy could profit from tolls, and, of course, Jews had to pay a special toll. So the great god Mammon probably played as great a role as Justitia in these cases. More fundamentally, we also have to remember that in both of these cases Goethe and the Privy Council were acting to protect Jews in the context of existing law rather than expanding their rights. Of course, Goethe was fully capable of violating existing rights of the duke's subjects,[8] but he generally had an antipathy to doing so if it could be avoided. The incident with the insulted Jews was not the last time that Goethe protected the rights of someone he found distasteful. In a famous episode after the surrender of the revolutionaries in besieged Mainz he prevented bystanders from venting their rage against one of the Jacobin leaders, since the terms of the surrender called for an amnesty for them. Goethe describes intervening on behalf of the prisoner and preventing violence against him, and it is in this context that he uttered his well-known and sometimes distorted pronouncement: "It is simply part of my nature: I would rather commit an injustice than bear disorder."[9] In the incident involving the insulted Jews, too, Goethe abhorred disorder, especially when it threatened the economic well-being of the duchy. And, ultimately, this abhorrence meant that the individual rights of (favored) Jews were protected.

Introducing *new* rights was, however, an entirely different issue. And Goethe's attitude to granting fundamental rights to Jews brings us back to where Goethe's prejudice toward Jews was founded, the Frankfurt ghetto. Life in the *Judengasse* has been described as Hell.[10] It is said to have been the most densely populated place on earth in the eighteenth century. The narrow street was enclosed by thirty-foot-high walls that made the stench and bad air almost unbearable. To accommodate the increasing population (and the city authorities did everything possible to prevent such an increase), the Jews had to build upward along this one street; if the houses got higher than the walls, they were allowed no windows that would have let the Jews look out onto the Christian neighbors, which, of course, exacerbated the problem of poor ventilation. Sanitary conditions were almost disastrous. Restrictions were rigid: the Jews were not allowed to leave the ghetto in the evenings or on Sundays or Christian holidays, and when they did so at other times, they were prohibited from taking strolls in the city or moving in groups of more than two (though this latter restriction was apparently enforced unevenly). Gutzkow later wrote that in Frankfurt the principle was "Wherever there is a green space, no Jew is allowed."[11] Jews had to wear a yellow ring and special cap. There were the most bizarre and humiliating rules: Jews could not touch the food at the open market or have Christian wetnurses; they were allowed Christian servants only on the Sabbath. A few of the most absurd restrictions were weakened in the course of the eighteenth century, but most remained in force right up to the end of Frankfurt's status as a Free Imperial City in 1806 — in other words, change was forced on the Christian majority of Frankfurt from outside, by the French occupiers. Frankfurt is thus viewed as a particularly vicious example of anti-Semitic attitudes, and conditions for Jews in Frankfurt were much worse than those of other German Jews, so that Gutzkow wrote that

Goethe's contempt for Jews was "inoculated in him at birth and nurtured by Frankfurt custom."[12]

After the Napoleonic occupation of Frankfurt and the end of the empire in 1806 the Jews of Frankfurt enthusiastically hoped that their unequal status would end; after all, Jews in the Napoleonic territories of Westphalia, Bavaria, and Baden were given full status as citizens under French influence. The Frankfurt Jews were disappointed. The Napoleonic grand duke of Frankfurt and prince primas of Germany, Dalberg — a friend of Goethe's during the days when Dalberg was governor of Erfurt — was favorably inclined toward the Jews but felt that emancipation had to await their assimilation into the Christian populace; in other words, their Jewishness, explicitly viewed by Dalberg as "foreign," "oriental," had to be eliminated before they could be integrated.[13] It was a typical Enlightenment position, directed against what was seen as "superstition," i.e., orthodox Judaism; Dalberg favored the reform party in the Frankfurt Jewish community and opposed the Orthodox establishment. The Christian populace of Frankfurt generally did not share even this "enlightened" prejudice; theirs was of the older sort, and they did not want any changes, particularly since change might have forced the Christians to face competition in the business world. So Dalberg's supposedly "enlightened" anti-Semitism and the Frankfurt burghers' traditional anti-Semitism found themselves in general agreement that emancipation was the wrong course. The new "Judenstättigkeit" [right to dwell] of early 1808 brought little progress vis-à-vis the old one from almost two hundred years earlier. The Jews of Frankfurt were deeply disappointed in Dalberg, on whom they had pinned their hopes for emancipation, and appealed directly to Napoleon for relief. The new ordinance evoked passive resistance in the ghetto; Ludwig Börne, who grew up in the *Judengasse* and was one of the most prominent advocates of emancipation, later described the conflict as "the Jewish revolt,"[14] and some of the city authorities saw it as an outright revolution.

This is the context in which we have to read some intemperate letters that Goethe wrote to Bettina von Arnim in Frankfurt in the first half of 1808. Goethe was informed by his mother of the debate over the new "Stättigkeit," and he showed a lively interest in it, asking Bettina to send him documents from both sides of the debate. In Braunschweig a Geheimer Finanzrat [privy financial councilor], Israel Jacobson, published a defense of the rights of Frankfurt Jews. His pamphlet sparked a stormy debate in Frankfurt,[15] adding to the discontent in the ghetto, so that the city moved quickly to prohibit any further public discussion of the issues surrounding the new ordinance.[16] Goethe comments on the dispute between Jacobson and the government under Dalberg: "The Brunswick Jewish messiah [Jacobson] might very well look at his people as it ought to be and become, but the Prince [Dalberg] cannot be blamed for treating this race as it really is, and as it will be for quite some time."[17] Goethe is referring to Dalberg's opinion, mentioned earlier, that the Jews had to become enlightened and cultivated before they could be legally emancipated and freed from the ghetto. This opinion of Dalberg's and Goethe's was not only illiberal and ungenerous; it had been proven wrong by the events of 1796. One hundred eighty houses in the ghetto burned down after the French bombardment, so the authorities had to allow many Jewish families to rent from Christians in the city. Börne reports that as soon as the Jews were liberated from the humiliating and miserable conditions in the ghetto, "they gained in respectable mores, in sociability, they improved themselves, sought scholarly knowledge, and cultivated everything that one can expect from educated people."[18] In other words, the de facto partial emancipation — the liberation from the ghetto — led to cultivation of the Jews, rather than the other way around, as Dalberg and Goethe would have it. Their position, restricting the Jews to the ghetto in the most demeaning imprisonment until they achieved cultivation, would have made emancipation impossible. Incidentally, in 1796 the Jews argued that their obvious improvement after the fire spoke for eliminating the ghetto; but they argued unsuccessfully: the *Judengasse* was rebuilt, and they were forced to move back in. Remarks that Goethe made when visiting the city in 1797 indicate that he favored reconstructing the *Judengasse* rather than allowing the Jews to continue to live among Christians.[19]

But back to 1808. On April 20 Goethe writes again to Bettina about Jacobson's brochure and an opposing one: "It was pleasant to see that the Finance Councilor Jacobin son of Israel was put in his place so well. Do you know who wrote the little book? . . . Unfortunately, it is not as quickly paced, bold and funny as it should have been in order to ridicule that pious humanitarian driveler once and for all for all the world to see."[20] The term *Humanitätssalbader* (which I have translated as "pious humanitarian driveler") speaks volumes for the gulf between Goethe's classical ideal of *Humanität* and his attitude to Jewish emancipation — indeed, to any civil rights. When Goethe plays with the name Israel Jacobson and calls him "the Jacobin son of Israel" ("den . . . Jacobinischen Israels Sohn"), he implies a political connection between revolutionary ideals and Jewish emancipation that was not altogether far-fetched, since it was Napoleon who brought Jewish emancipation to Germany; and despite his admiration for Napoleon, Goethe associated Jewish emancipation with political radicalism and abhorred it even more.

The Congress of Vienna envisioned retaining and unifying the Napoleonic emancipation measures, but during the Restoration the reaction against Jewish rights set in with a vengeance. The title of one of the brochures of 1816 is representative: *Die Rechte des Christenthums und des deutschen Volkes verteidigt gegen die Ansprüche der Juden und ihrer Verfechter* (The Rights of Christianity and the German People Defended against the Claims of Jews and their Advocates);[21] rising nationalism viewed Jews as an alien element. Another such polemic "on the Jewish threat to the well-being and character of the Germans," was penned by the Heidelberg Professor Jacob Friedrich Fries, who was then hired as a professor in Jena. He calls the Jews a dangerous "caste of brokers and dealers,"[22] "ruinous for our people, and petty thieves";[23] he wrote that in Frankfurt they had achieved control over half of all capital, and that soon the sons of the leading Christian families would have to become servants of the Jews. Goethe supported the appointment of Fries in Jena, and after reading his anti-Semitic polemics in the *Heidelberger Jahrbücher* (Heidelberg Yearbooks) he wrote to Boisserée: "All of [local] Jewry is trembling because their vicious opponent, whose acquaintance I have just made from the ninth issue [of the *Heidelberger Jahrbücher*], is coming to Thuringia. According to ancient laws, Jews are not allowed to spend the night in Jena. This praiseworthy ordinance will probably be enforced better in the future than it has been up to now."[24] These remarks show Goethe at his most adamant in his rejection of Jewish emancipation. It is no wonder that he explicitly refused to engage in the public debate on behalf of the Jews, though his opinions would have weighed heavily for their cause: "I am refraining from taking the side of any Jews or their friends," he wrote to Marianne von Willemer and her husband in Frankfurt.[25]

Saxe-Weimar confronted the issue of Jewish emancipation in 1823, eight years after the duchy had been elevated to the status of grand duchy and had gained significant new territories in which many Jews lived and in which first steps had been taken toward equal rights. Since the Jews in the older territories of Saxe-Weimar did not enjoy such rights, uniformity had to be ordained. On 23 June 1823 a *Judenordnung* [Jewish ordinance] was proclaimed that brought moderate Jewish emancipation and that met with stiff resistance in some quarters. Goethe was one of the opponents, though at this point he was no longer an active minister of state and could not do much damage. But he railed intemperately against the provision that Jews and Christians could intermarry. He had an "unpleasant conversation" with Chancellor von Müller "on intermarriage between Christians and Jews,"[26] which the latter recorded. "I had hardly entered Goethe's room," Müller reports, "when the old gentleman poured out his passionate rage against our new law regarding Jews, which allows marriages between these two related faiths. He foresaw the worst and most disastrous consequences of it, he claims that if the Superintendent-General has any character, he would have to lay down his post rather than marrying a *Jewess* in the church in the name of the Trinity. All *moral* sensibility in families — which rest on *religious* feeling — would be undermined by such a scandalous law, he said." This conservative Christian tone hardly fits our image of the great pagan Goethe, a contradiction on which Müller remarks: "The thing that was very remarkable in his zeal against the Jews was a profound respect for positive religion, for existing state institutions, which shone through all of his comments despite his free-thinking spirit. 'Do we really want to be in the vanguard of *absurdity* here, to be the first to try out everything grotesque?' he said, among other things."[27] Goethe's advocacy of strict separation of Christians and Jews, incidentally, follows a tendency that we find around the same time in the *Wanderjahre;* speaking there of the utopian colony, one of the normative characters says that the children of the community will be taught about the Christian religion and its founder. "In this spirit, which could perhaps be called pedantic, but which should be recognized as consistent, we do not tolerate Jews among us, for how should we let them take part in the highest culture, when they deny its origin and heritage?"[28] This bizarre justification of the separation of Jews and Christians — made even more embarrassing by the equally bizarre defenses of it by scholars — was at the very least ambiguous, as Goethe had to know. The passage is a fictive reflection of the writer's political attitude to Jewish emancipation.

Goethe has been criticized repeatedly for his attitude to Jews. But his opposition to legal emancipation is surely as significant as his personal prejudice; in fact, he differed from enlightened contemporaries more in his resistance to Jewish rights than in his anti-Jewish sentiment. I would suggest that Goethe's political rejection of civil rights for Jews ought to figure at least as importantly as his prejudice when considering later Jewish attitudes toward him. After all, it could be said that the weak sense for civil and human rights in the German political tradition enabled the Holocaust as much as or even more than German anti-

Semitism. It is illegitimate to equate traditional anti-Semitism with the biologistic, virulent modern brand, or Goethe with modern totalitarianism. But the Holocaust can no longer be wished away when we consider these issues, and the continuities in these kinds of mentalities cannot be overlooked, either. My thesis is that after the genocide against European Jewry, Jewish readings of Goethe's political activities and thought sometimes took on a decidedly critical tone. It is precisely in those works by Jewish Goethe scholars in which Jewish issues are addressed that critique of his politics is most pronounced. In fact, the biographical interpretation of Goethe's political activities as privy councilor and of his political opinions serves as a sort of displacement of the biographers' grappling with Goethe's rejection of Jewish emancipation.

It is well known that German Jews sought assimilation through participation in the Goethe cult, as George Mosse and, especially, Wilfried Barner have shown.[29] Perhaps because of this assimilationist thrust, most of the many biographies of Goethe by Jews contain little significant mention of the Jewish issue and only a sketchy depiction of Goethe's activities as privy councilor. The new biographism began in earnest in 1895 with no fewer than four works: by Karl Heinemann, Eugen Wolff, Richard M. Meyer, and especially the influential Albert Bielschowsky. These biographers had access to almost all the relevant information, in published documents, on Goethe's anti-Semitism and his opposition to emancipation.[30] But much of his activity as privy councilor was also known by this time,[31] including some of the most important infractions against civil and human rights, such as the dismissals of Fichte and Oken, and his rejection of freedom of the press; after all, Heine had discussed the case of Fichte, and Börne coined the term *Fürstenknecht* [lacky of the prince] for Goethe in 1835. So critique of Goethe's political activities would have been possible in Goethe biographies around 1900, even without archival work.

There are, of course, huge differences among the Jewish Goethe biographies with respect to these political questions. At the one pole we find Ludwig Geiger, son of a famous Berlin rabbi and founder and long-time editor of the *Goethe-Jahrbuch* (Goethe Yearbook). In 1910 Geiger published not only a biography of Goethe but also a chapter on Goethe in his book *Die deutsche Literatur und die Juden* (German Literature and the Jews). He is almost the only Goethe biographer who confronts the Jewish issue at any length, and in spite of his harmonizing tendency he hardly suppresses the shadowy side. Geiger comes to the obvious conclusion that Goethe "did not like the Jews in general" and mentions as evidence Goethe's rejection of equal rights for Jews in

Saxe-Weimar, his remark about the law prohibiting Jews from staying in Jena, and his support of the opponents of the Jews in the Frankfurt debates. But Geiger then draws attention away from these issues and points to Goethe's respect for Spinoza and cultivated Jews, which supposedly prevented the poet from assenting to prejudices and from voicing "malicious accusations, which were still expressed in Goethe's time"[32] — a judgment for which there is a certain justification when one thinks of openly anti-Semitic figures such as Fichte. Geiger thus ends up defending Goethe's attitude to Jews, and he also avoids significant criticism of the privy councilor, although he mentions that Goethe was against freedom of the press.[33] In one sentence, however, Geiger brings together Goethe's general political principles and his rejection of Jewish rights when he writes of Goethe's attitude toward mixed marriages: "Such heated comments can be explained just as easily by his antipathy to liberalism as by his antipathy to Jews."[34] It thus seems that Geiger's perception of Goethe's anti-Semitism opens his eyes at least partially to general questions of human rights in Goethe's opinions and practice.

Bielschowsky, on the other hand, has nothing to say about Goethe and Jews, though his biography is twice as long as Geiger's.[35] And although he treats Goethe's official activities in the first Weimar decade in a separate chapter and discusses his attitude toward the French Revolution, political conflicts in Saxe-Weimar and the question of civil and human rights are overlooked; Goethe appears, as in almost all biographies, by Jews or non-Jews, as a paternalist reformer and enlightened advocate of the lower classes against the interests of the nobility and the irresponsibility of the duke — perspectives that are essentially half-truths. Bielschowsky's obfuscation is clear in his treatment of Fichte and Oken; he mentions them, but not that they were dismissed. The great aesthete of the George circle, Friedrich Gundolf, who was subjected to especially venomous caricatures of his Jewishness, avoids the topic of Goethe and the Jews and recounts Goethe's official activities in only one paragraph, where they appear simply as a prelude to Goethe's trip to Italy.[36] We find similar argumentation in Eduard Engel, who in 1909 wrote two articles on Goethe as *Politiker* [politician] and as *Beamter* [official], neither of which moves beyond panegyric glorification.[37]

Before the Second World War, then, the desire for assimilation seems to have been too strong for Jewish Goethe biographers to develop a keen sense of Goethe's political attitude to Jewish emancipation, and I think it is no accident that Goethe's general political illiberalism was also ignored; we saw that the only significant biographer who addressed the question of Jewish emancipation (Geiger) also expressed a reserved critique of Goethe's political stance. The political Goethe myth rested in these years on the assumption that there were no significant political conflicts in Saxe-Weimar, only social reforms with the good of the people in mind. And as far as I can tell, that was not a specifically Jewish myth.

After the Second World War we find a completely different situation. The most important political critiques of Goethe were launched by Jews. A famous Germanist with partly Jewish parentage, Richard Alewyn, after being forcibly retired from his Heidelberg professorship in 1933 and enduring an unhappy exile in New York, returned to Germany after the war and during the 1949 Goethe commemorations coined the famous phrase "Between us and Weimar lies Buchenwald. We simply can't get around it."[38] This formulation has been repeated again and again, particularly in the commemorative year 1999 to the extent that the old guard in Weimar complained of a "Buchenwaldization of Weimar." But in 1999 no less than in 1949, a clean opposition was set up between Buchenwald and Weimar — in Alewyn's words, "There is only Goethe and Hitler, humaneness and bestiality."[39] Alewyn explicitly assumes that Goethe stands above politics, as high as the stars. While it would be foolish to equate Weimar and Buchenwald, the stark opposition of bestiality and humanitarianism ignores Goethe's fulminations against the "Humanitätssalbader" who would force Jewish emancipation on Christian Germany; it also ignores Goethe's general disdain for human and civil rights. Alewyn had been sensitized to the contrast between humanitarian ideals and modern totalitarianism; but because he leaves Goethe's political life out of the equation, he ignores the contrast between these ideals and the reality of Goethe's political activities, not to mention Goethe's regressive attitude to Jewish emancipation.

Other Jewish writers were much more historically grounded and provided the major impetus for political critique of Goethe after the Second World War. The first is a group of Jewish scholars around the legendary Gerhard Scholz, who returned from Swedish exile in 1946 to take over the Goethe institutions in Weimar.[40] He conducted a course in 1950 that produced some of the leading Germanists in the GDR and then launched an exhibition that brought together some documents that showed the shadowy side of absolutist rule in Weimar. Scholz never published much himself, however, and the rest of this group — among them Edith Braemer, Ursula Wertheim, Heinz Stolpe, and

Hans-Günther Thalheim — never worked specifically on Goethe's political activities, focusing instead on political aspects of his works. And Scholz was, in any case, pushed aside rather early by Helmut Holtzhauer, who did not continue this approach of applying the Marxist critique of absolutism to the Duchy of Weimar in the Classical period. Thus, the work of this group remains more or less without consequence except for the individuals involved in it.

I can only mention in passing the study of Goethe by the Viennese Jewish expatriate psychoanalyst in New York, Kurt R. Eissler; this tome certainly represented a new and potentially unsettling view of Goethe, but it hardly had political implications — and, in any case, it had little effect in the world of Germanist scholarship until it was translated into German in 1983, twenty years after it was first published.[41] A much wider impact was made by Richard Friedenthal, of a wealthy Berlin Jewish family, a minor writer who conversed with such luminaries as Stefan Zweig. He had to leave for England in 1938 and remained there for the rest of his life. In the same year as Eissler's book, 1963, Friedenthal's iconoclastic Goethe biography caused outrage among Germanists in Germany. Political critique is palpable everywhere in the book, even in areas that seem at first blush unpolitical, such as the so-called *Genietreiben* [youthful pranks] of Goethe and Carl August, which Friedenthal sees in the long tradition of princely arbitrariness and abuse of the populace (219, 221). He draws attention to Goethe's mistrust of the lower classes (371), recites the whole roster of abuses in German absolutism (374 ff.), and does not shy away from saying that Goethe lived in the past, politically speaking. Almost offhandedly, Friedenthal remarks in the context of Jewish admirers of Goethe that the writer was "no philosemite . . . as was Lessing; in questions of equality and civil rights he favored emancipation of the Jews just as little as he favored freedom of the press."[42] In personal remarks in his afterword, too, Friedenthal suggests that his experiences of anti-Semitism and the Holocaust deepened his sensitivity to Goethe's political conservatism. Though he never mentions that he is a Jew, Friedenthal points to his personal experience as the fundament for his biography, moving effortlessly from the First World War to the Second:

> Whoever had to dig into the loose chalk soil of the Champagne in 1915 at almost the same spot as Goethe, "for an early burial," as he said [in *Campagne in Frankreich 1792*], will see such a campaign with different eyes, and so it goes with many things. If one then survives the early burial, which later, too, often seemed imminent, then one gains a different outlook on life and literature. One will cultivate a

certain irony or humor, without which such times can hardly be mas-
tered. Thus, I think that besides my study of the sources, a great deal
of life experience can be found in my book.[43]

There is, indeed, a great deal of irony in Friedenthal's book, and he di-
rects it often at the political Goethe.

That was 1963, rather early in a turbulent decade and also early in
the history of politically critical Goethe scholarship. A few years later
appeared the now famous — or infamous — *Klassik-Legende,* another
legendary Wisconsin Workshop, but here we find hardly any substan-
tive critique of Goethe's political activities as privy councilor or his attitudes to human rights.[44] More significant in this respect was,
undoubtedly, Hans Mayer's slim 1973 *Goethe: Ein Versuch über den
Erfolg* (Goethe: An Essay on Success). Mayer stresses the contradictions, the discrepancies, and the failures in Goethe's life and works. His
political critique is more pronounced than Friedenthal's; of course, he
sees the same phenomena from a decidedly Marxist perspective, sometimes excessively stressing class conflict and Goethe's supposed failure
to support the aspirations of his own class. Only a thorough reading
makes clear what the social histories of literature in the 1980s owe to
this book. And only in the last pages does Mayer address Goethe's rejection of Jewish emancipation; like Friedenthal, he does not mince
words. After he quotes the infamous passage from the *Wanderjahre* in
which the narrator admits that the exclusion of Jews from the utopian
project might seem "pedantic," he quotes the response of an early
Germanist, Ferdinand Grogorovius: "That is not only pedantic, we
must call out to Goethe with deep regret, but also very mean-spirited
and barbaric for someone who claims to be a humanist."[45] In the case
of Mayer, like Friedenthal, I would suggest that his Jewish perspective
plays a role in his general political critique of Goethe. Mayer does not
say this explicitly in his book; at most, a passage like the following
could be interpreted in this way: "Goethe as *Bildung* [formative influ-
ence] and *Besitz* [cultural heritage] — all that is gone. Goethe as *Innerlichkeit* [inwardness], doesn't hold up: in a prison cell, in mortal
danger. . . ."[46] This line could even be seen as a critique of those Jews
in the 1920s and 1930s who hoped for salvation from the tide of fascism through Goethean humanism. The contradiction between this
humanism and the reality of the political Goethe became fully clear, I
would suggest, only after the failure of democracy in Germany to prevent the most horrid genocide of the twentieth century, and it became
clearest to those in the outsider position as Jews.

We can only hope that we are not facing a new *Gründerzeit* [period of building up a new Reich such as after 1871] in which these contradictions will disappear again. Goethe scholarship became quite critical in the 1970s and 1980s; among the biographers I would mention Karl Otto Conrady. Nevertheless, there is a renewed tendency to hold Goethe up as a political model; Katharina Mommsen attempted last year, like Thomas Mann in an earlier commemorative year and Ekkehart Krippendorff in 1988 and 1999, to make Goethe into a democrat, if only a sort of virtual or inward one.[47] It is, I think, thanks in large part to the efforts of two Jewish scholars, Richard Friedenthal and Hans Mayer, that Goethe's political contradictions will never again be fully eradicated, even if they had to prevail against an earlier Jewish (and non-Jewish) myth and experience a traumatic awakening.

Notes

[1] Viertes Buch; Johann Wolfgang Goethe, *Sämtliche Werke nach Epochen seines Schaffens: Münchner Ausgabe,* ed. Karl Richter et al., 20 vols. in 33 parts (Munich: Hanser, 1985–99), henceforth abbreviated *MA.*

[2] "Der Eindruck, den ich in früher Jugend in meiner Vaterstadt empfing, war mir ein mehr erschreckender. Die Gestalten der engen und finsteren Judenstadt waren mir gar befremdliche und unverständliche Erscheinungen, die meine Phantasie beschäftigten, und ich konnte gar nicht begreifen, wie dieses Volk das merkwürdigste Buch der Welt aus sich heraus geschrieben hat. Was sich allerdings in meiner früheren Jugend als Abscheu gegen die Juden in mir regte, war mehr Scheu vor dem Rätselhaften, vor dem Unschönen. Meine Verachtung, die sich wohl zu regen pflegte, war mehr der Reflex der mich umgebenden christlichen Männer und Frauen. Erst später, als ich viele geistbegabte, feinfühlige Männer dieses Stammes kennen lernte, gesellte sich Achtung zu der Bewunderung, die ich für das bibelschöpferische Volk hege, und für den Dichter, der das hohe Liebeslied gesungen hat." 1811; *Goethes Gespräche. Eine Sammlung zeitgenössischer Berichte aus seinem Umgang: Auf Grund der Ausgabe und des Nachlasses von Flodoard Freiherrn von Biedermann, ergänzt und herausgegeben von Wolfgang Herwig* (Zurich: Artemis, 1965–87), 2: 669.

[3] In *Brief des Pastors zu *** an den neuen Pastor zu **** and in *Zwo wichtige bisher unerörterte Biblische Fragen* Goethe was "nicht weit davon entfernt, offen gegen den Anti-Semitismus Front zu machen"; in *Das Jahrmarktsfest zu Plundersweilern* we find an "ironische Abfertigung des antisemitischen Ideologen." Norbert Oellers, "Goethe und Schiller in ihrem Verhältnis zum Judentum." *Conditio Judaica. Judentum, Anti-Semitismus und deutschspra-*

chige Literatur vom 18. Jahrhundert bis zum Ersten Weltkrieg. Inter-disziplinäres Symposion . . . , ed. Hans Otto Horch and Horst Denkler, 2 vols. (Tübingen: Niemeyer, 1988), 1: 108–30, here 123–24.

[4] "Was hast du zu den Morgenstunden [von Mendelssohn] gesagt? und zu den jüdischen Pfiffen mit denen der neue Sokrates zu Wercke geht? Wie klug er Spinoza und Lessing eingeführt hat. O du armer Criste wie schlimm wird dir es ergehen! wenn er deine schnurrenden Flüglein nach und nach umsponnen haben wird! Machst du gegen Anstalten?" To Friedrich Jacobi, 1 December 1785, in *Goethes Werke,* hrsg. im Auftrage der Großherzogin Sophie von Sachsen, 133 vols. in 4 parts (Weimar: Böhlau, 1887–1919); vols. IV/51, 52, 53: *Nachträge und Register zur IV. Abteilung: Briefe,* ed. Paul Raabe, 3 vols. (Munich: Deutscher Taschenbuch Verlag, 1990), IV/7 (1891): 131 (henceforth abbreviated WA). Goethe called Mendelssohn's book "das Jüdische neuste Testament" (to Herder, 20 February 1786, WA IV/7: 182). Ludwig Geiger appeared to have no knowledge of these letters, because he portrays Goethe's relationship with Mendelssohn in the most positive light. See "Goethe und die Juden," in Geiger's *Die Deutsche Literatur und die Juden* (Berlin: Reimer, 1910) 96.

[5] To Johann Jost Textor, 8 August 1782, WA IV/6 (1890): 32–33.

[6] *Goethes amtliche Schriften: Veröffentlichung des Staatsarchivs Weimar,* [vols. 1–4:] *Goethes Tätigkeit im Geheimen Consilium,* ed. Willy Flach [vols. 2–4:] Helma Dahl (Weimar: Hermann Böhlau, 1950–87) 1: 395–99.

[7] "Es scheint mir daher eine Art von Satisfaktion [i.e., for the insulted Jews] um so nötiger als diese Geschichte in eine Zeit fällt, wo man Sorge tragen muß den Weeg über Weimar allen und ieden Passagieren sicher und angenehm zu machen." *Amtliche Schriften* 1: 398.

[8] See W. Daniel Wilson, *Das Goethe-Tabu: Protest und Menschenrechte im klassischen Weimar* (Munich: Deutscher Taschenbuch Verlag, 1999), esp. chs. 1 and 2.

[9] "Es liegt nun einmal in meiner Natur, ich will lieber eine Ungerechtigkeit begehen als Unordnung ertragen." *Belagerung von Mainz, MA* 14: 549.

[10] For the following see Paul Arnsberg, *Die Geschichte der Frankfurter Juden seit der Französischen Revolution. Hrsg. vom Kuratorium für Jüdische Geschichte e.V., Frankfurt am Main,* ed. Hans-Otto Schembs (Darmstadt: Eduard Roether, 1983) 60 ff.; I[sidor] Kracauer, *Geschichte der Juden in Frankfurt am Main: Hrsg. vom Vorstand der Israelitischen Gemeinde Frankfurt/ Main,* 2 vols. (Frankfurt/Main: Kauffmann, 1925, 1927) 2: 217 ff.

[11] "Wo ein grüner Raum, kein Jude." Qtd. Arnsberg 129.

[12] "Die Abneigung Goethes gegen das Judentum, eingeimpft schon durch die Geburt, anerzogen durch die Frankfurter Sitte . . . ." Qtd. Arnsberg 129.

[13] Arnsberg 159–60.

[14] "Die jüdische Revolte," qtd. Arnsberg 193.

[15] Arnsberg 197.

[16] The edict was read aloud in the synagogue on 27 February 1808 (Arnsberg 196).

[17] "Dem Braunschweigischen Juden Heiland [Jacobson] ziemt es wohl sein Volk anzusehen, wie es seyn und werden sollte; dem Fürsten Primas [Dalberg] ist aber auch nicht zu verdenken, daß er dieß Geschlecht behandelt wie es ist, und wie es noch eine Weile bleiben wird." To Bettina Brentano, 3 April 1808, WA IV/20: 42. Cf. Alfred D. Low, who defends Goethe's point of view: *Jews in the Eyes of the Germans: From the Enlightenment to Imperial Germany* (Philadelphia: Institute for the Study of Human Issues, 1979) 71.

[18] "[gewannen sie] an bürgerlicher Sittlichkeit . . . , an Lebensart ihre Qualität zu steigern, wissenschaftliche Kenntnisse sich anzueignen und alles das zu kultivieren, was man von gebildeten Menschen erwarten kann." Qtd. Arnsberg 77; see also the contemporary report of the city "Bauamt," Kracauer 2: 335.

[19] "Über die Judengasse, das Aufbauen des abgebrannten Teils und ihre etwaige Erweiterung nach dem Graben zu wäre zu denken und darüber auch allenfalls ein Gedanke zu äußern." *MA* 4.2: 635 (*Auf einer Reise in die Schweiz über Frankfurt, Heidelberg, Stuttgart und Tübingen im Jahre 1797*); cf. Arnsberg 80. In the same text Goethe writes of Heilbronn, "Es werden keine Juden hier gelitten," and a few lines later he says that Heilbronn "auf gemeine bürgerliche Gleichheit fundiert ist"; Klaus H. Kiefer remarks in his commentary to this passage that this equality "schloß — wie scheinbar selbstverständlich — die jüdische Bevölkerung aus" (*MA* 4.2: 651, 1183). Indeed, for Goethe, in contrast to many of his contemporaries, the denial of Jewish emancipation was "selbstverständlich."

[20] "Es war mir sehr angenehm zu sehen, daß man den Finanzgeheimeräthlichen, Jacobinischen Israels Sohn so tüchtig nach Hause geleuchtet hat. Können Sie mir den Verfasser der kleinen Schrift wohl nennen. . . . Leider ist das ganze nicht rasch, kühn und lustig genug geschrieben, wie es hätte seyn müssen, um jenen Humanitätssalbader vor der ganzen Welt ein für allemal lächerlich zu machen." WA IV/20: 50.

[21] Fritz Hartung, *Das Großherzogtum Sachsen unter der Regierung Carl Augusts 1775–1828* (Carl August. Darstellungen und Briefe zur Geschichte des Weilmarischen Fürstenhauses und Landes. Im Auftrage der Weimarischen Gebietsregierung hrsg. von Erich Marcks. II. Abt.) (Weimar 1923) 457.

[22] "Über die Gefährdung des Wohlstandes und Charakters der Deutschen durch die Juden"; "Mäkler- und Trödlerkaste," Ernst Ludwig Theodor

Henke, *Jakob Friedrich Fries: Aus seinem handschriftlichen Nachlasse* (Leipzig: Brockhaus, 1867) 157.

[23] "Volksverderber und Brotdiebe," qtd. Arnsberg 126.

[24] "Die sämmtliche Judenschaft erzittert, da ihr grimmiger Gegner, den ich so eben aus dem 9ten Heft kennen lerne, nach Thüringen kommt. In Jena darf nach alten Gesetzen kein Jude übernachten. Diese löbliche Anordnung dürfte gewiß künftig hin besser als bisher aufrecht erhalten werden." WA IV/27 (1903): 64. On Goethe's participation in the appointment of Fries and on the later measures against him, see the references in *Amtliche Schriften* 4: 54 and in F. Hartung 483; see also Arnsberg 126.

[25] "Ich . . . enthalte mich aller Theilnahme an Juden und Judengenossen," 11–17 July 1817, WA IV/28 (1903): 183 (first publication: 1878). Cf. Arnsberg 126.

[26] Goethe's diary: "Abends Canzler von Müller, über Christen- und Juden-Heirathen, unerfreuliche Unterhaltung" 23 September 1823, WA III/9 (1897), and in an earlier conversation with Müller in April 1823: "Landtags-verhandlungen, besonders wegen der Juden," Gespräche 9 (1897).

[27] "Ich war kaum . . . in Goethes Zimmer getreten, als der alte Herr seinen leidenschaftlichen Zorn über unser neues Juden-Gesetz, welches die Heirat zwischen beiden Glaubensverwandten gestattet, ausgoß. Er ahndet die schlimmsten und grellsten Folgen davon, behauptet, wenn der General-Superintendent Charakter habe, müsse er lieber seine Stelle niederlegen als eine *Jüdin* in der Kirche im Namen der Heiligen Dreifaltigkeit trauen; alle *sittlichen* Gefühle in den Familien, die doch durchaus auf den *religiösen* ruhten, würden durch ein solch skandalöses Gesetz untergraben. . . . Was in seinem Judeneifer recht merkwürdig war, ist die tiefe Achtung vor der positiven Religion, vor den bestehenden Staatseinrichtungen, die trotz seiner Freidenkerei überall durchblickte. 'Wollen wir denn hier überall im *Absurden* vorausgehen, alles Fratzenhafte zuerst probiren?' sagte er unter andern." 23 September 1823, Biedermann/ Herwig 3.1: 581.

[28] "In diesem Sinne, den man vielleicht pedantisch nennen mag, aber doch als folgerecht anerkennen muß, dulden wir keinen Juden unter uns; denn wie sollten wir ihm den Anteil an der höchsten Kultur vergönnen, deren Ursprung und Herkommen er verleugnet?" III, 11, *MA* 17: 633; cf. the commentary by Gonthier-Louis Fink, 1193–94.

[29] George L. Mosse, *German Jews beyond Judaism* (Bloomington: Indiana UP; Cincinnati: Hebrew Union College Press, 1985); Wilfried Barner, *Von Rahel Varnhagen bis Friedrich Gundolf: Juden als deutsche Goethe-Verehrer*, Kleine Schriften zur Aufklärung 3 (Wolfenbüttel: Lessing-Akademie; Göttingen: Wallstein, 1992); On Goethe's attitude to Jews see also Barner, "150 Jahre nach seinem Tod: Goethe und die Juden," *Bulletin des Leo Baeck Insti-*

tuts 63 (1982): 75–82; Günter Hartung, "Goethe und die Juden," *Weimarer Beiträge* 40 (1994): 398–416; Hartung, "Judentum," *Goethe Handbuch,* vol. 4: *Personen, Sachen, Begriffe,* ed. Hans-Dietrich Dahnke and Regine Otto (Stuttgart: Metzler, 1998) 581–90 (with bibliography).

[30] When I quote from the volumes of the Weimar Edition that contain diaries and letters (sections III and IV), I have also given the dates of publication, but I have indicated, in the case of volumes that appeared after 1895 and in which the items cited appeared earlier, the date of original publication. In this way it will be clear which documents were available to the biographers discussed here.

[31] In 1914 a few official writings were published in vol. 53 of WA, sect. I (Works), but isolated documents had been published in 1874, 1878, 1882 and 1893. On the publication history of the official writings, see Volker Wahl, "Amtliche Schriften," *Goethe Handbuch,* vol. 3: *Prosaschriften,* ed. Bernd Witte et al. (Stuttgart: Metzler, 1997) 797–819.

[32] Goethe "liebte . . . die Juden im allgemeinen nicht"; "böswillige Anklagen . . . , die noch zu seiner Zeit vielfach laut wurden." Ludwig Geiger, *Goethe. Sein Leben und Schaffen: Dem deutschen Volke erzählt* (Berlin: Ullstein, 1910) 460–61.

[33] *Ibid.* 381.

[34] "Solche heftige Äußerungen waren ebenso erklärlich durch seine, sowohl dem Liberalismus wie den Juden abholde Gesinnung." *Ibid.* 382.

[35] Albert Bielschowsky, *Goethe: Sein Leben und seine Werke,* rev. Walther Linden, 2 vols. (Munich: Beck, 1928; 1st ed. 1895).

[36] Friedrich Gundolf, *Goethe,* 13th ed. (Berlin: Bondi, 1930) 261 (1st ed. 1916).

[37] Eduard Engel, "Der Politiker Goethe," *Vossische Zeitung,* Sonntagsbeilage Nr. 30 (25 July 1909); "Der Beamte Goethe," *Velhagen & Klasings Monatshefte* 23.2 (1909) 576–81.

[38] "Zwischen uns und Weimar liegt Buchenwald. Darum kommen wir nun einmal nicht herum."Alewyn, "Goethe als Alibi?" (introductory lecture in a course on Goethe at the University of Cologne, where Alewyn had just begun teaching). *Goethe im Urteil seiner Kritiker: Dokumente zur Wirkungsgeschichte Goethes in Deutschland,* ed. Karl Robert Mandelkow (Munich: Beck, 1984), 4: 335; the following quotations are from the same page).

[39] "Es gibt nur Goethe und Hitler, die Humanität und die Bestialität."

[40] Information on this group is sketchy; I owe some of these facts to Jochanan Trilse-Finkelstein of the Jüdischer Kulturverein Berlin, and some of them to Ingeborg Cleve of the Universität des Saarlandes, who is working on a history of the Weimar cultural institutions in the GDR period.

[41] K[urt] R[obert] Eissler, *Goethe: A Psychoanalytic Study, 1775–1786* (Detroit: Wayne State UP, 1963). Translation: *Goethe: Eine psychoanalytische Studie, 1775–1786.* ed. Rüdiger Scholz, 2 vols. (Basel: Stroemfeld/Roter Stern, 1983; Munich: Deutscher Taschenbuch Verlag, 1987).

[42] "Keineswegs Philosemit . . . wie etwa Lessing; in Fragen der staatsbürgerlichen Gleichberechtigung war er ebensowenig für Emanzipation der Juden wie für Pressefreiheit." Richard Friedenthal, *Goethe: Sein Leben und seine Zeit* (Munich: Piper, 1963) 499–500.

[43] "Wenn man sich 1915 an nahezu derselben Stelle wie Goethe in der Champagne in den lockeren Kreideboden hat eingraben müssen, 'zur voreiligen Bestattung,' wie er sagte, so sieht man einen solchen Feldzug mit anderen Augen, und so geht es mit vielen Dingen. Hat man die 'voreilige Bestattung' überstanden, die auch noch später nicht selten drohte, so ergibt sich eine andere Haltung zum Leben wie zur Literatur. Man wird eine gewisse Ironie walten lassen dürfen oder auch Humor, ohne den solche Zeiten kaum zu bewältigen sind. So steckt in meinem Buch auch, wie ich glaube, neben vielem Quellenstudium eine nicht unbeträchtliche Menge von Lebenserfahrungen" (738).

[44] *Die Klassik-Legende: Second Wisconsin Workshop,* ed. Reinhold Grimm and Jost Hermand (Frankfurt/Main: Athenaeum, 1971); cf. Klaus L. Berghahn, "Das Andere der Klassik. Von der 'Klassik-Legende' zur jüngsten Klassik-Diskussion," *Goethe Yearbook* 6 (1992): 1–27.

[45] "Das ist nicht nur pedantisch, muß man Goethe mit tiefem Bedauern hier zurufen, sondern auch sehr engherzig und für einen Humanisten barbarisch." Hans Mayer, *Goethe: Ein Versuch über den Erfolg* (Frankfurt/Main: Suhrkamp, 1973) 102–03.

[46] "Goethe als *Bildung* und Besitz, das ist dahin. Goethe als Innerlichkeit, das hält nicht stand: in der Zelle, in Todesgefahr, als Schutz gegen Verdinglichung" (107).

[47] Katharina Mommsen, *Goethe und unsere Zeit: Festrede im Goethejahr 1999 zur Eröffnung der Hauptversammlung der Goethe-Gesellschaft im Nationaltheater zu Weimar am 27. Mai 1999* (Frankfurt/Main: Suhrkamp, 1999); Thomas Mann, "Goethe und die Demokratie," in his *Goethe's Laufbahn als Schriftsteller: Zwölf Essays und Reden zu Goethe* (Frankfurt/Main: Fischer, 1982) 283–308; Ekkehart Krippendorff, *Wie die Großen mit den Menschen spielen: Versuch über Goethes Politik* (Frankfurt/Main: Suhrkamp, 1988) and *Goethe: Politik gegen den Zeitgeist* (Frankfurt/Main: Insel, 1999).

The Insufficient as Event: Goethe Lesson at the Frankfurt School

Karla L. Schultz
University of Oregon

> I once teased Benjamin in a conversation about his predilection for remote and esoteric themes and asked just when he might write an interpretation of *Faust*. He parried: when it would appear in serial form in the *Frankfurter Zeitung*.[1]
> — Theodor W. Adorno

A WITTY POSTCARD OF FRANKFURT shows a gigantic Goethe casually reclining across his hometown's late-twentieth-century skyline. The model for the pose is, of course, Tischbein's famous painting of Goethe from the 1780s, with the poet gazing across the Campagna di Roma spread at his feet. But there is a small oddity in the adaptation. In the Tischbein rendering Goethe's right foot is firmly planted on the ground. In the postcard — conspicuous, casual — it dips into the flow of the river, creating a wake, a disruption, a pause. Adorno would have liked this detail. In his discussions of Goethe's language he often speaks of its *Rauschen* [streaming quality], punctuated by breaks that allow sediments to wash up. These sediments, "dregs of absurdity,"[2] do not quite fit, strike a discordant note. They alter, briefly, the auditory flow, poke eddies in the ideational content. Though they participate in the streaming, they also stir it up, give it texture from below.

Aside from brief references scattered throughout his work,[3] Adorno wrote two essays on Goethe, both of which appeared in *Noten zur Literatur* (Notes on Literature). One, "Über den Klassizismus der 'Iphigenie'" (On the Classicism of "Iphigenie"), was written in 1967 amid the growing student revolt; the other, "Die letzte Szene des 'Faust'" (On the Final Scene of "Faust," 1959) amid Germany's postwar economic boom.[4] Seemingly removed from these contexts, they address what Adorno considered a truly performative kind of enlightenment: unforced, humane speech and the aesthetic illumination of hope. The Iphigenie essay, with its theme of *Humanität*, thus is oriented toward the secular, the Faust commentary toward the metaphysical. Each examines key notions associated with a certain tradition: the idea of humanity, placed on the banners of a new class as the bourgeois era commenced (*Iphigenie*, 1787, was put into final form right before the French Revolution), and the idea of transcendence as transmitted by the Judeo-Christian faith (with transcendence reconceived and secularized by German Idealism. *Faust II* was finished in 1831, the year of Hegel's death). In both instances Adorno holds that Goethe's language, understood as communicative medium, falls short of these ideas. As aesthetic performance, however, it expresses each to a remarkable extent.

What is also remarkable is that Adorno, intransigent critic of the bourgeois-metaphysical tradition, takes up Goethe on his return from Nazi-imposed exile. As if he wants to reclaim a heritage, the German Jew Adorno turns to Germany's cultural icon. But he reads it against the grain. He meditates on *Faust* amid fashionable proclamations of despair (the existentialist pose of the fifties); turns to *Iphigenie*, a "veritable nuisance" of a play shelved by the rebellious 1960s. In each particular context Adorno had become a nuisance himself. He had refused to join the self-pitying attitude of postwar German intellectuals when he returned, and he refused, taken aback by the violence, to participate in the student uprising.[5] Instead, he immersed himself in texts. Let me begin with the *Iphigenie* essay.

Always the contrarian, Adorno meant his reading of *Iphigenie* to show how neither the clichés of the establishment nor the slogans of the rebels had taken in the lesson of the play. It was a lesson in the falsity and truth of *Humanität*. He starts out by sketching the evolution of Goethe's language within the historical context of the late 1700s:

> What his artistic work required him to practice was natural speech. The generation of his youth, and he along with it, had been seduced by naturalness, but naturalness, as the abstract negation of unnaturalness, had since then become unnatural. . . . Through its own concept, natural speech becomes tempered speech, nonviolent speech (*NII* 161).

Written between the rebellious Storm-and-Stress movement and the French Revolution, the drama's measured form practices nonviolence and indicates, for a brief historical moment, the natural language of a nonviolent *Humanität*.

The tempestuous diction of the Storm and Stress did have good political reasons, Adorno writes, but had remained negative-abstract, meaning that it had been forced by a subjective, purely oppositional will, not by the requirements of the object: the idea of a nature that would be free of violence, externally *and* internally. This double aspect of natural language — liberation from social *and* psychological oppression — is central to Adorno's language criticism overall. Throughout his writings he emphatically criticizes the battle cry to meet violence with violence, and not just in regard to student revolts. In regard to Goethe and the form that the theme of *Iphigenie* demanded he writes: "Language now finds its autonomy not in self-assertion but in responding attentively to the matter at hand" (*NII* 161).

But the matter at hand was not an easy one. It was, conceptually put, Goethe's negotiation of humaneness "through the experience of its antinomy" (*NII* 157). The essay sifts through a stack of such irreconcilable opposites on the level of the plot, in history, in consciousness, in language. The plot contrasts two mythical people, one supposedly civilized, the other allegedly barbaric. They meet but do not mingle; the Greeks return home, the Scythian Thoas is left behind. In terms of Goethe's historical moment, the antinomy rested in the promise of an encompassing sociality on which the new era was not making good. Those considered "other" continued to be excluded, underlining "the dilemma of a situation in which humanness emerged and was cut off at the same moment" (*NII* 160–61). Goethe inscribed this discrepancy into his play:

> He was disgusted by the bourgeois who sets himself up as a hero; he had a sense of the dark secret of a revolution and an allegedly emancipated consciousness that, as in France around 1789, has to present itself through declamation because it is not completely true, because in it *Humanität* becomes repression and interferes with full humanness (*NII* 161).

In artistic terms, the negotiation of the human/humane results in a concealing, falsely reconciliatory move that, however, encounters resistance. This means that the play's communicative-semantic dimension tries to cover up the antinomy, makes declarations. Yet its expressive audial-rhythmic dimension, the linguistic streaming punctured by dissonance and silence, indicates that the move was hasty, forced. Adorno thus distinguishes between the subjective, idealizing untruth of the medium (i.e., a negative-abstract, grand and intention-ridden vocabulary) and its concrete-objective truth (the nonconceptual rhythm and sound of it). We could put it this way: the willed content prematurely announces the realization of the idea, while the material form makes the idea appear only as potential — weighted as it is with the sediments of human suffering that brought forth the idea to begin with.

Adorno calls the play modern, because it stages, at the eclipse of the Enlightenment, the dialectic between civilization and barbarism in a new form. He draws attention to the internal brittleness of this form, which pushes toward formal autonomy because the speaking subject, alienated and estranged, still objectifies itself in the language but does not participate in any objective sociality:

> Goethe had to deal with the problem peculiar to a literature thrown back on subjective experience: that of objectifying itself without participating in any objectivity that would serve as its foundation. . . . The substitution of form for a content antagonistic to the subject is already exposed in *Iphigenie* (*NII* 159).

Where the language of the drama forgets this tricky dialectic it starts to clatter classicistically, becomes hollow and smooth. Adorno cites the final scene, in which the Greek princess Iphigenie unrolls her long, all-too-beautiful river of words, at the end of which Thoas the barbarian is left behind:

> He is not permitted to participate in the highest *Humanität* but is condemned to remain its object, while in fact he acts as its subject. The inadequacy of the resolution, which achieves only a fraudulent reconciliation, manifests itself aesthetically. . . . The wires become visible. . . . The masterpiece creaks, and by doing so indicts the concept of a masterpiece (*NII* 166).

On the other hand, where the language becomes conscious of the dialectic, it frees itself also in rhythm, and reveals a glimpse of utopia:

> [The monologue of Orestes' madness] gives rise to an image of unrestricted reconciliation, beyond the construction of *Humanität* as the middle way between the absolute and blind nature. Here, truly, Goethe leaves classicism as far behind as his meter, in a reprise of the free verse of his early period. "All of us here have been set free of enmity" (1288). . . . Orestes' vision transcends anything that could have been imagined in Greek terms (*NII* 166).

In Adorno's interpretation it matters that the vision takes place on Scythian ground, which in history eventually became Russian Orthodox. It is the place of the "other," the non-Western faith, the alien and strange. The Greeks, at first eager emissaries of Western culture, now helplessly ecstatic in the figure of the mad Orestes, are made to speak differently. His monologue invokes peace after ancient bloodshed, alludes to mystical illumination, resounds with echoes of the doctrine of the apocatastasis, of the redemption of even radical evil, of utter sinfulness. What is invoked here is the heresy of the *hetero*dox, the *other* faith. "It is this vision that demolishes the special preserve Goethe had elsewhere, for the sake of Iphigenie's *Humanität*, established for culture" (*NII* 167). Adorno's essay includes vivid echoes of his and Horkheimer's philosophy of history, set forth in *Dialektik der Aufklärung* (Dialectic of Enlightenment).[6] It also includes, via two extremes — Thoas the civilized barbarian and Orestes the ecstatic Greek — the spirit of Walter Benjamin's meditation on the baroque (in *Ursprung des deutschen Trauerspiels* [Origin of the German Mourning Play]): that antinomic ideas may be circumscribed in a contextual constellation of their extremes.[7]

The Greeks in the play consider themselves more human/humane than the Scythians, because they consider their own civilization superior — indeed, as the only one worthy of the name. Even when they are on foreign ground, their language is their prerogative: they talk too much and profess too quickly. The averred/aspired state of a shared humanity in which *all* will participate is sublimated into the conviction of a proprietary humaneness — denied barbarians and "others." "The social co-efficient of language, that of a cultured upper stratum, is an index of the particular, exclusive quality of *Humanität*" (*NII* 163). Goethe's own phrase of the "diabolically humane Iphigenie" gives an inkling of this. In Adorno's synoptic view the subjectivist, class-based confrontation with the "other" occurs over and over again, imprinting the prevailing race, gender, and class relations into so-called classical or universal texts. The Greeks' attitude toward Thoas in *Iphigenie*, Adorno writes, is not much different from late nineteenth-century European imperialism,

> which transposed the class struggle into a struggle between nations or blocs, down to the current opposition between highly industrialized and undeveloped peoples, making it invisible. . . . There is no counter-evidence that can allay the spontaneous reaction to *Iphigenie* that Thoas is being dealt with in an ugly way (*NII* 164).

He sees in Thoas not the taciturn, stammering "barbarian," i.e., someone not in control of the (ruling) language, but the only humanely acting and humanly speaking figure. Goethe's syntax brings out his truly civilized speech, as it does the civilizing aspect of the play overall:

The form of every sentence is accomplished with a well-considered just proportion of formulation, oddly coupled with a warm, encompassing streaming. . . . When, antithetically, the Scythian king is silent or uses few words, . . . his silence works toward civilization in its own right, negotiated down from a raging outburst (*NII* 158).

Thoas, one might say, is someone who keeps his word doubly. He speaks little so as not to let his language gallop away, and he keeps his word to Iphigenie and lets her go. His humane humanness keeps the words in check *and* sets them free into deed in a conscious act of *not* following his passion, of *not* making use of the power he has as king. In short, he remembers chaos and brutality — the overcoming of which is the condition for the possibility of his act.[8]

Orestes, by contrast, is less civilized. He regresses, taking a visionary stance. In his mad delusion he is open to a humaneness that transcends the limits of reason and restraint. His monologue conjures up the vision of a reconciliation that encompasses all, that is driven by a desire to include everyone, even the condemned. At least, that is the tendency of his speech. Adorno concludes that the play stops short of true radicality. It ultimately recurs to the traditional equation of justice equals revenge: "Utopia is charged with its impossibility. . . . The curse on Tantalus remains in force" (*NII* 167).

The essay's argument plots two extremes as the outer reaches of *Humanität*: madness and silence. They circumscribe a humaneness conceived *ex negativo*, i.e., as the despairing vision of a history that was/will be different and a deed that is congruent with the word. In both cases the ferments of enlightenment are at work: a crazy (unorthodox) imagination and nonviolent speech, each one embodied in bourgeois reason's opposites, the mad mystic and cultural other.

In each instance the language of the play makes room, recedes. With Orestes the rhythmic flow breaks up, with Thoas it breaks off. Goethe's achievement was to make the language of the time capacious and generous enough to let such ruptures stand. Yet, in the plot — the rational, intentional dimension — Orestes, sane again, rejoins his family, and Thoas, doubly left behind, remains the stranger and primitive. This is why Adorno calls the play's communicative content "*Humanität*'s apology for its immanent inhumanity" (*NII* 165).

Put yet another way, the content of *Iphigenie* commits itself to only half of humane humanness (rational justice and eloquence), whereas the fullness of humanity appears in their negative extremes, in silence and crazy visions. Only by its outer fringes — in the figures of the rambling madman and the terse, ominous stranger — does the concept of humanity suggest a whole. It is the non-conceptual dimension of the play that alludes to this possibility, with its breaks and blanks, cross currents, and wakes embedded in the "warm and encompassing streaming" of a medium made newly resonant. For Adorno, it was Goethe's innervation of the promise of the age. Not the promise of humanity made whole, but the prerequisite to the promise, a language reflective as well as self-reflective of its constraints:

> Goethe's drama was finished in the same year as *Figaro*, and Goethe's text is a continuation of the text of the *Magic Flute*. In the objectless and conceptless language of Mozart a lucidity that is clearly completely enlightened is combined with a sacred element that is completely secularized, an element concealed within the murmuring of Goethe's objective and conceptual language (*NII* 170).

Some of Adorno's most moving observations on the metaphysical dimension of language are inspired by literary endings. I am thinking of his "Short Commentaries on Proust" and his "Notes to Kafka." His Faust essay is no exception. Its subject matter is the last scene of *Faust II* — more precisely, some oddities in the language of this scene. He comments specifically on just a few lines, usually singling out no more than a phrase, a word, or even just a syllable. His approach is minimalist in the extreme. Or is it, in actuality, a macro-approach? The details of Goethe's language appear caught in wide loops and arches, in an associative thought process that expresses itself through allusions and startling juxtapositions. If it were not such heresy, I would liken his way to a cowboy flinging a lasso: the loop, broad and slightly irregular, is tossed deftly through the air to capture the animal's footing at its surest and swiftest — the point where it touches / now leaves the ground. The loop descends, the object is brought home.

How to bring home metaphysical hope is the question that spurs on the Faust essay. The countercurrent to the question is Adorno's sense for its presumptuousness.[9] A radio lecture from the early 1950s puts the need for attending to the detail in ethical terms (the worldly version of metaphysics). Adorno writes that literary criticism will have force only where it understands how each rightly and wrongly put phrase contributes to the course of humankind. While he acknowledges the pervasive commodification of culture, he implores critics to take culture's "useless" products such as artworks seriously, because they testify to the lives of the actual human beings inscribed in them (and whom the social totality considers equally "useless" because they, too, are singular). What is necessary, Adorno suggests, is a reading of literary forms that is mindful of the history that produced them yet resistant to that history's perpetuation: "Only that critic would do justice to his task whose thoughts register something of the shock inflicted on the ground on which he moves."[10] And yet, the hasty declarations of nihilism, of existential anguish and despair so fashionable in the Germany of the fifties seem to him a mockery, coupled as they were with an economic reconstruction that defied, by its sheer bustling busyness, the memory of recent events. The essay begins with an observation and an emotion: "It appears that the current situation calls for alexandrinism, interpretive immersion in traditional texts. Modesty and shame make one recoil from expressing metaphysical intentions directly ... Auschwitz as boundary" (my translation).

The loop Adorno tosses is wide, configuring the Jews of Alexandria two thousand years ago with recent Jewish history. Then, too, there had been survivors, texts that had been passed on, texts that were waiting to be reread. I am extrapolating this trajectory from the first passage, which is a veritable tour de force of allusion. It also contains a barely concealed agitation. Adorno knows that he has become Jewish but without the proper faith. Let me insert an imaginary footnote in the text: It was Philon Judaeus of Alexandria, the Judaeo-Hellenic philosopher, who had pleaded with the emperor Caligula to stop the persecution of the Jews when they refused to erect his image in their synagogues. When his plea was rejected, he wrote a defense, which was read in the Senate after Caligula's death. Philon's teachings comprised the core of Alexandrinian theology, thoroughly influencing subsequent developments such as Neo-Platonism. His philosophy, based on biblical as well as Hellenic thought, embraces as the ultimate purpose of life the direct vision of God. But because the spiritual and the material world are radically different and do not touch, Philon taught that mediators negotiate between the two, corresponding in shape to both the Jewish angels and the Platonic ideas. Their common substance is Logos.

In Adorno's essay the material/immaterial word, the *logos incarnate,* is the foot of the animal "hope" in flight, now touching, now leaving the ground. It is spirit as well as the mark on the page, illusion as well as the trace of a human hand. It is not absolute truth; it is, rather, a kind of vulnerable document open to interpretation. He reflects on what sustains interpretive immersion in texts:

> Interpretation does not seize upon what it finds as valid truth, and yet it knows that without the light it tracks in the texts there would be no truth (*NI* 111).

The passage concludes with a remark that used to run like a red thread through his exchanges with Walter Benjamin:[11]

> To regard profane texts as sacred texts — that is the answer to the fact that all transcendence has migrated into the profane sphere, and survives only where it conceals itself (*NI* 111).

Transcendence in hiding. The lesson that Goethe's text demonstrates is about the truth of the detail. In the last scene of *Faust II* profane details, "sediments of the absurd," survive in colloquialisms and dialect traces, in adjustments of rhythm and rhyme, in incongruities with the play's overarching idea — all the while being pushed, prodded, and coaxed toward that which they are not: chips of the sublime. They offer, one might say in the context of the scene, a passive, weighty resistance on their way to heaven. Even the angels complain. The essay singles out *Nüchternheit*, sobriety vis-à-vis the sublime, as characteristic of Goethe's language. It resists the logic of purity. Adorno cites the instance of the angels, who sing as they carry Faust's remains heavenward:

> Lifting an earthly rest
> Pains us, Almighty,
> And were it made of asbestos,
> It's not clean and tidy.

The scene is sublimely humorous for its incongruity. Faust's remains have the weight of an earthly life attached to them, just as language — even as it strives to express the most esoteric of notions — remains a thoroughly material medium. Adorno writes: "Humanely, language lets the non-identical, the heteronomous alone. It does not sacrifice it to the seamless unity of an idealistic principle" (*NI* 118). He describes Goethe's achievement as having produced an art that remained porous to the material elements of language, that did not solidify into the principled, closed discourse of idealism. Rightly called beautiful, his language, in effect, resembles "the feeling of breathing freely in fresh air" (*NI* 115).

Against the monumentality and universality attributed to Goethe by a chauvinist tradition, Adorno the returning exile pits what he terms his *Großheit* [grandeur] and, as precondition, its *Begrenzung* [limitation]. *Großheit* is an odd term in German, specific to a philosophical tradition, and stands out in Adorno's vocabulary. A relational concept, it is marked by what it surpasses, "its relationship to the finite keep[ing] it from evaporating into empty cosmic enthusiasm" (*NI* 115). The essay locates the transcendent aspect of this greatness concretely: in the mobilizing and liquidizing of the natural setting by theatrical magic and song, by the woodland lurching forward, and the Pater profundus invoking the torrents of cascading water as an allegory of almighty love. It is as if the scenery, divided hierarchically and ascending in levels, were enacting its own creation: "The being of the landscape pauses, a figure of its becoming" (*NI* 116). The Hegelian Adorno calls this coming to self-consciousness of nature via language and song the promise of a nature rising beyond itself, without forgetting where it came from.

He locates the limitation or *Begrenzung* for such "magical" language in its concrete social aspect, that is, in its bourgeois mediation. All magic has its price. Regarding Goethe's treatment of Gretchen, for example, he provides a scathing critique of the patriarchal callousness, the philistinism that marks the category of *das Bürgerliche* [the bourgeois], saturated as it is with masculinism and misogyny. Gretchen, like Thoas, is treated shabbily. The language gives it away:

> Gretchen is praised with petty condescension as the "the good soul who forgot herself only once." To demonstrate his own broadmindedness, the commentator remarks that the number of nights of love is not computed in heaven, and in doing so he calls attention to the philistinism of the passage, which splits hairs in excusing the one who has had to suffer the full humiliation of masculine society while her lover, the assassin of her brother, is dealt with far more magnanimously. Rather than gloss over what is bourgeois in bourgeois fashion, one should understand it in relationship to something that would be different. It is this relationship that defines Goethe's humaneness (*NI* 117).

We could say that it was his class and gender bias that Goethe did *not* excise from his language that gives it its historical truth. The reason at work in texts is always limited, specific, and embodied. The *logos incarnate* is never pure. But that also means that it carries within itself the potential for its transcendence. Adorno, the philosopher of determinate negation, offers this defense on reason's behalf:

> Bourgeois reason is both universal reason and a particular reason, the reason of a transparent world order and the particular reason of a calculus that promises the rational man a secure profit. The universal reason that would supersede this particular reason is formed from it; the good universal would be realized only in and through particular situations in their finiteness and fallibility (*NI* 117).

This is moving testimony to the specificity of truth and to the significance of the profane. In the Iphigenie essay I singled out the figures of Thoas and Orestes; in the Faust essay I also want to draw attention to two figures: to Gretchen as the bourgeois-mediated representative of the "eternal feminine" (a figure of hope) and to Abraham, the mythical patriarch and representative of tradition (a figure of continuity). Neither, of course, appears as a dramatic figure in Goethe's scene. There are no dramatic figures. They have disappeared, vanished into the language of holy beings. They are invoked, then dropped again in the music's flow. Who is speaking? Gretchen, as Faust's guilt and redemption, is a distant memory and, as Adorno points out, an instrumentalized memory at that. Abraham, mentioned in the stanza of the Mulier Samaritana, appears at first sight to be treated similarly: "One reads — again for the sake of the verse, again an extreme case of making a virtue out of necessity — 'Abram' instead of 'Abraham' (line 12046)" (NI 114). The elision, however, is the result of a formal constraint, which, in contrast to the editorial on Gretchen — a semantic, content-driven statement — has its own inherent dynamic. The content is mired in ideology ("the good soul who forgot herself only once"), whereas the form pushes toward transcending convention. It makes what is familiar strange, hence new to sensory (aesthetic) perception. "Abram," the shortened form forced by the verse, opens up a new vista, prehistory brought close in the estrangement of the name. The archaic comes alive in the present:

> In the illumination of the exotic name, the familiar Old Testament figure, shrouded in innumerable associations, is abruptly transformed into the Oriental nomadic tribal chieftain. The memory that is faithful to him is seized and wrenched out of the canonized tradition . . . it acquires color and contour (NI 114).

Startlingly, a connection appears to Philon Judaeus, to the vision of God, to medieval Jewish mysticism. Adorno notes that in *Faust*, the German cultural icon, "the chosen people is Jewish, just as the image of beauty in the third act is Greek." The icon is a multicultural composite, a layered edifice. It is layered like the natural scene depicted. But the new, "natural" view of Abram, arising from the most remote layer, is also the most spiritual. Accompanied by the chanting of the "Chorus mysticus," the ecstatic Jewish inflection of which Adorno describes as "the cries of a Hassidic voice, exclamations from the Cabalistic potency of *gevurah* [the one representing power and severity]," it transcends the Catholic mise-en-scène, breaks it open.

If the breaks and pauses in *Iphigenie* appear to reach below the surface of language and wash up sediments, the colloquialisms and archaisms in the final scene of *Faust II* seem to reach above and beyond it. Adorno, who never tired of probing the insufficiency of language, finds that in Goethe this insufficiency became event. By attending to his craft, Goethe innervated the hope and shame of his era, expressing the striation of tradition as well as its false consolidation, conveying Faust's costly redemption as well as the scene's magnificent grace. "The metaphysics of *Faust* is not the effortful striving to which a neo-Kantian reward beckons somewhere in infinity but the disappearance of the natural order in a different order" (*NI* 119).

His art made German a porous language, allowing fissures and breaks to startle recollections of what had been forgotten. It also made it a fluid, musical language, much of which was to its poetic detriment by the time Goethe worked on *Faust II*. An instrumentalizing bourgeois enlightenment had appropriated the discourse for facile communication. The occasional starkness of the late Goethe's style, the juxtaposition of elevated and pedestrian phrases, of colloquial casualness and esoteric pathos all show the contradiction Goethe faced "when a reified, facile discourse invaded expressive discourse." But he did not battle it nor turn away from it (as did later generations of modernists); rather, "his restitutive nature attempt[ed] to awaken that sullied language as a literary language" (*NI* 112). For the time being, he kept it liquid enough to allow for musicality, sturdy enough in detail to allow for transcendence.

Adorno's remarks — and the essay is really a loose series of remarks — come full circle (better yet, full spiral) at the end. He began with an implied trajectory of Jewish history from Alexandrian to Nazi-imposed exile, with an implicit admonishment to safeguard the Jewish tradition of interpretation, of the illumination of texts. He ends with an analogous trajectory, this time of Goethe's life-long work on *Faust*, understood as a search for unconditional love remembered. Or was it one's own early writing remembered, one's mark of entry into the world inspired by such love? Adorno's concluding sentences suggest as much. They suggest a nonpatriarchal, joyously erotic trust in finding what reason and logic had forgotten. Strangely, it seems Goethean and Cabalist in one, extremely natural and extremely spiritual. Yet it acknowledges the permanent gulch carved by historical events, the actual fires that destroy humans. The idea of *Faust*, he writes, may be progressive purification, but it is a meager idea compared to the moment when, in an affront to logic whose radiance heals all logic's acts of violence, the memory of Gretchen's lines in the dungeon dawns on us, as if across the eons, in the invocation of the Mater gloriosa as the *Unvergleichliche* [incomparable one] there speaks from it, in boundless joy, the feeling that must have seized the poet when, shortly before his death, he reread on the boards of a chicken coop the poem, "Wanderers Nachtlied" [Wanderer's Nightsong], he had inscribed on it a lifetime before. That hut too has burned down. Hope is not memory held fast but the return of what has long been forgotten (*NI* 120).

I said earlier that in the *Faust* essay Adorno knows that he has become Jewish but without the proper faith. I am trying to suggest that Adorno, perhaps the least religious, the most adamantly secular of the Frankfurt School, became Jewish by history as well as choice. He had been profoundly moved by Benjamin's messianism and deeply impressed by Scholem's Zionism but kept his distance in matters of faith. If he had to choose, he would side with the Enlightenment (and with Goethe), which was the newer, darker, muddied side of the illuminative tradition. He conducted and wrote extensive studies of anti-Semitism and pointed to the scars it had gouged in the social fabric. He also drew attention to the scars left by poverty and fear. He called the callous oblivion to oppression and exploitation, to cruelty and repression that is present in obedient discourse the yellow spot,[12] the blind spot of the cultural conscience. But he did not consider himself Jewish by nature; he became Jewish through solidarity and moral conscience. Unlike Horkheimer, who converted to Catholicism toward the end of his life, Adorno remained agnostic. Both he and his wife, Gretel, expressly put down their wish to have neither a priest nor a rabbi present at their grave.[13]

Hope, the secular version of faith, arose from actual experiences in the world, from the love of/for another human being and the associative capacity of the mind. There is a section in *Negative Dialektik* on place names that calls the wonder of sensory experience remembered a metaphysical experience but cautions that such experience not be turned into something abstract, not be made part of a system.[14] And in a diary note jotted down before a trip a few years before his death we read: "The night before the trip I dreamed: that I will not let go of metaphysical hope is not because I love life so much but because I would like to wake up with Gretel."[15] It was the concrete attachment, not an overarching idea, that had to suffice for instilling the trust in going on.

What he learned over a lifetime — studying Judaism by analyzing fascism, rereading German poetry by living in exile, writing negative dialectics by meditating on metaphysics — was that a freely lived life, a porous resonant language, a shared human bond still were outrageous, impossible privileges, as contingent as ever on societal relations. They had not become natural rights, as the bourgeois revolutionaries had declared in 1789; never had been biological rights as, perversely, the Nazis claimed in 1933; and they certainly were not consumer rights, as the tide of capitalist advertising insinuated. They also could not be achieved by throwing Molotov cocktails in the streets, by pitting violence against violence. For the Adorno of the late 1960s it seemed time again for alexandrinism.

Notes

[1] Adorno's remark, reprinted in the recent one-volume edition of his *Noten zur Literatur*, ed. Rolf Tiedemann (Frankfurt/Main: Suhrkamp, 1991) 698, appeared as a note appended to his Faust essay when it was first published in the journal *Akzente*. It is a poignant reminder that the life of one of Goethe's most brilliant readers, like so many others, had been cruelly cut short.

[2] Theodor W. Adorno, *Ästhetische Theorie*, ed. Gretel Adorno and Rolf Tiedemann (Frankfurt/Main: Suhrkamp, 1977) 506.

[3] There are numerous references in *Aesthetic Theory* (1970), an interpretation of "Wanderers Nachtlied" in the essay "Über Lyrik und Gesellschaft" (1957), and brief remarks in the musical essays, such as "Spätstil Beethovens" (1937). We also find bits and pieces in the Adorno/Benjamin correspondence from the 1930s, in particular in an exchange on Benjamin's letter collection *Deutsche Menschen*, where Adorno notes their agreement on Goethe's special "technique of crossing the abstract with the concrete."

[4] Adorno, *Noten zur Literatur*, 129–38 and 495–514. Each essay was positioned at the beginning of a volume, the Faust piece introducing volume II and the Iphigenie essay volume IV. My quotations are taken from the English translation, which collects the original four volumes into two: Theodor W. Adorno, *Notes to Literature*, trans. Shierry Weber Nicholsen (New York: Columbia UP, 1991, 1992); they are indicated by *NI* and *NII* in the text.

[5] Though Adorno agreed with the objectives of the student movement, he could not condone the means: "I would have to put the lie to my entire life — the experiences under Hitler and what I observed in Stalinism — if I did not resist the vicious circle of using violence against violence. I can imagine meaningful, change-effecting praxis only as non-violent praxis." From

"Autobiographie aus Zitaten," in *Theodor W. Adorno: Gesammelte Schriften. Dossier* (Frankfurt/Main: Suhrkamp, 1978), my translation.

[6] In this philosophy the seemingly positive poles of a conceptual binary (such as enlightenment/myth, culture/nature, civilization/barbarism, language/body) carry their "negative" pole along within and turn into their opposite once they are declared simply "positive." In their dialectical conception of history Horkheimer and Adorno argue that nature's "power" over man, at first mimetically placated, then manipulated and repressed, is transformed, via the social division of labor and the idea of property, into the ruling subject's domination of nature — a process that perpetuates the fear/violence vis-à-vis the subject's own passions and the human beings perceived as "other." Culture reverts to nature, enlightenment to myth, instead of creating the conditions that would permit humane interaction.

[7] Walter Benjamin, *Ursprung des deutschen Trauerspiels* (Frankfurt/Main: Suhrkamp, 1978) 17.

[8] I extrapolate this aspect from the text, since it corresponds to the argument of *Dialectic Enlightenment*. One of the sections in the "Notes and Drafts," called "The Importance of the Body," states: "Europe has two histories: a well-known, written history and an underground history. The latter consists in the fate of the human instincts and passions which are displaced and distorted by civilization." Max Horkheimer and Theodor W. Adorno, *Dialectic of Enlightenment,* trans. John Cumming (New York: Continuum, 1972) 231. Conversely, Thoas's humane comportment in Goethe's drama is based — in the spirit of true enlightenment — not on repression but on the knowledge about the brutal counterpart to such comportment, the *in*humane possibility.

[9] The last section of *Negative Dialectic* speaks to the conundrum. Adorno passionately, cautiously defends enlightenment, which for him means dialectical thought, but he cautions of its totalizing tendency: "Enlightenment leaves just about nothing of the metaphysical truth content, or, to use a recent term of musical presentation, presque rien. That which retreats gets ever smaller, just as Goethe described it by naming an extreme in his parable of the little box in the New Melusine; it gets ever more inconspicuous. This is the epistemological and historical reason why metaphysics emigrated into micrology. It is the refuge of metaphysics from totality. No absolute may be expressed other than in the fabric and categories of the immanent, while neither the immanent in its contingency nor its full, encompassing concept must be deified. . . . Perhaps [metaphysics] is possible only as a legible constellation of the existent. . . . To become writing it must know the art of making a wish." Theodor W. Adorno, *Negative Dialektik* (Frankfurt/Main: Suhrkamp, 1966) 399, my translation.

[10] Theodor W. Adorno, "On the Crisis of Literary Criticism," *Noten zur Literatur,* 664.

[11] See *Theodor W. Adorno, Walter Benjamin, Briefwechsel 1928–1940,* ed. Henri Lonitz (Frankfurt/Main: Suhrkamp, 1994).

[12] Robert Hullot-Kentor, in his translation of Adorno's programmatic "The Essay as Form," renders the metaphor "der gelbe Fleck," used by Adorno for the gadfly function of the essayist, as "the yellow star" — a pointed reminder not only of the Jewish cultural position as outsider but of the German National Socialists' identification, persecution, and destruction of Jews in the Holocaust. Adorno, "The Essay as Form," trans. Bob Hullot-Kentor and Frederic Will, *New German Critique,* 32 (1984) 152.

[13] See Rolf Tiedemann, "Gretel Adorno zum Abschied," *Frankfurter Adorno Blätter III* (Munich: Text + Kritik, 1992) 150.

[14] Adorno, *Negative Dialektik* 366–67.

[15] *Frankfurter Adorno Blätter III,* 151.

Contributors

EHRHARD BAHR is professor of German at the University of California-Los Angeles. His research and teaching interests include German literature since the eighteenth century (especially Lessing and Goethe), exile literature and modernism, literary theory and criticism, and German-Jewish relations.

KLAUS L. BERGHAHN is the Weinstein-Bascom Professor of German and Jewish studies at the University of Wisconsin-Madison. His research and teaching interests include German literature and culture since the eighteenth century, history of criticism, German-Jewish relations, and history of anti-Semitism. His most recent publications are as editor of *The German-Jewish Dialogue — Reconsidered* (1996), *Grenzen der Toleranz: Christen und Juden in der deutschen Aufklärung* (2000), and as editor of *Friedrich Schiller: Über die ästhetische Erziehung des Menschen* (2000).

HOPE HAGUE is a graduate student in German at the University of Wisconsin-Madison and is writing her dissertation on intergenerational narratives of the Third Reich and the war years in German youth literature of the 1970s and 1980s.

BARBARA HAHN is professor of German at Princeton University. Her areas of interest include genre theory, intellectual history, feminism, German-Jewish culture, and German literature from the late eighteenth to the twentieth century. Her publications include: coeditor of *Von einer Welt in die andere: Jüdinnen im 19. und 20. Jahrhundert* (1993), *Frauen in den Kulturwissenschaften: Von Lou Andreas-Salomé bis Hannah Arendt* (1994), *Rahel Levin Varnhagen: Briefwechsel mit Pauline Wiesel* (1997), and editor of *Pauline Wiesels Liebesgeschichten* (1998).

JOST HERMAND is the William F. Vilas research professor of German culture at the University of Wisconsin-Madison. His publications on related topics include: editor of *Das junge Deutschland* (1966), coeditor of *Die Klassik-Legende* (1971), editor of vol. 6 of *Heinrich Heine: Sämtliche Werke* (1973), *Streitobjekt Heine: Ein Forschungsbericht 1945–*

1975 (1975), *Der frühe Heine: Ein Kommentar zu den "Reisebildern"* (1976), coeditor of *Heinrich Heine: Poetry and Prose* (1982), coeditor of *Heinrich Heine: The Romantic School and Other Essays* (1985), editor of *Geschichten aus dem Ghetto* (1987), *Mehr als ein Liberaler: Über Heinrich Heine* (2nd ed. 1992), *Deutscher, Jude oder Franzose: Heinrich Heine im internationalen Kontext* (1995), *Judentum und deutsche Kultur: Beispiele einer schmerzhaften Symbiose* (1996), and coeditor of *Heinrich Heine's Contested Identities: Politics, Religion, and Nationalism in Nineteenth Century Germany* (1999).

GISELA HOECHERL-ALDEN is the language program director and a lecturer in German at the University of Pittsburgh. Her dissertation was on "Germanisten im 'Niemandsland': Die exilierten Akademiker und ihre Wirkung auf die amerikanische Germanistik (1933–1955)." Her teaching and research interests include literature and culture of the nineteenth and twentieth centuries, intellectual history, German-Jewish exile studies, and issues of second-language acquisition.

ROBERT C. HOLUB is professor of German at the University of California-Berkeley. His most important publications include *Heinrich Heine's Reception of German Grecophilia* (1981), *Reception Theory: A Critical Introduction* (1985), *Reflections on Realism: Paradox, Norm, and Ideology in Nineteenth Century German Prose* (1991), *Jürgen Habermas: Critic in the Public Sphere* (1991), *Crossing Borders: Reception Theory, Poststructuralism, Deconstruction* (1992), and *Friedrich Nietzsche: The Timely Philosopher* (1995).

CHRISTOPH KÖNIG is Privatdozent at the Humboldt Universität Berlin and head of the Arbeitsstelle für die Erforschung der Geschichte der Germanistik at the Schiller-Nationalmuseum/Deutsches Literaturarchiv in Marbach, Germany.

BRENDA MACHOSKY is a graduate student in comparative literature at the University of Wisconsin-Madison and is writing her dissertation "The Phenomenology of Allegory."

MARCEL ROTTER is a graduate student in German at the University of Wisconsin-Madison and is writing his dissertation "'Ätzende Striche — beißende Worte': Propagandistische Motive in Text und Bild vom zweiten Kaiserreich bis zum Kalten Krieg."

KARLA L. SCHULTZ is professor of German at the University of Oregon. She has written widely on the interface of modernism and critical theory, love poetry and gender, the contemporary lyric, and Adorno's concepts of mimesis and modernity.

W. DANIEL WILSON is professor and chair of German at the University of California-Berkeley. He has published extensively on the literature, culture, and history of the eighteenth and early nineteenth centuries: the writer and the state, enlightened absolutism, opposition and dissent, German culture and the French Revolution, gender studies, history of the family. His most recent books include *Unterirdische Gänge: Goethe, Politik und Freimaurerei* (1999) and *Das Goethe-Tabu: Protest und Menschenrechte im klassischen Weimar* (1999).

Index

Adorno, Theodor W. 77, 118, 165; critique of violence, 166, 167, 178, 178n. 5; on Goethe's greatness and limitation, 173–174; on *Humanität* in *Iphigenie*, 166–171; and Jewish history, 172, 175, 176–177; Jewish identity of, 166, 172, 176–177; on metaphysical hope in *Faust*, 171–177

Alewyn, Richard 126, 129, 137n. 10, 139n. 22, 156

Allgemeine Zeitung des Judentums 87

Altmann, Alexander 23

American Association of Teachers of German (AATG) 123

Arendt, Hannah 130, 142n. 45

Arndt, Karl J. R. 137n. 11

Aschheim, Steven 16, 17

Atkins, Stuart 126

Auerbach, Berthold 17, 97

Bab, Julius 82n. 44

Bahr, Erhard 27

Barner, Wilfried 26, 49, 88, 118n. 2, 154

Bartels, Adolf 88

Baumann, Carl 137n. 7

Benjamin, Walter 91, 95–97, 98, 165, 169, 173, 177

Berg, Caroline von 33

Berghahn, Klaus L. 133

Berlin literary circles 88

Berlin salons x, xi, 31–32, 33–34, 46

Bernays, Jacob 67

Bernays, Michael xi

Bielschowsky, Albert xi, 16, 17, 85, 88, 90, 92–93, 98, 155

Bildung: concepts of, x, 17, 22–23, 24–25, 85, 99; and emancipation, 6, 16, 26, 92; and Jewish-German assimilation, xii, 24, 67, 85, 87; and spiritual leadership, 127–28, 158

Bildungsbürgertum xi, 16, 63, 79, 81, 83, 85, 86, 88, 91

Binz, Carl 110

Blume, Bernhard 131, 132, 133, 138n. 14

Blumenthal, Käthe 143n. 58

Boas, Franz 144n. 61

Bollack, Jean 67

Börne, Ludwig 25, 45, 54–56, 58, 150, 151, 154

Bradley, Lyman 144n. 60

Braemer, Edith 156

Brecht, Bertolt 91, 125

Brentano, Bettina (Bettina von Arnim) 5, 6, 13n. 5, 19, 150–51

Brinkmann, Karl Gustav von 32–36, 42

Brühl, Carl 109

Buber, Martin 99

Burschenschaften 45, 46, 52

Bursian, Conrad 88

Carl August, Duke of Saxe-Weimar 5, 147, 157

Chamberlain, Houston Stewart 19

Christiani, Rudolf 47, 50

Cleve, Ingeborg 163n. 40

Congress of Vienna 6, 152

Conrady, Karl Otto 159

Dalberg, Karl von 5, 150, 151